Jan Sebastian Zipp

PROGRAMMING CREATIVITY

Semantics and Organisation of Creativity Within IT Enterprises

[transcript] Culture & Theory

Jan Sebastian Zipp
Programming Creativity

Culture & Theory | Volume 280

Jan Sebastian Zipp, born in 1985, is based at the Tübingen AI Center, the competence centre for machine learning jointly operated by the University of Tübingen and the Max Planck Institute for Intelligent Systems. Prior to that, the cultural scientist worked for several years at IBM Research in Zurich while doing his doctoral thesis at Zeppelin Universität. His research focuses on artificial and human creativity, innovation management, digitisation and the future of work..

Jan Sebastian Zipp

Programming Creativity

Semantics and Organisation of Creativity Within IT Enterprises

[transcript]

Dissertation of Zeppelin University
First reviewer: Prof. Dr. Karen van den Berg
Second reviewer: Prof. Dr. Tasos Zembylas
Date of disputation: March 3, 2020

Bibliographic information published by the Deutsche Nationalbibliothek
The Deutsche Nationalbibliothek lists this publication in the Deutsche Nationalbibliografie; detailed bibliographic data are available in the Internet at http://dnb.d-nb.de

Cover layout: Maria Arndt, Bielefeld
Printed by Majuskel Medienproduktion GmbH, Wetzlar
Print-ISBN 978-3-8376-6316-7
PDF-ISBN 978-3-8394-6316-1
https://doi.org/10.14361/9783839463161
ISSN of series: 2702-8968
eISSN of series: 2702-8976

Printed on permanent acid-free text paper.

Contents

ABSTRACT

This dissertation examines the concept of creativity in large IT (information technology) companies in times of digital change and related phenomena such as changes in methods of working and the allegation of artificial creativity. Based on the assumption that the related creativity narrative occupies a prominent position in the creativity discourse, the question is asked what the IT specifically means when it refers to creativity or acts in the name of it. On the basis of a diachronic analysis, the prerequisites and developmental steps of the specific creativity narrative in IT could be examined. This shows that both the geosocial characteristics of the Silicon Valley and the self-image of IT are mutually influenced by- and influencing the narrative. In addition to the constitutive effect of the space and an interplay of different distinct aspects, the main constitutive elements are in particular the affinity for quantification, the connection to counterculture and the associated understanding of technology. In addition, the analysis of the representation and organisation of creativity as a social practice shows that the creativity narrative within IT is characterised by its own logic, which is persuaded both externally and internally of the uniqueness and predominant character of IT. The narrative plays a decisive role as a justification for this and at the same time became the key understanding of a notion of creativity due to the significance of IT. Finally, the role of the creativity narrative in maintaining and expanding total structures within IT is examined. Here the creativity narrative functions as a vehicle to conceal the total structures and to further consolidate them through the desire for performance and confirmation. To overcome this, there is no direct solution, but a change of perspective. With a view to the aesthetic, a different understanding of creativity is thus possible and conceived as an attempt to elude an understanding of creativity.

1 PROLOGUE – PROGRAMMING CREATIVITY

In May 1991, ecologists in New York's Hudson River discovered a peculiar alteration in the river's habitat. A new species of shellfish appeared that originally only occurred in the Asian part of Russia but expanded globally since the 19th century: the zebra mussel. This invasive species quickly spread along the Hudson's stream, displacing native species to a point where some of them were on the verge of extinction. With the zebra mussel as the predominant species, the number of individual native life forms was temporarily reduced to only 1% of their pre-invasion population.[1] The former diverse ecosystem gradually evolved into a so-called monotypic habitat, meaning a place where an invasive species supersedes or hinders the growth of other species, in particular native ones.[2] From the surface of the water, this process goes unnoticed. It is silent and quiet, but rapid and steady.

In the context of Saussure' s distinction between a signified and a signifier,[3] the habitat – whether diverse or monotypic – represents a *signifier*

1 David L. Strayer, Nuria Cid and Heather M. Malcom, "Long-term changes in a population of an invasive bivalve and its effects", *Oecologia* 165, no. 4 (2011): 1063-1072, doi: https://doi.org/10.1007/s00442-0101792-0, p. 1065.

2 Enacademic, "Habitat", *Enacademic*, [accessed 7th April, 2019], https://enacademic.com/dic.nsf/enwiki/776335#cite_note-4.

3 Ferdinand de Saussure, *Course in General Linguistics* (London: Peter Owen, 1974), p. 67. Saussure inspired the majority of contemporary semiotic research; his explanation is inadequate by modern standards, however, because his definition of *the sign* excludes many elements that are understood as part of semiotics according to the current state of research. Cf. Umberto Eco, Einführung in die Semiotik (München: Wilhelm Verlag, 2002), p. 28. Within this thesis, Saussure's concept of signs is used in the knowledge that many experts regard his work as the foundation of semiotics (still called *semiology* by Saussure). As such, however, it was significantly improved and refined within the framework of semiotics (e.g. by Eco or Roland Barthes).

here, capable of inheriting a variety of different species that echo, in consequence and again according to Saussure, different meanings of the *signified*. Remaining in this metaphorical image for another while, creativity resembles the Hudson. Just as the river originally harboured many *species*, so did creativity harbour many *species of meaning*, which, through its lexical uncertainty and definitory imprecision saw a multitude of meanings expressed in itself. And just as the diversity of living creatures and plants in the Hudson were now displaced by the invasive zebra mussel, a discursive narrative appropriated the shell of creativity, hence creativity as a sign, transforming it almost into a *monotypic sign* through its predominance of meaning. What is implied here as the predominant species is the narrative of creativity by large tech companies.[4]

This in itself is by no means novel or even unique, though, for each discourse knows the interpretive sovereignty of a dominant participant to a greater or lesser extent. Unlike other discourses, however, the discourse on creativity is of rather unprecedented supremacy. Because the concept of creativity's career is breath-taking to begin with. The notion has long ceased to be a hype but become an imperative matter of course and a social norm.[5] The same goes for IT: hardly any area of everyday life, work or other social reality is not either directly affected by IT or at least by the technologies it develops. The boundaries between the digital and the analogue are gradually blurring and dissolving.[6]

In addition to these two rather evident (and often discussed) phenomena of creativity and IT, the subject of this thesis is particularly acute with regard to two other areas in which both concepts – IT and creativity – are deeply entangled and have a crucial part to play. These discursive phenomena have been

---

4 These *large tech companies* are in particular those American companies that have significantly shaped the technical development of the last decades and are now considered to be among the most powerful companies in the world, such as Amazon (rank 1), Apple (2), Alphabet (3), Microsoft (4) or Facebook (6). For the sake of simplicity, the term *IT* is commonly used when referring to these companies and in particular its logic. Cf. Roland Lindner, "Amerikas Tech-Giganten demonstrieren ihre Macht", *Frankfurter Allgemeine Zeitung*, last modified 1st August, 2019, https://www.faz.net/aktuell/wirtschaft/diginomics/us-konzerne-feiern-apple-ist-wieder-eine-billion-dollar-wert-16311893.html?printPagedArticle=true#pageIndex_0.

5 See chapter 4.1 for a more detailed account and explanation.

6 See chapter 4.2.

emphasised not only by researching the topic, but also by several years of experience at IBM (the International Business Machines Corporation) Research in Zurich, Switzerland. One is the *changing conditions of work and labour*. New concepts of working and producing arose in the wake of arcade games and the "computer revolution"[7] in the 1970s and 80s, which moved constantly further away from the process of physical production itself. The so-called platform economy systematically further develops this logic by no longer even dealing directly with immaterial labour or any type of production, but rather with connecting different *things* that already have been created. In short, the IT supplies the infrastructures and the tools to carry out work in times of the digital. But creativity is the ability to use and exploit these tools and infrastructures. New opportunities that arise thanks to IT are only actually activated and implemented through creativity, according to the liberal economic tenor.[8] Simultaneously, concerns are repeatedly expressed from various perspectives about how the current transformation of work and society itself could lead to the loss of many jobs.[9] Following the logic of a creativity imperative, *to be creative* became a strategy to overcome that threat. But with the advent of the phenomenon of supposedly artificial creativity, this potential solution has also started to falter. Debating the questions of whether artificial intelligence can be creative or not further expands the discourse on creativity in IT by adding an ontological perspective concerning possible differences and similarities of human and computational concepts of creativity. Although this is still a matter of semantic constructs, the discourse is turning towards the *big picture* on the future of humankind by incorporating more and more discursive strings coming from various domains ranging from the arts, humanities, psychology, to engineering and computer sciences.[10] Combining these aspects creates the image of a mixture of uncertainties and sub-complex terms in which contradictory and ambiguous pairings of concepts such as utopias and dystopias, progression and depression, freedom and control, individuality and totalitarianism exist in parallel and amplify each other.

---

7 Steven Levy, *Hackers* (Sebastopol: O'Reilly, 2010), p. 371.

8 Amid these developments, a number of discourses are resonating, some of which exist much longer than the digital transformation or the computer revolution. For a more accurate description, see chapter 4.3.

9 Cf. Carl Benedikt Frey and Michael A. Osborne, "The future of employment: How susceptible are jobs to computerisation?" *Technological Forecasting and Social Change* 114, January (2017): 254-280, doi: https://doi.org/10.1016/j.techfore.2016.08.019.

10 See chapter 4.4.

All this happens with unprecedented speed but occurs in a comparatively subtle way. The effects of the digital are physically expressed on a smaller scale: whereas the transformation of society first became visible with the construction of huge factory complexes at the outset of industrialisation, today's façades of co-working spaces in already existing buildings fit seamlessly into the overall impression of a street's scenery, just like the cyclist who delivers food and the neighbour who, as a second job after work, now commutes even longer by car to bring passengers to their destination. Each of these short examples embodies a narrative of creativity characterized predominantly by IT. They demonstrate both the current volatile nature of the discourse on creativity in IT as well as its close connection to social practices. Moreover, the discourse is of a reciprocal nature: whereas the concept of creativity is linked to discourses regarding authorship and originality, an entrepreneurial logic framed the perception of creativity in IT. For a better understanding of all these discursive movements, a further integration and consideration of IT's notion of creativity in related debates may seem to be of great value.

However, the issue remains as to what is specifically supposed by IT when large tech enterprises refer to or act in the name of creativity. This raises the following number of questions: how and why did the semantics of an IT-specific creativity narrative emerge? How did it develop and organise itself? What is its purpose? How is creativity epitomised externally and how does it differ from the internal organisation within IT, hence, how aware is IT of its own creativity narrative? How does the narrative distinguish itself from other narratives and where does it make use of them?

For these reasons, it appears essential to examine the meaning, content and developed conjunctures, the performative portrayal and socio-historically situated practices of creativity within large IT enterprises. This dissertation equally aims to close this prospected research gap by carefully examining the research question formulated above, as well as by preparing the foundations for further research and creating alternative ways of connection that take greater account of IT's influence on the notion of creativity.

2 DESIDERATUM OF RESEARCH

Starting with this chapter, I will consider the notion of creativity to clarify its meaning in the context of this work. As will be shown, it is in the very essence of creativity as a concept not to attempt to define it, but rather to approach a general understanding of it. In order to then be able to adequately locate the work within the scientific discourse, I present what knowledge of the given research object is already available to build on. Since the concept of creativity in IT operates in the context of inter- and intradisciplinary discourses, it appears to be a necessity to also mention contributions from other disciplines in order to outline the discourse on creativity in IT as a whole and to further reveal the presumed research gap.

2.1 CONCEPTUAL CLARIFICATIONS

As with other concepts, creativity remains hard to define. A tremendous number of possible approaches are faced with rather vague definitions that differ as the case arises. The conceptualisation of creativity is heterogenous and varies across disciplines, professions, languages – and its terminology itself. For the discourses related to the notions of creativity show that *creativity* is superordinate to a *family of concepts*;[1] including but not limited to buzzwords like *innovation* and *disruption*, misleading and ambiguous terms like *singularity* or, in an extended way of understanding, also *art* and *artistic*.[2] Due to the semantic ambiguity of creativity, these concepts appear to be interchangeable

1 Zygmunt Bauman uses a similar approach of including neighbouring terms into a "family of concepts" when he introduces his understanding of "culture". Cf. Zygmunt Bauman, *Liquid Life* (Cambridge: Polity, 2005), p. 52.

2 Cf. Karen van den Berg, "Kreativität. Drei Absagen der Kunst an ihren erweiterten Begriff", in *Rationalität der Kreativität? Multidisziplinäre Beiträge zur Analyse der Produktion,*

in some statements.[3] Accordingly, an approach to the concept of creativity proves to be rather complex. At the same time, there is a certain risk of misinterpretation since it usually remains unclear whether a statement about innovation, for example, is made in the knowledge of a *family of concepts* – i.e., whether it includes creativity – or not. As early as 1992, in its section on the concept of creativity the Dictionary of Philosophy states that not everyone is referring to the same facts when arguments are expressed in the name of the concept of creativity.[4] In order to avoid a sub-complex approach, the above-mentioned notions related to creativity, hence its *family ties*, cannot and will not be completely excluded within this work.

Despite the term's variety of possible semiotic expressions however, the distinction between the *shell* and the meaning of the concept of creativity does not necessarily imply entirely arbitrary meanings. Rather, it is to be assumed that a fundamental and common understanding exists, on the basis of which possible narratives and interpretations are competed for. For this, Gallie coined the notion of an *essentially contested concept*, meaning that differently used terms "subserve different though of course not altogether unrelated functions".[5] It hence considers an open concept – such as creativity is – from certain angles, through which a term is further specified beyond its core meaning – albeit "an unequivocal meaning as between its different (contestant) users"[6] exists.

It is in the very nature of an essentially contested concept that it inherits diverging disputes "which, although not resolvable by argument of any kind, are nevertheless sustained by perfectly respectable arguments and evidence".[7]

Organisation und Bildung von Kreativität, eds. Stephan A. Jansen, Eckhard Schröter and Nico Stehr (Wiesbaden: VS Verlag, 2009).

3 For example, a specific notion of creativity can be (intentionally or unintentionally) implied when talking about innovation.

4 Cf. Joachim Ritter, (1992), p. 1194.

5 Walter B. Gallie, "Art as an essentially contested concept", *Philosophical Quarterly* 6, no. 23 (1956): 168, doi: https://doi.org/10.2307/2217217. Gallie provides the examples of "work of art", "democracy" and "Christian doctrine" for which different schools, groups, parties or communities (among others) exist in parallel. Whether a concept is *essentially contested* depends on five different characteristics that all must apply. In short, it must be appraisive (1); must have an internally complex character (2); is initially variously describable (3); is modifiable or *open* in character (4); and parties involved must be aware of a concept's contention (5). Cf. ibid., p. 171f.

6 Ibid., p. 175.

7 Ibid., p. 169.

With respect to the concept of creativity, the narratives within art and computer technology, for example, would represent individual perspectives that are "perfectly genuine"[8] and justified in themselves. The concept of creativity thus contains partial sub-concepts whose meanings and relationship are theoretically controversial among one another yet based on the same core content. Gallie's idea, although referring to contentions, therefore assumes a certain equilibrium between the respective points of view, not least because each perspective considers its own narrative to be correct, making the actual dominance of a single narrative within the framework of this theory rather unlikely:

> "Each party continues to maintain that the special functions which the term [...] fulfils on its behalf or on its interpretation, is the correct or proper or primary, or the only important, function which the term in question can plainly be said to fulfil. Moreover, each party continues to defend its case with what it claims to be convincing arguments, evidence, and other forms of justification".[9]

Simultaneously, certain members of individual disciplines are well aware of their own limited points of view of creativity as a term. For example, the neuropsychologist Henrik Walter acknowledges that only a part of creativity, namely the process, can be comprehended by his discipline. However, since creativity is not only a "purely individual psychological"[10] phenomenon but is also defined by the recognition of the creatively new, a definition would lie outside the area of competence outlined by neuroscience. Therefore, it seems vital to first present the term's context and to clarify its semantic origin as well as its development before the influence of IT on a fundamental and not only subject-specific basic understanding (in Gallie's sense) of the concept of creativity can be considered in more detail.

Research into creativity was originally established in the field of psychology. After a first appearance by name in 1931 by E. D. Hutchinson[11], the concept of creativity became widely known only after the psychologist J. P. Guilford postulated creativity as a separate field of research in the area of intel-

8 Ibid.

9 Ibid., p. 168.

10 Henrik Walter (2006), p. 595.

11 Eliot D Hutchinson, (1931). Materials for the study of creative thinking. *Psychological Bulletin*, 28(5), p. 392–410.

ligence research in 1950. At a psychology congress as early as 1960, Guilford then claimed that every human being is creative. Only a few years after the broad introduction of the concept of creativity, it was thus already fundamentally democratized in the field of psychology by its most prominent expert to date.

Starting from there, the concept has had an almost unprecedented career in the last decades. Creativity seems to be composed by various notions and related terms (such as *innovation* or *ingenuity*) that are affected by several scientific disciplines and societal fields. In the following, a general overview of research on creativity as well as the paths to it will therefore be presented in order to identify relevant connections to IT with the aim of making a concept of creativity operational for the subsequent analyses regarding a specific creativity narrative of IT.[12]

2.2 CURRENT STATE OF THE DISCOURSE ON CREATIVITY IN IT

The projected dissertation aims to contribute to creativity research at a time when both the creative imperative and the digital transformation meet in the phenomenon of artificial (i.e., or computational) creativity. This *uncreative art*[13] leads back to the ontological question of what constitutes human creativity in the first place and how *natural* (hence: human) and artificial (hence: computational) creativity might differ from each other. In the subsequent attempt to operationalise the concept of natural creativity to its artificial equivalent, the already diffuse discourse on creativity was extended by further narrative perspectives from various special discourses: The being and becoming of humans in times of digital transformation and the advent of smart machines

---

12 Within this work, the term *narrative* is used in a somewhat expanded format. The concept does not only refer to the story-telling ductus (of creativity), but also to its inner impetus. It therefore includes the question of how creativity in IT is conceived, understood and implemented beyond the outward representation. In other words, the term narrative involves both an external descriptive narrative and an inward-looking organisational narrative by means of operationalising the concept of creativity.

13 This was the title given to the concept of artificial creativity in a welcoming lecture on the topic of the same name at the Humboldt Institute for Internet and Society. Cf. Humboldt Institute for Internet and Society, *Digitaler Salon: Zahlen, die malen*, YouTube, posted by Humboldt Institute for Internet and Society, 5th February, 2019, https://www.youtube.com/watch?v=t74H1OVFW-I.

are two examples being discussed and negotiated along to a general debate on the capacity to be or act creative.

Hence, the notion of creativity in IT affects several scientific disciplines and societal fields. The range of contributions to the topic is correspondingly broad: Teresa M. Amabile, decades-long researcher on creativity, points out that if strides are to be made in the sciences, humanities, and arts, a far more detailed understanding of the creative process must be arrived.[14] These strides have actually been made in "an ever-expanding variety of disciplines"[15] but in particular in the field of psychology: amongst other approaches, neuroscientists approximate a mapping of how and where creative cognition is processed in the human brain[16] while further research points to the neurophysiological origin of creativity, demonstrating a connection between daydreaming and creativity.[17] Although science is thus able to get closer towards an understanding of *how* creativity is processed in the human brain, it remains a question *what* creativity actually is.[18] Artificial creativity is an often-involved aspect in thereof resulting debates, which is why IT enterprises attempt to understand artificial creativity by approaching human creativity from different perspectives, such as psychology and neurosciences. With the proclamation to make substantial progresses in the field of artificial creativity[19] the IT sector itself is confronted with a need of comprehension regarding creativity in order to understand and value what *kind* of substantial progress is meant specifically and how it could be evaluated. Answers seem to be a good way off: at the very beginning of her book on computers and creativity *The*

---

14 Teresa M. Amabile and Beth A. Hennessey, "Creativity", *Annual Review of Psychology* 61, January (2010), https://ssrn.com/abstract=1601146.

15 Ibid.

16 Rex E. Jung, Brittany S. Mead, Jessica Carrasco and Ranee Barrow, „The structure of creative cognition in the human brain", *Frontiers in Human Neuroscience* 7: July (2013): 330, doi: 10.3389/fnhum.2013.00330.

17 Scott B. Kaufman, "Dreams of Glory", *Psychology Today*, last modified 11th March, 2014, https://www.psychologytoday.com/us/articles/201403/dreams-glory.

18 Cf. Margaret A. Boden, *The Creative Mind: Myths and Mechanisms* (London: Routledge, 2004).

19 Cf. Amílcar Cardoso, Tony Veale and Geraint A. Wiggins, „Converging on the Divergent: The History (and Future) of the International Joint Workshops in Computational Creativity", *AI Magazine*, Fall 2009, pp. 15-22.

Creative Mind: Myths and Mechanisms, Margaret A. Boden claims that "human creativity is something of a mystery, not to say a paradox".[20]

Boden explicitly does not refer to the usage of creativity here, but to its apprehension. Interest into the latter was pushed aside over time, especially since the end of the 1990s and progressively in the first years of the new millennium. Increasingly, management literature on the subject of creativity – and thus the applicability, the organisation of creativity in the entrepreneurial environment – is booming. The underlying economic connotation of the term creativity perceives the term as a resource that can be transformed into an acquirable skill that consequently ought to be scaled and exploited in the most efficient way.[21]

In this respect, economist Richard Florida can be seen as having been highly successful in promoting this approach with his influential book *The Rise of the Creative Class* from 2002. Florida famously argues that it is the "creative class" that drives regional economic development and essentially determines its prosperity and future viability. This led to a situation where the economic interpretation became the dominant discursive reading of creativity – and with it the exploitation of creativity as a concept in the pursuit of a mere economic ideology of progress, as the rapidly emerging critical response to this understanding of creativity puts it: Cultural scientist and artist Marion von Osten was among those introducing the concept of the *creative imperative*, hence the dictum of not just *aspiring to be creative*, but the *urge to be creative*.[22] Artists, designers, architects, journalists and their kind become the dominant class to strive for. Where the difference between the ability to be creative and the aspiration to be creative already reveals the fundamental desire to promote and make use of creativity, the creative imperative excels in exceeding this desire by making creativity an obligation. A desirable option turns into a requirement without reproach: To not desire to be creative and to not exploit one's own creative potential, as sociologist Andreas Reckwitz presents it in a pointed way, strikes him as an absurd intention "just as it may have been the intention at other times not to be moral, not to be normal or not to be au-

20 Boden, *The Creative Mind: Myths and Mechanisms*, p.1.

21 Peter Koslowski, *Einführung*, in: Abel, G. (Ed.). *Kreativität* (Hamburg: Felix Meiner, 2006), p. 1083.

22 Marion von Osten, *Unberechenbare Ausgänge*, in G. Raunig; U. Wuggenig (Ed.), *Kritik der Kreativität* (Wien: Turia + Kant, 2007)

tonomous".[23] As early as the 1990s, managerial literature prepared the ground for this obligation to be creative. In his well-known book *Leading Change*, for example, American economist and professor of leadership management John Kotter sees the will of management to change not as one possibility among many, but as a necessity without an alternative, due to the increasing speed of newly emerging difficulties and challenges.[24]

Despite such literature, however, the imperative to be creative remained cloaked in a cover made of the inevitable desire to be creative, as expressed not least by many guidebooks and advice literature that assess and promote the aspiration to be creative in a throughout positive and, in this sense, inherently under-complex way. As a result, creativity in general, but especially within the business sphere, would be "thoroughly misunderstood", according to journalist and curator Thomas Edelmann: Instead of creativity, this society constantly indulges in the myth of the amateur, i.e., those "idiotic imitators" of what has already existed for a long time, as he puts it in direct words.[25]

From an economic perspective the *need to be creative* culminates in the ostensible standing rule that "creativity and innovation in any organisation are vital to its successful performance"[26], as stated in a comprehensive review on the state of both innovation and creativity in companies.

Following this economic logic, creativity must be thoroughly organised in order to be able to produce it and use it as fuel, as a quantifiable raw material. The organisation comprises both the geographical and architectural conditions of potentially creative ways of working as well as the selection, implementation and performance of respective types of work. The geographical focus on urban centres is specific at first, known as *creative cities*.

The term *creative city* is coined by Charles Landry, who engaged urban creativity through his studies in the UK and Germany in 1990 and 1994. According to Landry, the term was preconfigured in a 1988 agenda by former Australian Minister for Planning and Environment in Victoria, David Yencken, who suggested that a city should be emotionally satisfying and stimulate the creativity

23 Reckwitz, *Die Erfindung der Kreativität*, p. 9.

24 Cf. John Kotter, *Leading Change*, (Boston: Harvard Business School Press, 1996), p. 161.

25 Thomas Edelmann, *Kreativität ist nur ein Wort – Wie Design zum Vorbild wurde*, in: Jarchow, M. (Ed.). *Kreativität in Gestaltungsprozessen*, (Neumünster: Wachholtz, 2011), p. 21-40.

26 Neil Anderson, Kristina Potočnik and Jing Zhou, *Innovation and Creativity in Organizations: A State-of-the-Science Review, Prospective Commentary, and Guiding Framework*, Journal of Management 40, no. 5 (2014): 1297–1333, doi:10.1177/0149206314527128.

of its citizens.[27] Richard Florida then introduced the concept of *creative cities* as an essential component of his theory on the creative class. In it, the question of reciprocal effects and developments among cities and those active in the creative class is addressed.[28] Accordingly, the transformations of cities into creative hubs with an increased economic wealth is credited to members of the creative class, which are specifically known for their increased mobility. Other types of labour are initially excluded from this process. Due to the creative class' increased mobility, members would tend to concentrate in certain metropolises, so that the term *creative cities* essentially refers to densely populated, urban centres.[29] The transformation of cities is expressed through new forms and structures of work seeping into town pictures – such as the *co-working spaces*, which favour to be situated in *creative cities*.[30]

Yet, even before Florida further popularised the concept of *creative cities*, research had already been conducted on this topic. The study "The Creative Community – Leveraging Creativity and Cultural Participation for Silicon Valley's Economic and Civic Future" from 2001 is an example of how creativity was seen from an economic perspective around the turn of the millennium and how attempts were made to organise it. Furthermore, it is particularly important with regard to the topic of creativity in IT. For this reason, I will go into some relevant aspects of the working paper above mentioned in more detail. The study, prepared by the think tank "Collaborative Economics", explores the questions of why it is important for Silicon Valley to become a so-called *creative community* and what constitutes such a community in the first place. In a further step, the study is intended to contribute to the creation of an index capable of "the identification and development of quantitative measures of progress".[31] Although suggestions are made on how to measure creativ-

---

27 Cf. Charles Landry, *The creative city: A toolkit for urban innovators*, (London: Earthscan, 2012).

28 Cf. Richard Florida, *Cities and the Creative Class* (New York: Routledge, 2005).

29 Stefan A. Jansen, *Magnetismus der Metropole als Stätte der Kreativen. Ein Überblick bildungs-, migrations-, politikökonomischer Analysen zur Dynamisierung von Metropolen*, in: Jansen, S. A.; Schröter, E.; Stehr, N. (Ed.). *Rationalität der Kreativität?*, (Wiesbaden: VS, 2009), p. 67-92.

30 The concept of co-working spaces and its connection to the specific creativity narrative of IT is examined in more detail in chapter 6.1.2

31 Kim Walesh & Doug Henton, *The creative community-leveraging creativity and cultural participation for Silicon Valley's economic and civic future*, (San Jose: Collaborative Economics, 2001), p. 1.

ity (for example, through cultural participation or cultural outcome) the very last sentence of the paper then reads "How would you measure progress?", identifying a difficulty in grasping creativity as a measurable resource.[32] Although the (quantitative) measurability of creativity was defined as a goal, the actual implementation of such a measure therefore remained largely undefined. Furthermore, the study is noteworthy for a number of reasons that, collectively, once again highlight the complexity and definitional ambiguity of the concept of creativity – especially with regard to the IT economy, as in this case by focusing on the Silicon Valley. The study first noted that there is an opportunity:

> "to spark a "Regional Renaissance" in Silicon Valley that evolves Silicon Valley into the world's first true Creative City-Region, where creativity leads not only to continued technological excellence, but to artistic, cultural, and civic innovation. The region can be the first in history to consciously develop and connect creative capacity across business and cultural realms."[33]

Interestingly, Silicon Valley as of 2001 is not yet considered truly creative by the authors of this study. To gain this attribution, a region like Silicon Valley requires not only technological innovation, but also cultural creativity. It is therefore remarkable that different forms of creativity are distinguished, which are capable of combining their respective capacities, but do not mean the same and are represented by different groups. More precisely and based on the works of the urbanist Peter Hall, the study distinguishes between *Technological and Business Innovation* which "is about devising new products, services, technologies, industries, and ways of doing business" (such as the semiconductor, the entrepreneur, or the Internet), *Artistic and Cultural Innovation* because creativity "is also (sic!) about advancing the fine and the performing arts, literature, commercial arts, popular culture, and avocational or amateur arts" (such as new forms of literature, music, or other forms of aesthetic expressions) and *Civic Innovation* that "has produced a range of public innovations in the built environment and in social institutions" (such as the subway, social security, or democratic institutions).[34] This distinction once again underlines the application-oriented character of the study, giving the authors

32 Ibid., p. 15.

33 Walesh, *The creative community-leveraging creativity and cultural participation for Silicon Valley's economic and civic future*, p. 1.

34 Ibid., p.4.

the advantage of being able to limit themselves to examples of results relating to the respective manifestation of creativity. According to the authors, however, it is especially the combination of all three distinguishable types of creativity that seems to be crucial "for securing the Valley's long-term economic and civic achievement"[35] so that "the joint evolution of technological and cultural creativity may prove not just interesting but essential".[36] To address the question of feasibility the study continues to refer to Peter Hall, whose "landmark book" *Cities in Civilization* strives to answer the question "What makes for a creative city?".[37] Despite the same wording, Hall never had the impact Florida received shortly after. Interestingly, Richard Florida does not refer to Peter Hall at any point in *The Rise of the Creative Class*. Only in a note at the end of the book Hall's *Cities in Civilization* is mentioned as marginalia, which shows that Florida at least took note of Hall's works.[38] In Florida's even more resembling subsequent book *Cities and the Creative Class* there is no more reference to Hall to be found.

The study, which aims to transform Silicon Valley into the first truly creative region, retains Hall's work in its formulation of "common factors of creative cities" at which a distinction between cultural and technological creative cities is consequently maintained.

Conditioned by the advent of the creative imperative, creativity was highlighted as a central skill of the working subject so that the concept could fundamentally break free from its mystically transfigured heritage represented by a cult of genius.[39] Instead, it has been commodified by the economic mindsets inherent in the creative industries: The study on creativity in Silicon Valley discussed above, emphasises that "we often think of creativity as the province of the exceptional individual – the creative genius", however "research and experience also show that everyone has the ability to create and that creativity is also a collaborative process".[40] Paradoxically and despite the democratic

---

35 Ibid.

36 Walesh, *The creative community-leveraging creativity and cultural participation for Silicon Valley's economic and civic future*, p. 3.

37 Ibid.

38 Richard Florida, *The Rise of the Creative Class, Revisited* (New York: Basic Books, 2012), p. 451.

39 Hannes Krämer, *Praktiken kreativen Arbeitens in den Creative Industries*, in: Göttlich, U.; Kurt, R. (Ed.). *Kreativität und Improvisation*, (Wiesbaden: Springer VS, 2012), p. 109.

40 Walesh, *The creative community-leveraging creativity and cultural participation for Silicon Valley's economic and civic future*, p. 5.

nature of this universal capacity, organising the narrative of creativity continues to be fuelled by the idea of an individual genius. In spite of the creative imperative's weight, the idea of individual genius has nonetheless surpassed the general democratisation of the term and continues to exist in parallel. IT comes to the fore here: for a long time, the late Steve Jobs was the archetype, but for some time now business blogs, pages on business success and the like have been referring to personalities such as Elon Musk or the Chinese entrepreneur and founder of Amazon competitor Alibaba Jack Ma. These narratives are usually loaded with references to the *natural*, unspoiled genius who left university after a short time to found a company, thus already carrying the knowledge for this endeavour within him or herself.[41]

Further attempts of explaining and approaching the concept of creativity derive from a contemporary *philosophical IT* that aims to evaluate and question IT's influences on both society and human beings. Protagonists are IT experts with roots in the counterculture of the 1960s and its related hacker movement, such as computer scientist and artist Jaron Lanier, renowned computer scientist and cultural journalist David Gelernter or the neuroscientist and founder of Palm Computing Jeff Hawkins, of which the latter addresses creativity as "a necessary component of prediction"[42] and thus "a challenge to the entire idea of building intelligent machines.[43] In the wake of these developments, there is a concern that artificial systems could harm humans if they were too autonomous and unconstrained. It is pointed out "that these systems are likely to behave in anti-social and harmful ways unless they are very carefully designed".[44] The IT sector itself takes these concerns quite serious and establishes countermeasures such as Google's ethics council. As a consequence, the company's set of principles includes clearly defined objectives for AI and

41 The extent to which the development of the European idea of genius is known, especially in Anglo-Saxon contributions, remains unclear. Presumably, however, no deliberate reference is intended. Cf. on this only Jochen Schmidt, *Die Geschichte des Genie-Gedankens in der deutschen Literatur, Philosophie und Politik 1750-1945*, (Darmstadt: Wissenschaftliche Buchgesellschaft, 1985).

42 Jeff Hawkins and Sandra Blakeslee, *On Intelligence* (New York: Times Books, 2004), p. 123.

43 Ibid.

44 Steve Omohundro, "Autonomous technology and the greater human good", *Journal of Experimental & Theoretical Artificial Intelligence* 26, no. 3 (2014): 303, doi: 10.1080/0952813X.2014.895111.

even identifies those applications Google will not pursue.[45] These formulations go back to a series of internal disputes that questioned the company's stand on ethics and its former official motto *don't be evil*, underlining the difficult and tense dynamics between IT, politics and society, which is therefore of importance with regard to the creativity narrative of IT.[46]

IBM, as a second example, underlines the importance of AI machines giving people good reasons to trust them – albeit the concept of trust is understood here as transparency and control.[47] This led to the creation of the "Partnership on AI" in 2017, which brings together 90 different institu-

---

45 These applications include AI technologies that "cause or are likely to cause overall harm", weapons, applications that "gather or use information for surveillance violating internationally accepted norms" and the rather openly formulated technologies "whose purpose contravenes widely accepted principles of international law and human rights". Cf. Google, "Artificial Intelligence at Google: Our Principles," *Google AI*, [accessed 9th April, 2019], https://ai.google/principles. Google also mentions that it wants to approach its aims with prudence and "humility". Cf. Ibid.

46 In particular, the dynamic refers to the field of tension between management and employees, politics and society - as can be seen from the background story of Google's *AI Principles*: already in 2006, Google received a lot of opposition from employees when it launched a censored version of its search engine in China, as employees saw the company's principles in terms that they "were supposed to make the world's information universally accessible, not suppress it", with the consequence of Google leaving the Chinese market in 2010. Yet, two months after a first version of the above listed principles were published, Google was said to try secretly again establishing a censored search engine (named Dragonfly) in China (which would have blacklisted terms like *human rights* or *air quality*) and again encountered massive opposition by employees when they learned about the previously leaked plan. Politically right-wing critics now also joined in and accused Google of being "un-American". In consequence, Google's CEO had to defend the company's stance on an official hearing, leading to senator Elizabeth Warren's "plan to break up Big Tech" and the American President Donald Trump tweeting "Google is helping China and their military, but not the U.S. Terrible!". Cf. Nitasha Tiku, "Three years of misery inside Google, the happiest company in tech", *Wired*, last modified 13th August, 2019, https://www.wired.com/story/inside-google-three-years-misery-happiest-company-tech/; Issie Lapowsky, "Elizabeth Warren fires a warning shot at big tech", *Wired*, last modified 8th March, 2019, https://www.wired.com/story/elizabeth-warren-break-up-amazon-facebook-google/.

47 IBM, "Trusting AI", *IBM AI Research*, [accessed 7th May, 2019], https://www.research.ibm.com/artificial-intelligence/trusted-ai/.

tions (with Apple, Amazon, Google, Facebook, IBM, and Microsoft as founding partners).[48]

Most often, however, the narrative of creativity in IT and its attributed effects on both the individual and society are reported rather affirmatively from IT and its related associations and groups of interest. *Fast Company magazine*, for example, a magazine focusing on technology, business and design, published a whole issue entitled "How to Unleash Creativity".[49] Leaders of IT companies seem to confirm the relevance of creativity for their corporations. Bill Gates, founder of Microsoft, gave a radio speech with a very similar title already a few years earlier (*Unleashing the Power of Creativity*)[50] and Ed Catmull, president of Pixar Animation wrote a book about his company entitled "Creativity, Inc.".[51] Catmull in particular, but Gates and others in general too, hence use the discursively prevailing positive image of creativity to project it onto their IT companies with the help of an image transfer.

In direct contrast to this affirmative perspective, diametrically opposed mindsets exist. On the one hand, these are IT entrepreneurs who have an affinity for technology and deal with concepts in the field of post- and transhumanism, as well as the so-called technological singularity.[52] On the other hand, there is an academic community that takes a much more critical stance on the tech scene and its current technological developments.

In the presence of large IT companies and somewhat overwhelming technologies, certain IT experts such as Jaron Lanier feel an unease, stating no-

---

48 Eric Horvitz and Mustafa Suleyman, "Introduction from the Founding Co-Chairs", *Partnership on AI*, last modified 28th September, 2016, https://www.partnershiponai.org/introduction-from-the-founding-co-chairs/.

49 Fast Company, http://www.fastcompany-digital.com/fastcompany/201404?pg=1#pg1.

50 Cf. Bill Gates, "Unleashing the Power of Creativity,"*National Public Radio*, last modified 19th September, 2005, http://www.npr.org/templates/story/story.php?storyId=4853839.

51 Edwin Catmull, *Creativity, Inc.: Overcoming the Unseen Forces That Stand in the Way of True Inspiration* (New York: Random House, 2014).

52 The concept of technological singularity describes a predicted point at which machines and AIs can independently develop themselves further, which, due to the expected exponential development, will then lead to a very rapid, radical change in the history of mankind. Cf. Ben Goertzel, "AI Can Help Create a Better World – If We Build it Right", *SingularityHub*, last modified 13th August, 2018, https://singularityhub.com/2018/08/13/ai-can-help-create-a-better-world-if-we-build-it-right./.

tions like "You alone are Google over all the kingdoms of the earth".[53] US-based economist Shoshana Zuboff asks whether technology could replace humans and stated: "a sense of doom and helplessness has planted itself in our public conversation".[54] Most recently, Zuboff described the current state of affairs as the *age of surveillance capitalism*, stating: "the entangled dilemmas of knowledge, authority, and power are no longer confined to workplaces as they were in the 1980s. Now their roots run deep through the necessities of daily life, mediating nearly every form of social participation".[55] In her work, Zuboff explicitly mentions large IT companies such as Google as usurpers for surveillance capitalism: IT not only prepares the stage for the project of digitisation, but also creates a world in which they are in charge and act as both creators and administrators. Zuboff asks about "the very possibility of a human future in a digital world".[56] According to her, the current logic of IT supports the "rapid mutation into a voracious and utterly novel commercial project"[57] that she calls *surveillance capitalism*, making her one of the fiercest (and most vocal) critics of the IT sector.

Hence, the bewilderment about technological developments ranges from categorical demonization to apologetic deification. Standpoints rarely seem to be in the balanced middle, but rather at the outer edges of two extreme poles.

Yet in works on social creativity research, IT in general and large tech companies and their protagonists in particular are perceived only as marginal discursive actors.[58] Besides, the concept of creativity is being discussed in

---

53 Jaron Lanier, "Whoever owns our data will determine our fate",*Frankfurter Allgemeine Zeitung*, last modified 24th April, 2014, https://www.faz.net/aktuell/feuilleton/debatten/the-digital-debate/almighty-google-whoever-owns-our-data-will-determine-our-fate-12908348.html.

54 Shoshana Zuboff, „The human factor", *Frankfurter Allgemeine Zeitung*, last modified 18th July, 2014, https://www.faz.net/aktuell/feuilleton/debatten/the-digital-debate/digital-economy-the-human-factor-13050472.html.

55 Shoshana Zuboff, *The age of surveillance capitalism: the fight for a human future at the new frontier of power* (New York: PublicAffairs, 2018), p. 7.

56 Ibid., p. 10.

57 Ibid.

58 An exception might be the research on so-called collective creativity, where growing interdisciplinarity is taken into account to shift focus from research from individual creativity towards collective. Cf. Satu Parjanen, "Experiencing Creativity in the Organization: From Individual Creativity to Collective Creativity", *Interdisciplinary Journal of Information, Knowledge, and Management* 7 (2012).

a rather figurative sense and is more likely to tacitly resonate than to be discussed explicitly in social analyses that take greater account of the phenomenon of digitisation. Here, too, IT remains in the rough when digitisation in the broader sense is indeed identified as a constitutive-transformative process for today's societies, whereas digital technologies in bond with their creators always remain comparatively abstract and approximate (*the* digital transformation; *the* technology), though, as the following paragraphs outline.

Marion von Osten analysed the coherence between the new economy and creative industries, but this aspect only contains a partial area of overall IT.[59] Von Osten challenges the existence of the creative industries: although they are an intended requirement and an area of political visions, creative industries are, in her view, yet to come. They are only rudimentarily established in certain countries like Germany or Great Britain, the source of a discourse on creative industries – despite its attempt to privatise the cultural sector in every respect.[60] However, she is not directly connecting the concept of creative industries with a narrative of creativity in IT, neither does she discuss individual protagonists from the IT sector directly.

Sociology in particular diagnoses the present as a period of social change and fundamental transformation and ascribes a leading role in this to digitisation (and its semantic equivalents, such as *technology*). However, the role of IT companies as well as their leading figures themselves fall short of analysing the impact of digital transformation. Andreas Reckwitz indeed considered these in his analyses. He mentions Steve Jobs and Marc Zuckerberg by name and concedes them the ability to act as *stars* and *creative folks* in one of his most influential works known in English as *The Invention of Creativity: Modern Society and the Culture of the New*.[61] Nonetheless, he only symbolises them as rare examples of businessmen becoming famous within the scope of an extended *system of celebrities* and does not take their field of expertise, the IT sector, into considerable account.[62] Following on from *The Invention of Creativ-*

---

59 Marion von Osten, „Unberechenbare Ausgänge", in *Kritik der Kreativität*, eds. Gerald Raunig and Ulf Wuggenig (Wien: Turia + Kant, 2007).

60 Ibid.

61 Andreas Reckwitz, *Die Erfindung der Kreativität* (Frankfurt am Main: Suhrkamp, 2012), p. 264f. The English version has first been published in 2017.

62 Reckwitz separates the historical formation towards an omnipresent creative need into four single phases. The last of them starts in the 1980s by virtue of the creative industries, a psychology on creativity and a *system of stars*, among other aspects. Although he thus involves a wide spectrum to establish a hegemonic notion of creativity, he ex-

ity,[63] Andreas Reckwitz attempts a general theory of a contemporary form of society, which he calls the *Society of Singularities*. The claim to develop a general theory on the state of society is sufficient to subject the work to a closer examination in order to illustrate the role of IT in this. Reckwitz considers the concept of singularity almost as a neologism but at least as a very scattered term, regarding the term of singularity as unused.[64] In particular, Reckwitz does not deal with Ray Kurzweil's quite prevalent connotation of singularity. Instead, he only mentions (in a footnote) that the term is used differently by him than in the context of research into artificial intelligence or transhumanism as represented by Kurzweil.[65] Reckwitz' main thesis presumes a social structural change takes place in late modernity, where the social logic of the general loses its predominance to the social logic of the particular.[66] Accordingly, we no longer live in industrial capitalism, but in cultural capitalism.[67] In the mode of singularisation, life is not simply lived. It is *curated*. The late modern subject performs the seemingly special self, with other people acting as audiences.[68] However, and still according to Reckwitz, not only individuals or things but also collectives become singularised.[69] The social logic of the particular affects all dimensions of the social: things and objects as well as temporalities.[70] For Reckwitz, this is without precedent in world history:

---

cludes influences of the rise of the Internet from his study and disregards most relevant aspects of the related IT industry – despite its significant rise in this period of time. Reckwitz has neither taken a possible affiliation of the IT sector to the creative industries nor the importance of IT protagonists for the concept of an extended *star system* (system of celebrities) into account. Ibid. pp. 52f.

63 To a certain extent, Reckwitz sees his current work as a continuation of his work on the invention of creativity since the structural features he examines were already present in the first work. According to Reckwitz, however, the focus changes: whereas the historical genealogy was at the centre in his book on creativity, it now has a social-theoretical claim. Cf. Andreas Reckwitz, *Die Gesellschaft der Singularitäten* (Berlin: Suhrkamp, 2017), p. 24.

64 Moreover, and despite his claim to use an *unused* term, Reckwitz adds more examples and states that he explicitly does not refer to the historical dictionary of philosophy or to the poststructuralist school of Derrida, Deleuze, Nancy and Negri. Cf. ibid., p. 47.

65 Cf. ibid., p. 11.

66 Cf. ibid.

67 Cf. Reckwitz, *Die Gesellschaft der Singularitäten*, p. 8.

68 Cf. ibid., p. 9.

69 Cf. ibid., p. 57.

70 Cf. ibid., p. 12.

the social logic of singularity since the 1970s and 1980s completely contradicts what has been the core of modern society for over 200 years.[71]

Reckwitz identifies two areas as the causes of this: the economy and technology. The creative economy became the leading industry, and with the digital revolution *a technology* became dominant that is no longer merely standardised.[72] Reckwitz abstractly sticks to the concept of *technology* (Reckwitz uses the singular), without admitting any responsibility to the companies behind these technologies (here deliberately thought in the plural to cope with the complexity of the digital and its numerous creators). To some extent, *the technology* is now present in Reckwitz' approach of a general theory and subject to negotiation – but without the designers of these technologies having a say in the discourse about their creations and their impact on society. IT hardly appears as an actor.

Sociologist Dirk Baecker attempts a similar path to that of Reckwitz and tries to create an *experimental balloon to diagnose the current state of society* [73] – a society that doesn't know what's happening to it.[74] Because, Baecker says, there's a lot at stake. For him, the contemporary digital change is the fourth profound change after the *adventures* of oralisation, literacy and literarisation, all of which were no less overwhelming to society.[75] But as Reckwitz, Baecker does not directly address the role of IT companies themselves (let alone the specific narrative of creativity), although he attests society a progressive attitude in relation to technology and therefore considers a large number of IT-relevant issues in 26 theses.[76]

These examples indicate how the influence of IT is underrepresented in past and current socio-theoretical studies. They either deal individually with digitisation, AI, creativity or IT, or combine these topics, such as AI with creativity (artificial creativity) or digitisation, AI and IT (e.g., Zuboff's *surveillance capitalism*) or creativity with IT and digitisation (economic-affirmative

71 Cf. ibid., p. 14.

72 Cf. ibid., p. 16.

73 Dirk Baecker, *4.0 oder die Lücke die der Rechner lässt* (Merve Verlag: Leipzig, 2018), p. 10.

74 Ibid., p. 266.

75 Ibid., p. 10.

76 As an example, Baecker specifically deals with the issue of communicating with machines. He argues that there is no longer any discussion today of how artificial intelligence can copy and surpass human intelligence. Instead, the specific intelligence of machines can be networked and interconnected with the different kinds of intelligence of bodies, brains, consciousness and society. Ibid., p. 17.

and organisational perspective). Beyond the latter, however, creativity in IT is not given much attention, especially not from a rather critical, at least not affirmative perspective on digitisation and its effects on society and the individual, even though the synergy effects of creativity and the creations of IT in particular are growing in analytical popularity, as demonstrated not least by the above-mentioned debates on creative industries. Many of the contributions played a decisive role in shaping the discourse on creativity and digital transformation – without the anticipated specific and decisive narrative of creativity for IT advancing from the indistinct into the open.

2.3 HYPOTHESES

The state of research on creativity and IT shows that both concepts (the latter is not limited to companies or protagonists but includes technological products and services) have a significant influence on the current way of being, working and thinking in Western cultures and beyond. Both terms simultaneously represent hope and belief in progress as well as concern and a certain discomfort. With reference to the previous chapter, it becomes apparent how both the concept of creativity and IT (or rather the technologies they create) dominate the discourses about the present being in Western societies. The sheer presence of both concepts would hardly exclude the possibility of them overlapping or being conditional in one way or another. However, this is neither reflected nor considered sufficiently in current literature. It is therefore the aim of this thesis to uncover the creativity narrative in IT, i.e., the semantics and organisation of creativity within IT enterprises.

A fundamental assumption is at the heart of this, which forms the foundation of the subsequent analyses in the sense of a main hypothesis, which reads as follows:

The narrative of creativity in large IT companies equals the predominant meaning of the term creativity.

I therefore proceed from the assumption that both concepts (IT and creativity) are in fact not only interdependent, but that IT has contributed significantly to the current imprinting of a general understanding of creativity and is still doing so.

Five further hypotheses can be identified in this core hypothesis, which together are capable of providing a more precise account of causes and effects of the main hypothesis:

1) Creativity has gone from hype to a matter of course and is less present within the discourse in a literal sense but rather subtle and tacit.
2) Due to its technical developments the IT remains omnipresent, hence IT's narrative expression and self-understanding is still the dominant understanding of creativity.
3) For the creativity narrative in IT, creativity is a precondition for quantifiable success. What success means is defined by IT.
4) Moreover, creativity is a purposive vehicle for a logic that acts totally in its core.
5) In IT, creativity is staged in a unique way and thus masks the uniforming nature of IT.

3 METHODOLOGY – HEURISTIC TENDENCIES WITHIN THE DISSERTATION

This dissertation examines and analyses the narrative of creativity in IT from a discourse analytical perspective. The thesis is therefore not intended to make a further attempt at defining a concept of creativity and neither aims to extend the numerous already existing proposals on creativity. It rather aims to expose the processes of (1) how creativity is *organised* and (2) how it is *understood* in large tech companies. This *organised* and *understood* thus means the expression and the corresponding effect of a discursive truth through a certain narrative.[1] As creativity is an evaluative term, it does not describe the term to a (supposed) quality of human and organisational action. Further, it has an ambiguous meaning since it is used with reference to very different theoretical understandings and discourses. The question of what creativity is does therefore not seem to be a suitable one, since questions about the "what" evoke rather essentialist answers. The interpretative and evaluative attribution of approaching the concept of creativity represents a suitable vehicle to abandon the deterministic question of *what* creativity is. Instead, the questions of *how-*, *when-*, *by whom-* and *why creativity* move in order to capture the practical situation (i.e., the actors, institutions and constellations) and the discursive context.

1 For a more accurate comprehension, an analogy to artificial creativity research can be made, as an early approach towards the term defined artificial creativity in a way that places the impression of creativity above the question of what creativity actually is: "Computational Creativity is the study and simulation, by computational means, of behaviour, natural and artificial, which would, if observed in humans, be deemed creative. Cf. Anna Jordanous, "A Standardised Procedure for Evaluating Creative Systems: Computational Creativity Evaluation Based on What it is to be Creative", *Cognitive Computation* 4, no. 3 (2012): p. 248, doi: https://doi.org/10.1007/s12559-012-9156-1.

This kind of approach pursues an approximation rather than a clarity of definition. This is an essential reason for the decision to discursively grasp the phenomenon of creativity in IT.

Therefore, and before the methodical approach as well as the further structure of this thesis are to be presented, I would like to emphasise the reasons that lead to a discourse analytical approach, as they can help to arrange and hence narrow down the otherwise very broad field of topics that are affected by my carried-out procedure.

3.1 WHY DISCOURSE

The discursive approach to the concept of creativity in IT has certain advantages in itself. The concept of creativity is as diffuse as it is ubiquitous. It is overly complex in its number of possible understandings, as well as underly complex in these very understandings – at least if it is meant to be a common and collective one. The meaning and entanglement of creativity in IT is therefore not comprehensible if only referring to *the* discourse on creativity in IT. This is also due to the fact that secondary literature was unable to generate a handy concept of discourse from Foucault's writings. Discourse analysis enables a multiplying view; therefore, it becomes possible to perceive the complexity of the concept of creativity with regard to IT. Discussing discourse analysis, the term toolbox sometimes comes up from which the appropriate tools can be chosen and used.[2] Over time, the toolbox became larger

2 See Brigitte Kerchner and Silke Schneider, „'Endlich Ordnung in der Werkzeugkiste'. Zum Potenzial der Foucaultschen Diskursanalyse für die Politikwissenschaft - Einleitung", in *Foucault: Diskursanalyse der Politik*, in eds. Brigitte Kerchner and Silke Schneider (Wiesbaden: VS Verlag für Sozialwissenschaften, 2006), p. 9. This source can also be found in a footnote section at Klaus Röhl, "Diszipliniert Foucault: (K)ein Hammer, genannt Diskurs", *RSOZBLOG.de, Weblog von Prof. em. Dr. Klaus F. Röhl, Ruhr-Universität Bochum* (blog), last modified 16th March, 2015, https://www.rsozblog.de/diszipliniert-foucault-kein-hammergenannt-diskurs/#fn4-3465. However, Röhl himself considers it interesting how the Foucault reception converges over such standard quotations, by mostly referring to (and quoting) themselves, therefore creating core sentences of secondary origin. Cf. ibid.

and more versatile. The initially vague methodological approach to discourses evolved into a large number of analytical approaches.[3]

It therefore appears to be appropriate to initially address the concept of discourse in more detail. For both discourse and creativity are concepts of greater magnitude than could be left as such: the concept of discourse is all too diverse and fragmented that no more precise specification is needed, and the concept of creativity is too diffuse and charged to refer to something like *the* discourse on creativity in large IT enterprises without further remarks (this relates – as will be shown – not only to the quantities of discourses, but also to their quality, their type). For a better discursive orientation, the concept of discourse[4] itself will be dealt with as opposed to focusing on the analytical part of discourse. According to Gardt, the concept of discourse can be considered in three categories: theory, method and stance.[5] However, theory will only be of inferior relevance in this section.

Concerning the theory only the following: the discursive consideration of this work's topic is based on the concept of discourse introduced by Foucault.[6] This allows for a certain perspective that would not have been feasible or hardly accessible otherwise, as the discourse of creativity in IT does not only describe but determines. It defines and constitutes a social reality of

3 According to Keller, (private talk in Berlin) it is also allowed to select comparatively liberal from these offerings.

4 The concept of discourse within this dissertation essentially follows Michel Foucault's conceptions and subsequent research.

5 Andreas Gardt, "Diskursanalyse–Aktueller theoretischer Ort und methodische Möglichkeiten", in *Diskurslinguistik nach Foucault. Theorie und Gegenstände*, ed. Ingo H. Warnke (Berlin/New York: de Gruyter, 2007), p. 23. Gardt further notes that although the concept of discourse appears in very different research directions, there are various similarities among them. To him, a discourse is, in summary, a discussion of a topic that is reflected in statements and texts of all kinds, that is supported by more or less large social groups, that both reflects and actively shapes the knowledge and attitudes of these groups to the topic in question and thus has a guiding effect on the future shaping of social reality. Ibid., p. 26.

6 Jürgen Habermas in particular also uses the concept of discourse, but in a completely different way. According to Jürgen Link, two opposing concepts collide with a loud bang in the word discourse. With reference to Habermas and Foucault, he proposes to distinguish between *discourse (h)* and *discourse (f)*.

what a concept of creativity can be and has become.[7] It shapes the very thing it describes.[8]

Concerning the analysis and in order to create structure in the various strands of discourse related to creativity in IT, a further differentiation is needed. Following Jürgen Link, a distinction between special discourses and interdiscourses can be applied. The special discourse is oriented towards Foucault's understanding of discourse: it is about special areas of knowledge that regulate and institutionalize knowledge. Direct access to discourse is reserved for particularly legitimate actors.[9] A special discourse is predominantly a scientific discourse, such as the technical debate about the concept of creativity in the development of artificial creativity represents, whose technical language (i.e., knowledge) can only be legitimately pronounced by IT engineers and scientists. The example of artificial creativity, however, shows that the topic is not covered by one single special discourse. Instead, numerous special discourses address the concept in their respective angles. Together they form a heterogeneous and interdisciplinary *field*, with technical disciplines such as electrical engineering or computer science, as well as neurosciences or psychology and the popular scientific risk assessment of artificial creativity. In addition, a public awareness of the special discourses arises above a certain size. Due to the number and diversity of special discourses on one topic, they overlap and do not remain isolated. The discursive environment increasingly detaches itself from being single special discourses alone and extends into an interdiscourse.[10] The interdiscourse is hybrid and comprises the knowledge of individual special discourses. It is a streamlining, thus mediating type of discourse that is therefore able to produce common knowledge, used on a day-to-day basis. The interdiscourse forms the everyday subjective evaluation or descriptive expression of a term's presumed general understanding without

---

7 This argumentation follows Dietrich Schwanitz' notes on Foucault's discourse theory. However, the question of the extent to which discourses represent or constitute reality are treated with different accentuations depending on the definitions. Cf. Gardt, „Diskursanalyse–Aktueller theoretischer Ort und methodische Möglichkeiten", p. 27.

8 Jürgen Link, "Noch einmal: Diskurs. Interdiskurs. Macht", *kultuRRevolution. Zeitschrift für angewandte Diskurstheorie*, no. 11 (1986): p. 5.

9 Ibid., p. 4.

10 As already mentioned briefly, the term *interdiscourse* (*Interdiskurs*) is coined by the German literary scholar and discourse researcher Jürgen Link. Due to his research focus and collaboration with Siegfried Jäger, interdiscourse initially found particular use in historical discourse analysis and critical discourse analysis (CDA).

it being clearly defined or described. In addition to special discourses, society therefore needs an interdiscourse that (extremely selectively) reintegrates special discourses into the social debate. Interdiscourses are what cultures are based on.[11] Yet, special discourses do not cease to be obsolete under the roof of an interdiscourse but continue to exist as such. Rather, they affect the interdiscourse in a variety of ways, sometimes more, sometimes less intensive.[12]

Hence, if *the* discourse on creativity in major IT enterprises is mentioned without further explanation in the following course, it refers first and foremost to the interdiscourse, taking into account all special discourses as they too have a home in the concept of discourse presented here.[13] In addition, the interdiscourse not only accommodates all the participants of the special discourses but adds many other actors with different levels of knowledge about both the discourse itself and the respective specialist discourses. Similarly, observers and participants of the interdiscourse may have an affinity to certain special discourses without being part of these.

Discourse thus helps not only to uncover the semantics and organisation of creativity in IT, but also permits a particular reflection driven by a certain stance. For a more detailed explanation of *stance*, Gardt uses a dichotomy that Noam Chomsky has made his subject: the distinction between a descriptive and explanatory approach. Descriptive, for Chomsky, only refers to the surface structure of a phenomenon whereas an explanatory approach focuses on

11 Link, „Noch einmal: Diskurs. Interdiskurs. Macht".

12 There is, however, a third type of discourse in Links disposition, called the elementary discourse (*Elementardiskurs*). Waldschmidt et al. point out that in comparison to the other two types of discourses described by Link, the elementary discourse is not as elaborate as the descriptions of special- and interdiscourse, with a boundary to the concept of interdiscourse remaining indistinct to a certain degree. Cf. Anne Waldschmidt et al., "Discourse in Everyday Life – The Everyday Life of Discourse: Towards an Empirical Grounded Methodology of Discourse Research in Social Sciences," *Forum Qualitative Research* 8, no. 2 (2007). According to Link, the elementary discourse is fed both by of historical-specific knowledge with strongly reduced complexity and by anthropological everyday knowledge. For this dissertation, anthropological everyday knowledge is included within the concept of interdiscourse. This follows Siegfried Jäger (1997), who does not mention the third type of discourse at all but only distinguishes between special discourses and interdiscourses.

13 The awareness of the special discourse' participants of the possibility to simultaneously be participants of a superordinate interdiscourse is of course not necessarily given and cannot be assumed.

the underlying principles.[14] It is this reflexive focus on underlying principles that this dissertation strives for and the reason for using the following approaches, gathered under the discourse-analytical umbrella as a mixed set of methods.

3.2 APPROACH

In the following, the structure and the methodical approach of this dissertation is outlined. In Chapter 4, the context in which the topic is positioned is first laid out and explained. This will reveal the distinctive quality of the discourse on creativity in IT and at the same time underline the relevance as well as the contemporary nature of the topic.

Following the contextual positioning, the evolution of the concept of creativity in IT in relation to time will grasp the term in change by means of a diachronic analysis, exploring historical prerequisite[15] and identifying which ideas of creativity are used in IT and how they complement or replace each other. To this end, a distinction is made between the geosocial development on the one hand and the self-portrait of IT on the other hand. Silicon Valley can be identified as a geosocial nucleus and is examined here for its inimitable factors (by means of events, actors, political and social implications, to name but a few) that decisively determined the development of the creativity narrative in IT. Subsequently, the diachronic analysis detaches itself from the geographical location and focuses on those aspects in the course of time that have shaped the specific narrative beyond the influence of the Silicon Valley. These are rather external factors and developments in society as a whole all

---

14 For Chomsky, explanatory work is superior to 'only' descriptive work, because only then does linguistics become 'true science', as Gardt points out. Cf. Gardt, „Diskursanalyse–Aktueller theoretischer Ort und methodische Möglichkeiten." Cf. Noam Chomsky, "On the Nature, Use and Acquisition of Language, in *Mind and Cognition*, ed. William G. Lycan (Cambridge, Mass.: Basil Blackwell, 1990).

15 It should be noted that diachronic analysis is not synonymous with historical analysis. Diachrony is therefore not necessarily related to the past. A study that predicts the future development of a language can also be a diachronic one. It is hence not the goal to expose a formerly dominant understanding of creativity. Rather, the implications of the developments are to be made fruitful for current and future considerations of the concept of creativity in IT.

of which have had a constitutive effect on the logic of IT – and therefore on the creativity narrative as well.

After these two rather comprehensive subchapters, the direction is changed towards the export of the creativity narrative, and thus the process that represents the path to the IT narrative's predominant dictum of creativity. As a concluding diachronic part, the emergence and development of the phenomenon of artificial creativity will be presented in a concise manner and its influence on the conjuncture of the creativity narrative in IT will be analysed.

Following the diachronic analysis, the representation and organisation of the previously researched creativity narrative in IT will be analysed. In addition to a detailed analysis of material produced by IT itself that illustrate how IT uses and demands creativity as an attribute in equal measure, informal sources (i.e., sources other than IT's own discursive statements) are also examined, which reflect not so much the representation but the organisation of creativity in IT. This includes statements by former employees as well as press releases and other external reports. An essential methodological element contributing to this is the autoethnographic approach where I can draw on my insights, experience and observations with regard to creativity in IT during my more than 50 months at IBM Research.

Autoethnography as a research method is a quite young approach to qualitative research, rooting from the 1970s "insider ethnography" that focuses on researchers as members of a specific group.[16] But it was not until the late 1980s that an application of the term autoethnography became more and more common. Today, it is still a rather niche method, mostly used in the Anglo-Saxon research community of ethnographers. The main and obvious differentiation of autoethnography to ethnography is the added *auto*, the "I", the *self*. It uses self-reflection and personal experience "to describe and critique cultural beliefs, practices, and experiences",[17] revealing "personal investments, interpretations, and analyses"[18] in order to "connect the autobiographical and

16 David M. Hayano, "Auto-Ethnography: Paradigms, Problems, and Prospects", *Human Organization* 38, no. 1 (1979): 99-104, doi: https://doi.org/10.17730/humo.38.1.u761n5601t4g318v.

17 Tony E. Adams, Stacy Holman Jones and Carolyn Ellis, *Autoethnography: Understanding Qualitative Research* (New York: Oxford University Press, 2015).

18 Walter Goldschmidt, "Anthropology and the Coming Crisis: An Autoethnographic Appraisal", *Anthropologist* 79, no. 2 (1977): 293-308, doi: https://doi.org/10.1525/aa.1977.79.2.02a00060.

personal to the cultural, social, and political".[19] As with other (rather new and comparatively uncommon) methods, there are several possible approaches to autoethnography. For this dissertation, it is useful to separate between two types of autoethnographic methods: the analytic (1) and the evocative (2) approach.[20] While the latter seeks to evoke emotional responses, including "conflict-driven drama"[21] and is very much about the personal narrative of private accounts, the analytic approach focuses on developing theoretical explanations of broader social phenomena. Therefore, the analytical approach was chosen to be most suitable for this thesis.

In complement to the remainder of the methodological approach and in the course of my autoethnographic perspective, discussions were held with individual experts. The knowledge of meaning gained in these discussions is of interest here, through which subjective views or interpretations of the experts help to strengthen my line of argumentation.

In addition, I hope that by choosing this approach I will not only be able to bridge the research gap, but also, as mentioned in Chapter 1, provide a complementary perspective for future thinking on the phenomenon of creativity. This will be presented in a concluding discussion in which the explored and developed creativity narrative will be critically introduced to further discourses on creativity.

---

19 Carolyn Ellis, *The ethnographic I: A methodological novel about autoethnography* (Walnut Creek: AltaMira Press, 2004), p. xix.

20 Laura L. Ellingson and Carolyn Ellis, "Autoethnography as constructionist project", in Handbook of Constructionist Research in eds. J.A. Holstein and J.F. Gubrium (New York: Guilford Press, 2008)

21 It is a main goal of the evocative autoethnographic approach to put the readers in the shoes of the autoethnographer. Private struggles are translated into public concerns that become culturally essential. Cf. Arthur Bochner and Carolyn Ellis, *Evocative Autoethnography: Writing Lives and Telling Stories* (New York: Routledge, 2016), p. 87.

4 CONTEXTUAL AWARENESS AND PRECONDITIONS

In this chapter, the contextual framework of the discourse on creativity in IT is mapped out, showing both the further relevance of the topic and its influences and conditions on the part of society and the individual. Although context, what is presented here with reference to the creativity narrative in IT is equally influenced by that narrative as it has further reshaping effects on it. It is to be shown that the discourse on the concept of creativity in IT is framed by four time-specific distinctive characteristics. As will be shown, each characteristic is in itself of considerable significance to current and future societal development – in sum, however, they sketch the presumed inter-discursive scope of the creativity narrative that I expect to be an IT coinage. These characteristics are:

- first, the everlasting creativity as social norm (see chapter 4.1);
- second, the creation of a digital world (4.2);
- third, changing conditions of work and labour (4.3) and
- fourth, the dawn of creative machines (4.4).

All four factors are interrelated and, in some cases, are mutually dependent in their respective development. They reflect the unparalleled distinctness of the present. At the same time, my insight[1] into near, medium and long-term future IT developments indicate a tendency to rather downplay the impact of these characteristics on macrosocial developments even though they are

1 The assumptions I made cannot only be traced back to an internal IT perspective, but in particular to the practical examination of numerous economic, political, academic and educational institutions that visited the THINKLab at IBM Research - an intermediary between research and the "outside world" – in order to discuss current problems and questions and to gain insights into IBM's technology and mindset. This aspect is addressed only in brief at this chapter but is dealt with more specifically in chapter 6.

discussed and evaluated by experts and non-experts alike.[2] Since I expect the concept of creativity in IT to be a decisive driver for these four characteristics, they will be introduced below in order to frame and pave the way for the subsequent analytical process of exploring the distinct notion of IT's creativity narrative.

4.1 THE EVERLASTING CREATIVITY AS SOCIAL NORM

Asking US-American corporations about the meaning and purpose of a company, the official answer until 18th August 2019 would still have been based on Friedman's 1962 doctrine that "corporations exist principally to serve shareholders"[3] – that is, to make profit for those to whom these companies belong.[4] Due to increasing criticism of this orientation and fundamentally changing socio-economic conditions, this approach no longer seemed officially justifiable for "the most influential lobbying body for U.S. business interests, the

2 This paradoxically seeming claim will be further explored in the respective sub-chapters.

3 Thomas Koulopoulos, „181 CEOs of the Largest U.S. Corporations just altered the Role of Corporations for Decades to come", *Inc.*, last modified 19th August, 2019, https://www.inc.com/thomas-koulopoulos/181-ceos-of-largest-us-corporations-just-altered-role-of-corporations-for-decades-to-come.html?cid=hmside3.

4 Cf. Milton Friedman, *Capitalism and Freedom* (Chicago: University of Chicago Press, 2002). Milton Friedman's ground-breaking 1962 book *Capitalism and Freedom* is considered a major turning point in management literature, though it has since been subject to increasing criticism. In a nutshell, Friedman considers competitive capitalism and the free markets to be the most effective if not the only way to achieve political and personal (and of course economic) freedom. However, the positions negotiated in Friedman's book are by no means new but had been in practical use decades before. Nevertheless, Friedman laid the theoretical groundwork to which reference was still made in 1997 in the former proposal of the Business Roundtable. The criticism that CEOs in the new proposal are now considering and committing themselves to, at least in marketing terms, is of course older than Friedman's postulate *Freedom of the markets = personal and political freedom*. Industrialization, in particular, gave rise to a critique of capitalism that continues to this day, as it has for instance been presented in the form of Marxist theories. The Marxist school continues to evolve and is seeking (and finding) connections to rather contemporary currents, such as the work of Foucault, as attempted by the Italian philosopher Antonio Negri. Cf. Antonio Negri, *Marx and Foucault. Essays Volume 1* (Cambridge: Polity Press, 2017).

Business Roundtable".[5] The *Business Roundtable* consists out of 193 CEOs (Chief Executive Officers) who represent large companies such as Coca-Cola, Citigroup, Dow, FedEx, General Motors, Johnson & Johnson, KPMG, Mastercard, Pfizer, PricewaterhouseCoopers (PwC), Procter & Gamble, Siemens, United Airlines, Walmart, but also military corporations such as Lockheed Martin and Northrop Grumman as well as some of the largest global IT companies such as Amazon, Apple, Dell, Facebook, IBM, Oracle, SAP and Xerox.[6] The number and selection of enterprises shows that if all these corporations, despite their heterogeneity and different orientations, gather behind one lobbying body, it carries a lot of significance. From an economic point of view, it doesn't really get any more official and generally valid.

On 19th August 2019, 181 out of these 193 CEOs published a short account called "New Statements on the Purpose of a Corporation"[7] to meet the changing conditions on paper at least. The very first sentence of the very first paragraph reads as follows: "Americans deserve an economy that allows each person to succeed through hard work and creativity and to lead a life of meaning and dignity".[8] This means that whether military, IT, banking or beverage companies, they all see the main purpose of their very existence in creating an economic world in which all (American) people can be successful not only through their work (in order to lead a good and dignified life, it should be noted; not to enrich shareholders) but explicitly and literally through their own creativity. Remaining in this logic it follows that the entire economy mainly serves to provide jobs and enable the creativity of each individual.

In fact, the *Business Roundtable* is quite late in responding.[9] The extent to which a semantical notion of creativity[10] has already seeped into almost all areas of work and life without gaining any definitional sharpness can be seen,

---

5 Koulopoulos, "*181 CEOs of the Largest U.S. Corporations Just Altered the Role of Corporations for Decades to Come*".

6 Business Roundtable, "*Statement on the Purpose of a Corporation*", August 2019, https://opportunity.businessroundtable.org/wp-content/uploads/2019/08/Business-Roundtable-Statement-on-the-Purpose-of-a-Corporation-with-Signatures.pdf.

7 Business Roundtable, "Statement on the Purpose of a Corporation".

8 Ibid.

9 This applies both to developments and to the criticism directed at these developments.

10 The phrase semantical notion of creativity here means that only because creativity is of value as a communicative concept, it does by no means say anything about the actual relevance of creativity beyond linguistic use.

for example, in the assumption that creative craftsmen will have a clear advantage over their non-creative colleagues in finding their niches to work in the future like the following illustration shows: As role models for this, *good shoemakers* and *committed hatters* are given as examples in an interview with a subject-matter expert – but without the expert making it clear how creativity is to be understood in these cases and how creativity helps a shoemaker to became a *good* shoemaker.[11] Following John Dewey, Hans Joas describes creativity as a characteristic of human action and therefore as an everyday phenomenon.[12] His interpretation is not to be understood in the sense of a neoliberal idea but is based on Dewey's view that when people are confronted with problems, they begin to search for possible causes, means and solutions and in doing so become creative. Thus, creativity as described by the *Business Roundtable* is not seen as a mere everyday phenomenon that could help to solve problems, but, in contrast to Joas, as an unavoidable optimization tool. It seems to be indicated to somehow use the concept of creativity with a semantic indefiniteness, no matter if a however defined creative ability helps a shoemaker in her daily routine. What is more, the indefiniteness might even strengthen an argument due to its flexibility and semantic adaptability.[13]

This "paradox of creativity"[14] predominates within business literature, which indeed acknowledges and indicates the union between the concept of creativity and art (in a broader sense), but strives to detach creativity from the arts, thereby somehow democratising it: "On the face of it, 'creativity' seems like a skill useful only to artists, designers, writers, or marketers. Truth is – creative skills are indispensable for *all* professionals".[15] Hence, despite its scientific indetermination, the notion of creativity is widely perceived as an imperative dictum whose polarisation constrains opposing opinions. As introduced in chapter 2.2, it trickles down into many other fields of business

11 Nikolas Pelke, „Kreative Handwerker sind die Zukunft", Mittelbayerische, 16th July, 2018, https://www.mittelbayerische.de/region/nuernberg-nachrichten/kreative-handwerker-sind-die-zukunft-21503art1670797.html. [emph. in original].

12 Cf. Hans Joas, The Creativity of Action (Chicago: University of Chicago Press, 1996).

13 Cf. the reference to Saussure in chapter 1.

14 Gerald Raunig, „Kreativindustrie als Massenbetrug", in Kritik der Kreativität, in eds. Gerald Raunig and Ulf Wuggenig (Wien: Turia + Kant, 2007).

15 Michael Tomaszewski, "Creative Thinking: Definition, Examples & How to Boost Creativity Skills", *zety* (blog), 5th July, 2019, https://zety.com/blog/creative-thinking-skills .

and social aspects of life: a call for self-restraint and -regulation translates into a longing for self-formation and individual freedom.[16]

Within this environment, IT enterprises appear to act as a kind of lobbyist for its understanding of creativity, propagating creativity in fields that do not initially belong to its core areas. The software company Adobe, for example, has published a study on the role of creativity in education systems.[17] The study concludes that creative problem-solving competence pioneers the future, but outdated curricula lack imagination to pass on this competence.[18] The ubiquity of creativity (with its related family of concepts[19] as well as critical voices directed at them) with the resulting set of special- and interdiscourse indicates: creativity is not a hype anymore but a matter of course, a social norm that applies to many social fields.

4.2 THE CREATION OF A DIGITAL WORLD

Creativity as a social norm of the contemporary working world exists in the presence of the fundamental and universal process of the digital transformation. To refer again to a statement by Dirk Baecker, the *project of digitisation* has dramatic consequences for society just as the introduction of language, writing and book printing has.[20] Moreover, this transformation is taking place at

16 Isabell Lorey, "Vom immanenten Widerspruch zur hegemonialen Funktion. Biopolitische Gouvernementalität und Selbst-Prekarisierung von KulturproduzentInnen", in *Kritik der Kreativität*, eds. Gerald Raunig and Ulf Wuggenig (Wien: Verlag Turia + Kant, 2007).

17 Adobe, "Adobe Studie: Kreative Problemlösungskompetenz ist Wegbereiter der Zukunft, doch überholten Lehrplänen fehlt dafür die Fantasie", *Adobe Newsroom*, last modified 19th February, 2018, http://www.adobenewsroom.de/2018/02/19/adobe-studie-kreative-problemloesungskompetenz-ist-wegbereiter-der-zukunftdoch-ueberholten-lehrplaenen-fehlt-dafuer-die-fantasie/.

18 Cf. Ibid. Quite obviously, the study is backed by Adobe's financial and economic interests: among other findings, the study shows that "Global educators believe technologies like Adobe Creative Cloud can help students develop creative problem solving skills" and that "Educators that use Adobe Creative Cloud say creative problem solving often plays a role in their curricula, and their students are more prepared to put these skills to use".

19 Cf. chapter 2.1.

20 Dirk Baecker, *4.0 oder die Lücke die der Rechner lässt*.

an unprecedented speed and with unrivalled growth[21] with billions of people being connected via social media networks and massive investments to keep up with the pace of the digital transformation.[22] The transformative process itself is therefore sparked by technical innovations that, as Hans Ulrich Gumbrecht presumes "change – sometimes behind our backs, sometimes against our wills – the way we think, and with that the foundations of human existence".[23] In principle, the progress of civilization can originally be interpreted as a continuum: According to a quote by the philosopher Ernst Kapp on which Hans Blumenberg's work on the world's increasing mechanization refers to, the entire history of mankind, when examined closely, finally dissolves into the history of the invention of ever better tools.[24] This continuity seems to keep its validity, though, but is challenged in parts by the emergence of a parallel existing *digital otherness*. For Gumbrecht, the per se normal process of technologies that change epistemologies is now disrupted and "thinking is confronted with a maybe decisive and until recently not imaginable challenge".[25] This is due to the fact that technologies themselves became the backbone of a rather radical and all-embracing change, as "electronic technologies, which have long been seen as simple optimisations, are not just transforming the institutions of our communication in fundamental ways but also structures of society and politics".[26] Technical developments such as Personal Computers (PCs) and the Internet are creations of IT – and so is the creation of all things digital. The emerging *digital world* can therefore be seen as a creation of IT as well. The resulting central position of IT draws attention to

21 IBM, 2015. IBM also points out that the growth of data is exponential and accordingly incomprehensible to human minds (ibid.).

22 For schools in Germany alone, the costs of digitisation amount to 2.8 billion euros per year according to a study by the Bertelsmann Foundation. Cf. Dirk Zorn and Christian Ebel, "IT-Ausstattung an Schulen: Finanzierung ist eine milliardenschwere Daueraufgabe," *Bertelsmann Stiftung*, last modified 2nd November, 2017, https://www.bertelsmann-stiftung.de/de/themen/aktuelle-meldungen/2017/november/it-ausstattung-an-schulen-finanzierung-ist-eine-milliardenschwere-daueraufgabe/.

23 Hans Ulrich Gumbrecht, "Das Denken muss nun auch den Daten folgen," *Frankfurter Allgemeine Zeitung*, last modified 12th March, 2014, http://www.faz.net/aktuell/feuilleton/geisteswissenschaften/neue-serie-das-digitale-denken-das-denken-muss-nun-auch-den-daten-folgen12840532.html?printPagedArticle=true.

24 Hans Blumenberg, *Wirklichkeiten in denen wir leben: Lebenswelt und Technisierung* (Stuttgart: Reclam, 1981), p. 9f.

25 Ibid.

26 Ibid.

options for opportunities that indicate both a potential domination and lack of control. These are both eminently political and public issues with a corresponding large public resonance. It is a *res publica* in literal terms, as expressed in the title of the well-known digital conference *re:publica*, whose organisers and participants playfully use the selected name to indicate public participation in matters of digitisation. The topics range from questions about privacy on the Internet, participation in democratic processes and digital citizenship to ways of earning money by exploiting technology.[27] However, participants of *re:publica* have to pay less attention to the existing rules of the game and framework conditions developed by politics and society. Rather, they have to play by and consider IT's rules.

Because large IT companies are not only creators of the new digital world they also participate in it themselves. A condition that is not only perceived critically in Europe, but also in IT's home territory, the U.S. "Code is law"[28] concludes Harvard-based scholar and popular critical voice Shoshana Zuboff. And even when original decisions are made by people, it is all too often algorithms that ultimately decide whether a user's contribution can be published or not. Geographical classifications, national borders and regulations, distance and physical space by itself, physicalness and many other aspects that have been seen as immutable lose their validity in the digital sphere. The resulting opportunities (and responsibilities) have led IT companies to be accused of behaving like the barons and kings of a new world, which they themselves have created.[29] Even if more and more voices are joining the chorus calling for state regulation or even the breakup of entire companies, IT enterprises have so far only been obligated to themselves, without any higher authority that could judge them: "You alone are Google over all the kingdoms

---

27 Kai Biermann, „Zweifel als Motor des Fortschritts", *Zeit Online*, 14th April, 2010, https://www.zeit.de/digital/internet/2010-04/republica-2010-berlin.

28 Shoshana Zuboff, *The age of surveillance capitalism: the fight for a human future at the new frontier of power* (New York: PublicAffairs, 2018).

29 Olaf Groth in a panel discussion at the Robert Bosch-Stiftung in Stuttgart, 20th February, 2019. Cf. also: Shoshana Zuboff, she calls the "men at Google" today's "digital barons", referring to the infamous "Gilded Age robber barons" and stating: "Like the men at Google, the late-nineteenth-century titans claimed undefended territory for their own interests, declared the righteousness of their self-authorizing prerogatives, and defended their new capitalism from democracy at any cost" (p. 105). It is unclear if Groth borrows the term "barons" from Zuboff's work. However, the connotation is quite similar.

of the earth" states Jaron Lanier,[30] American computer scientist, composer and a founding father of the field of virtual reality on that point,[31] revealing a rather critical dimension of the discourse quite beyond the limits of polemics. Yet, the digital world is not only a tendentious slogan under which all relevant technologies gather in order to disrupt (for better, for worse) the existing order. At the same time, it is a parallel existence which will continue to grow and develop its own laws and legalities. As founder and sovereigns, IT companies will consequently have a major right to a say in the emergence of future values, norms and the determination of what is perceived as right and wrong. Even if individual governments or a federation of nations step up their efforts to regulate the services offered by IT companies, the latter will probably remain the operators and providers in the future as well.

4.3 CHANGING CONDITIONS OF WORK AND LABOUR

The nature of how people work and the conditions under which they do so is discussed and negotiated in an ongoing vivid and highly expressive discourse. For the French sociologists and economists Luc Boltanski and Ève Chiapello, the course of the discourse was more and more driven by the desire for social justice and the critique on the suppression of the autonomous subjects' self-activity, as they have examined in their book "The New Spirit of Capitalism" in 1999, by which they further accelerated this course over the last two decades through the influence of the book.[32]

On this basis, IT's developments have not only contributed to further changes in working conditions, for example through new tools. Rather, in the course of digitisation and the emergence of the digital world, the concept of work itself is in the process of being called into question and renegotiated. At first, however, people are confronted with very tangible problems: in their influential and frequently cited study of 2013, Carl Benedikt Frey and Michael

30 Jaron Lanier, "Whoever owns our data will determine our fate". A comparison with Foucault's concept of disciplinary power appears to be consistent here and is drawn on in the actual work.

31 Maureen Dowd, "Confirm or Deny: Jaron Lanier", *The New York Times*, last modified 8th November, 2017, https://www.nytimes.com/2017/11/08/style/confirm-or-deny-jaron-lanier.html.

32 Cf. Luc Boltanski and Ève Chiapello, *The New Spirit of Capitalism* (London / New York: Verso, 2007).

A. Osborne from Oxford University raise the claim to compare and examine how susceptible jobs are to computerisation, considering more than 700 occupations. Their then mentioned number of 47 percent of U.S.-based jobs being endangered by machines and algorithms in the next ten to twenty years has made a huge impact in both scientific and non-scientific communities. Seeing nearly half of all jobs at stake raises the question how people can distinguish themselves from machines and systems that apparently do tasks faster, cheaper and more efficient. *To be creative* has been a solution for this supposedly existential threat. This is pictured in various studies, such as a 2010 study in which the ability to act creatively is considered the most important attribute of a successful leader by 60 percent of 1541 executives from all over the world.[33] Figures by a 2012 study conducted by Adobe support this. According to this survey, eight out of ten people are convinced that creative potential must be released for future economic growth.[34] However, only a quarter of the respondents see their own creative potential fully utilised.[35] Hence, literature on *how to become creative* experiences a sustained boom (whereby this aspect refers back to the aspect discussed in Chapter 4.1, *The everlasting Creativity as Social Norm*). The demand to focus on creativity in order to be prepared for changing conditions of work is already reflected in the context of educational discourses, as the above-mentioned study commissioned by Adobe has demonstrated exemplarily. Thus, an IT journal contribution in the course of this study also considers creative abilities to play an essential role in order to survive in the future digital world of work, referring to an outcome of the study stating that job profiles in which it is important to continuously solve new challenges creatively are less affected by the trend towards automation.[36]

---

33 BJ Lombardo and DJ Roddy, "Cultivating Organizational Creativity in an Age of Complexity," *IBM Institute of Business Value*, last modified September, 2010, http://cdn.creativityatwork.com/wp-content/uploads/2011/08/IBM-creative-leadershipstudy-2011.pdf.

34 w. a., "Study Reveals Global Creativity Gap," *Adobe*, last modified 23rd April, 2012, https://www.adobe.com/aboutadobe/pressroom/pressreleases/201204/042312AdobeGlobalCreativityStudy.html.

35 Ibid.

36 Christian Schinko, "Kreativität als Schlüsselkompetenz der Zukunft: Schulen stehen unter Zugzwang", *Cancom info*, last modified 28th May, 2018, https://www.cancom.info/2018/05/kreativitaet-an-schulen-dasmuss-bei-der-foerderung-beruecksichtigt-werden/.

A quote by filmmaker, artist and internet pioneer Tiffany Shlain can be seen as an exemplary conclusion for the reasoning of using a notion of creativity as a distinct human factor, which therefore protects skilled people's jobs from becoming obsolete:

> "There's all this hysteria about AI taking over. But here's the thing: The skills we need most in today's world – skills like empathy, creativity, taking initiative, and cross-disciplinary thinking – are all things that machines will never have. Those are the skills that will be most needed in the future, too".[37]

Whether this assessment remains correct or not far into the future is almost impossible to predict on the basis of current knowledge and would inevitably remain pure speculation, although the determination in which the adverb *never* is used in this context should at least be called into question. From a discursive point of view, however, this question is not of great significance. Instead, it is of greater importance that the theoretical potential of AI already has the effect of strengthening the emphasis on creativity as a (manifestly acted) unique human characteristic. The answer to changing conditions of work and labour (further fostered by already given and potential AI developments) once again seems to be found in creativity as a social norm which is again further strengthened hereby.

4.4 THE DAWN OF CREATIVE MACHINES

But with both the promise and threat of allegedly creative machines, the distinctive human factor of being creative appears to be at stake as well, leading to another contextual aspect to be considered when dealing with the notion of creativity in IT: the possibilities and limitations of an artificial intelligence system to be by all or no means creative. The question of whether and how the possibility of artificial (or computational)[38] creativity could exist involves

37 Fisher, *Valley of Genius*, "The Endless Frontier" section, para. 2.

38 In research as well as in marketing both spellings exist for this phenomenon: either it is called artificial creativity, or computational creativity. Within this work I prefer to use the term artificial creativity to emphasize the linguistic opposition and the (presumed) difference to human respectively natural creativity. However, this equally includes computational creativity.

questions of what this implies for IT, society and the individual person. Computational creativity is therefore a subject of both semantic and ontological nature. In a recent panel on the topic of *Artificial Intelligence and Art*, a researcher of the Alexander von Humboldt Institute for Internet and Society (HIIG) describes the phenomenon of computational creativity "as uncreative art, which today is also to be found in music and literature",[39] deducing numerous fundamental questions about authenticity and authorship, originality, origin, aura and atmosphere, about art production or art reception, and finally about the creation of meaning and (human) values themselves. Yet, the scientist concludes, the "answer that we as humans are still superior in creativity, human interaction and reproduction and in working on so-called wicked problems is certainly a reassuring thought".[40] Given the significance of AI development, in whose waters the phenomenon of artificial creativity is to be found, such a reassuring answer seems to be of great importance: For Google's CEO Sundar Pichai, AI is "more profound than electricity or fire".[41] For Gerhard Vollmer, the idea of an artificial model of the mind can even be considered as one of the *insults of mankind*.[42] It thus ranks alongside illustrious *insults* such as the Copernican turn or the Darwinian system of evolution. Based on a thesis by Sigmund Freud, these *insults* are created when overturning scientific discoveries question people's self-concept – just as Copernicus brought about the cosmological insult by claiming the Earth (and thus humankind) was indeed not the centre of the cosmos.[43] Vollmer expands the count to a total of ten *insults*, beginning with the child, recognizing itself as

39 Humboldt Institute for Internet and Society, *Digitaler Salon: Zahlen, die malen*.

40 Ibid.

41 Harry McCracken, "Google CEO: AI is a bigger deal than fire or electricity," *Fast Company*, last modified 19th January, 2018, https://www.fastcompany.com/40519204/google-sundar-pichai-ai-is-a-bigger-deal-than-fire-or-electricity.

42 Cf. Gerhard Vollmer, „Die vierte bis siebte Kränkung des Menschen. Gehirn, Evolution und Menschenbild", http://www.gkpn.de/vollmer.htm. Vollmer hereby refers to a book by Sherry Turkle, in which she asked as early as 1984: "Are Smart Machines Alive?" Cf. Sherry Turkle, *The Second Self: Computers and the Human Spirit* (Cambridge: MIT Press, 2004), p. 33.

43 In addition, Freud considers a biological (Darwinism) and a psychological (triggered by himself) insult of mankind. Cf. Sigmund Freud, "Eine Schwierigkeit der Psychoanalyse", *Imago. Zeitschrift für Anwendung der Psychoanalyse auf die Geisteswissenschaften*, Bd. V (1917), 1–7.

part of the world, and ending with the still pending neurobiological dissolution of a body and mind's dualism. But before this final dissolution stands the prospect of artificial intelligence that attains and even surpasses a human's intellectual accomplishments – and therefore also the previous invulnerability to be creative. Paradoxically, an AI that outflanks the human mind would be the first insult that would not be due to a more precise observation or a better understanding (of nature and the environment, for example), but would be created by humans themselves.

The underlying ontological aspect in thereof resulting debates connects the pursuit for an understanding of both computational as well as human creativity. To get ahead, further deliberation on the very nature of creativity seems appropriate,[44] which is why IT attempts to understand computational creativity by conducting research on human creativity in close collaboration with different perspectives, such as psychology or neuroscience. Indeed, creativity is seen as a "final frontier"[45] from an IT's perspective, with human creativity as "something of a mystery, not to say a paradox".[46]

These four pillars, presented in chapters 4.1 to 4.4, thus form the backdrop on which a notion of creativity in IT is mapped and at the same time has a decisive influence on. The following diachronic analysis therefore proceeds in the knowledge of the characteristics of contemporary times presented here and seeks to provide evidence for the resulting presumption of an entanglement between the four aspects and a conception of creativity in IT.

---

44 Margaret A. Boden, „Creativity and artificial intelligence", *Artificial Intelligence* 103, no. 1 and 2 (1998): 347-356, doi: 10.1016/S0004-3702(98)00055-1.

45 Simon Colton and Geraint A. Wiggins, "Computational creativity: The final frontier?" in *Frontiers in Artificial Intelligence and Applications* 242, January (2012): pp. 21-26, doi: 10.3233/978-1-61499-098-7-21.

46 Margaret A. Boden, *The Creative Mind: Myths and Mechanisms.*

5 DIACHRONIC ANALYSIS

The following chapter examines the historical perspective and retraces the concept of creativity in large and dominant IT companies. It is shown when and which conjunctures concerning a notion of creativity appeared, what images of creativity were used and, most significantly, how notions of both creativity and IT were mutually shaping each other's perception in the flux of time.

In order to approach the complex emergence and development of the IT-specific narrative of creativity, it is initially important to identify the three main cornerstones that have emerged as such throughout the analytical process. These three cornerstones represent three main types of influences on the narrative: the unique characteristics of Silicon Valley (1), the social transformations and scientific currents of IT self-understanding (2), and the phenomenon of artificial creativity (3). The first two basic currents in particular – which I will discuss in subchapters 5.1 and 5.2, wherein individual evolutionary stages of the concept of creativity in IT are identified and analysed – are neither hierarchical nor isolated in relation to each other. Rather, they are interdependent, partially relate to each other or even overlap to a certain extent. In terms of a diachronic analysis, these conditions are highlighted and set in comparison to each other. An examination of computational creativity in the light of the creativity narrative in IT will conclude the diachronic approach with the chapter 5.3.

There is a wealth of material dealing with the history of IT and in particular the Silicon Valley. While researching this chapter, it became apparent that a surprisingly large number of sources include references to a notion of creativity or related terms such as innovation. This applies in particular to more recent sources that deal with the origins of today's IT. By their description, these sources thus help to shape the creativity narrative in IT.[1]

Due to the multitude of reports, analyses and story lines, not all available material can and will be covered within this chapter. This is further justified by the existence of certain redundancies, for example in the founding histories of many Silicon Valley companies, which may be of interest for socio-economic or economic historical reasons, but which do not offer any direct added value to the exploration of the creativity narrative beyond the consolidation of what is already extracted from other sources. In spite of this, a claim to depicting and analysing the most significant evolutionary strides and events of this particular narrative is possible, since certain historical strides can be seen as exemplary for the elaboration of the understanding of creativity. Regardless of the respective individual conditions of each case, this appears to be more purposeful with regard to the concept of creativity.

For the development of the creativity narrative in IT, events and persons are of importance that often have an iconic status within the tech scene but are hardly known outside of IT. It is therefore a purpose of this analysis to take these aspects into account along with the necessary framework conditions as well as stories and above all people who both internally and externally represent and decisively shape the specific narrative of creativity.

5.1 PROVENANCE – THE GEOSOCIAL SETTING OF THE SILICON VALLEY AS PLACE AND CULTURE

> "Creativity is high here – it's okay to have dreams and think about them and think maybe you could make them. Here more than other places."
> *Steve Wozniak*

> "At its core, Silicon Valley is a culture."
> *John Battelle*

1 Accordingly, the sources have been handled with caution, as it is sometimes difficult to distinguish between what took place originally and what is a contemporary attribution, triggered in particular by the boom in the concept of creativity and its significance for the self-understanding of IT, which is to be worked out in this chapter.

For this purpose, a focus will be on the region known today as Silicon Valley. That place, then, which is both geographically localisable and exists as an idea and social construct.[2] As will be shown, Silicon Valley is not just one of many places for the IT industry, but its origin and still decisive relevance for the self-image of IT. But contrary to what is often claimed, Silicon Valley is by no means just an idea and social construct. Already in 2000, MIT's Timothy Sturgeon dismissed "the notion that *anyplace can be Silicon Valley*" and that "industrialisation and urbanisation on the scale of Silicon Valley can be quickly induced in other areas".[3] He then continues:

> "Silicon Valley is nearly one hundred years old. It grew out of a historically and geographically specific context that cannot be re-created. [...] Silicon Valley was the fastest growing region in the United States during the late 1970s and early 1980s, but that growth came out of a place, not a technology. Silicon Valley's development is intimately entwined with the long history of industrialization and innovation in the larger San Francisco Bay Area".[4]

It is this *intimately entwined* history of innovation – and therefore creativity – that will be the object of investigation in this chapter. A historical reflection is not only valuable in order to understand the development towards today's creativity narrative. Rather, experts concerning the history of Silicon Valley have recognized "that the characteristics of early Bay Area electronics companies closely match the structure of industrial organization so widely hailed

---

2 The magazine "Medium", for example, makes a distinction between "Silicon Valley **the location** and Silicon Valley **the idea"** Cf. Alex Valaitis, "The Truth About Silicon Valley", *Medium*, last modified 25th February, 2018, https://medium.com/@Alex.Valaitis/the-truth-about-silicon-valley-7ba5de6c36a2 [emph. in original].

3 Timothy J. Sturgeon, "How Silicon Valley Came to Be" in*Understanding Silicon Valley: The Anatomy of an Entrepreneurial Region*, ed. Martin Kenney (Stanford: Stanford University Press, 2000), p. 47, [emph. in original].

4 Ibid. Sturgeon is not alone in this opinion. In an extensive article in the renowned journal MIT Technology Review, journalist Vivek Wadhwa explores the question of whether and how Silicon Valley has already been copied elsewhere or can be re-created. Large-scale efforts in New Jersey and Dallas, for example, are cited, but they remained unsuccessful. As for the uniqueness of Silicon Valley, the author states: "Sadly, the magic never happened—anywhere. Hundreds of regions all over the world collectively spent tens of billions of dollars trying to build their versions of Silicon Valley. I don't know of a single success". Cf. Vivek Wadhwa, "Silicon Valley can't be copied", *MIT Technology Review*, last modified 3rd July, 2013, https://www.technologyreview.com/2013/07/03/177476/silicon-valley-cant-be-copied/.

in Silicon Valley today, albeit on a much smaller scale".[5] Whether and how this also applies to IT's narrative of creativity and how it influenced and was influenced by the development of the *Silicon Valley logic* will be explored on the following pages.

The story of Silicon Valley has been told many times and from various angles.[6] These reports are valuable sources for the following analysis,[7] but whose aim however is not to provide a historical description of the Silicon Valley itself based on fixed dates and years. Rather, the role of creativity in the development of Silicon Valley will be explored, which – as will be shown – is a steady companion of this place's journey towards becoming the most defining technology hub and nucleus of a social norm. Historical hard facts therefore play a subordinate role in the following, if they are not of importance for the relationship between creativity and IT.

Silicon Valley is embraced by an auratic formation of myths, legends and facts that are promoted to a not inconsiderable extent by its own members – but also by outsiders such as *East Coast* journalists or academics working anywhere but in California. Together they form a highly loaded reading of Silicon Valley's history and present. The aspects presented within this chapter will outline why Silicon Valley as a place and idea can be considered a major constitutive element for the development of the creativity narrative in IT. For many Silicon Valley locals and storytellers, there are compelling reasons for the geosocial uniqueness of this area. Some of them are literally related to the geographical space itself, others refer to the idea and mindset behind. In addition, however, they are not only a blueprint for future evolutions on the narrative but remain current and valid to this day. More precisely and as briefly cited above, this means that "the characteristics of early Bay Area electronics companies closely match the structure of industrial organisation so

5 Ibid., p. 16.

6 In addition to the above-mentioned Timothy Sturgeon ("How Silicon Valley came to be", 2000), Stanford's Adrian Daub's "What Tech Calls Thinking" (2020) and Steven Levy's "Hackers: Heroes of the Computer Revolution" (2010) can be given as two examples for such stories about the Silicon Valley that will be discussed in more detail later.

7 From a discourse-analytical point of view, these sources are also of interest for the questions of when and, above all, who wrote them. Since these are discursively relevant sources, it is not only the content that matters, but also the originating author, who, depending on the person or institution, may attach greater value to a statement. If this is the case, the respective role or position of the source is also mentioned.

widely hailed in Silicon Valley today, albeit on a much smaller scale",[8] as the MIT-based historian Timothy Sturgeon puts it in his study on the origins of Silicon Valley. After conducting research, he concluded that "the key characteristics of Bay Area electronics, set in place so long ago, have proved to be readily 'scalable' as the industry has grown in the region".[9] For this reason they are considered in comparatively greater depth.

5.1.1 SEEDING THE CROPS – POLITICAL AND THEORETICAL FOUNDATIONS FOR A PLACE TO COME

The first of these main origins can be traced back to the year 1870. At this time California and the area of today's Silicon Valley were already part of the USA, but still influenced by the Spanish and later Mexican (from 1821) colonial rule (until 1846).[10] Through this influence the state of California agreed to prevent the enforcement of a covenant otherwise common in most states of the USA: the covenant not to compete. When in force, it "protect[s] a legitimate business interest of the employer" in that it "prohibits employers from suing former employees for going on to a competing company" [11] and thus prevents knowledge and intellectual property from migrating to another company. But while this is being enforced in most states of the USA, the covenant not to compete is not applied in

California, or, in the words of a Silicon Valley entrepreneur, it is "nonenforceable, period".[12] For Scott Hassan, former key developer at Google and founder[13] that is "a big deal. A lot less innovation happens on the East Coast

8 Sturgeon, "How Silicon Valley Came to Be", p. 16.

9 Ibid.

10 Officially, Mexican rule lasted until February 1848, but effectively ended two years earlier, in 1846, after a successful rebellion of American settlers proclaiming the California Republic. The USA initially supported the rebellion secretly, but the idea of a Californian republic was abandoned in the course of the Mexican-American War, which by then had erupted, and California became part of the USA.

11 Adam Fisher, *Valley of Genius: The Uncensored History of Silicon Valley (As Told by the Hackers, Founders, and Freaks Who Made It Boom)* (New York: Twelve, 2018), "Silicon Valley, Explained" section, para. 2.

12 Ibid. This entrepreneur is Brad Handler, known as an early employee of eBay. Cf. Richard Crawford '74, "Brad Handler '95 on eBay, Founding a Travel Empire, and Luck," *UVA Lawyer*, [accessed 19th April, 2019], https://www.law.virginia.edu/static/uvalawyer/html/alumni/uvalawyer/spr12/handler.htm.

13 Fisher, *Valley of Genius*, "Cast of characters" section.

because they believe in these noncompetes".[14] Well before the first tech companies were established in what later became Silicon Valley and long before today's IT enterprises were founded in garages, the soil for IT's contemporary concept of creativity was thus provided. A prerequisite for a highly competitive but also risk-taking environment was met, also promoting a culture of empowerment, which nowadays is so often tried to be imitated.[15] This "policy difference from hundreds of years ago"[16] is – in Steve Jobs' words – one reason why "people started breaking off and forming competitive companies, like those flowers or weeds that scatter seeds in hundreds of directions when you blow on them".[17] It is the "I-need-to-leave-my-big-thing-to-start-something-small story" that "became an imprint that got repeated and repeated and repeated".[18] It is important to note that the above mentioned statements about the non-compete clause date back to more recent times (the oldest is Jobs' quote, which is from the time between 1985 and 1995[19]) – including the link to creativity. Hence, the creativity narrative of IT contains established concepts of modern and therefore market-oriented economic theories that have been taken up by members of the IT world and used for their context.

5.1.2 ENGELBART – A FOUNDING FATHER OF SILICON VALLEY

This can be illustrated by the example of Doug Engelbart (1925-2013), who, according to IT insiders, had the idea of making computers accessible to all people already in 1962 – at least a decade before the advent of personal computers in the 1970s.

An explanation is needed as to why the figure of Doug Engelbart is addressed here in the section on Silicon Valley. After all, Engelbart could also be presented and discussed in the section on IT's self-image. Namely, because he became particularly famous for his contributions to the above-mentioned

14 Fisher, *Valley of Genius*, "Silicon Valley, Explained" section, para. 2.

15 Cf. Julia Löhr, "'Die Deutschen sagen immer nur: Oh Gottogott!'" *Frankfurter Allgemeine Zeitung*, 9th July, 2019, https://www.faz.net/aktuell/wirtschaft/diginomics/wirtschaftsminister-peter-altmaier-im-silicon-valley-16275487.html.

16 Fisher, *Valley of Genius*, "Silicon Valley, Explained" section, para. 2.

17 Ibid.

18 Ibid. How this imprint works will be shown in the later course of this chapter with a specific focus on the part of venture capital.

19 Cf. Adam Fisher, *Valley of Genius*, [accessed 20th April, 2019], https://www.valleyofgenius.com/secondary-sources.

development of the personal computer (PC), especially the computer mouse, and his spectacular and iconic way of demonstrating them. However, regarding the development of the creative narrative in IT, his influential role is not limited to the connection between creativity and the development of the PC but exceeds it: retrospectively, his personal motivation and modes of how and why he developed and implemented ideas were considered to be of greater relevance than the technical development steps he initiated. For the notion of creativity in Silicon Valley, however, Engelbart can be seen as both an archetypal and constitutive person, as will be shown below, which is why this section is located here. The author Adam Fisher can be named as a representative for this opinion, whose first chapter in his book on the history of Silicon Valley reads: "The Big Bang. Everything starts with Doug Engelbart".[20]

Engelbart, a former US Navy radar technician and engineer, presented his broad vision of *working machines* supporting the approach to complex problem situations. For this, he published a study that bears a title reflecting the breadth and the aspiration associated with it in a rather philosophical connotation. It is called: "Augmenting Human Intellect: A Conceptual Framework".[21] According to Engelbart, this augmentation shall lead to an increased capability of a "more-rapid comprehension, [...] in a situation that previously was too complex, speedier solutions, better solutions, and the possibility of finding solutions to problems that before seemed insoluble".[22] The study goes on to say that this will be done by "developing means to augment the human intellect. These 'means' can include many things – all of which appear to be but extensions of means developed and used in the past to help man apply his native sensory, mental, and motor capabilities" adding that an augmentation "can best be improved by considering the whole as a set of interacting components rather than by considering the components in isolation".[23] Hence, a conceptual framework is needed to pursuit the approach of this multisensory augmentation method. Engelbart goes on to outline a detailed description and visualization of how such a method might look like, or more specific, he envisioned how a physical *working system* is structured and organised step-

20 Cf. Fisher, *Valley of Genius*, "The Big Bang" section, para. 1.

21 Douglas C. Engelbart, „Augmenting Human Intellect: A Conceptual Framework", *Doug Engelbart Institute*, [accessed 22nd April, 2019], http://dougengelbart.org/content/view/138.

22 Ibid., http://www.dougengelbart.org/content/view/138/#1a1.

23 Ibid., http://www.dougengelbart.org/content/view/138/#1a3.

by-step, starting with the words: "Let us consider an augmented architect at work. He sits at a working station that has a visual display screen".[24] What follows is a blueprint for some of IT's most ground-breaking developments over the next years: a visual display and the computer mouse among other things. However, it is not only a blueprint for technical developments, but also for a style that will soon be representative of Silicon Valley's self-image: creating *ideas that change the world*, the *next big thing* with the *disruptive* and *transformative* power to make a difference how people act, live, work and think (to mention just a few recent buzzwords). Although engineer, Engelbart is not first presenting his technical innovation and what advantages this development could have. Accordingly, his paper is not about "how to build a small, personal computer". Rather, he conceives the subject from the rear and emphasises on the visionary but intangible character of his text. Engelbart is not asking about the applicability of a new technical idea, but for the means to support the human intellect – of which a smaller, more accessible computer can be one possible approach.

Engelbart's text is remarkable for several reasons. It is not only of importance for the development of Silicon Valley itself, but also for the intertwined evolution of creativity in IT, which can already be traced at this early stage and represents a first indication how creativity is conceived in IT not only at this time but also beyond. For Engelbart, the concept of intellect is also about creativity – in the literal sense of the word. Thus, he continues to write about the advantages of his *working machine* (i.e., the later PC): "You can integrate your new ideas more easily, and thus harness your creativity more continuously".[25] Even before the PC was designed and developed as such, the ability to foster ideas (i.e., the *new*) and creativity in people was already attributed to it. Due to Engelbart's high influence on future protagonists of Silicon Valley, it can be said that this aspect is of considerable value for the connection

24 The visualised description goes on to say: "some three feet on a side; this is his working surface, and is controlled by a computer (his "clerk") with which he can communicate by means of a small keyboard and various other devices. [...]. Now he enters a reference line with his pointer, and the keyboard. Gradually the screen begins to show the work he is doing". Cf. Douglas C. Engelbart, „Augmenting Human Intellect: A Conceptual Framework", [accessed 20th April, 2019], http://www.dougengelbart.org/content/view/138/#1a13.

25 Ibid., [accessed 20th April, 2019], http://www.dougengelbart.org/content/view/138/#2a2.

between PC development and the notion of creativity (for Apple in particular, this was of great importance; an issue that will be addressed later on).[26]

However, it is not only the actual content of the study that is of relevance here, but also the behaviour and biography of the person Doug Engelbart himself. In the years prior to publishing *Augmenting Human Intellect*, he studied electrical engineering at Berkeley out of the drive to do something good to the world instead of living a *normal* life:

> "In 1950 I got engaged. Getting married and living happily ever after just kind of shook me. I realized that I didn't have any more goals. I was twenty-five. It was December 10 or 11. I went home that night, and started thinking: *My God, this is ridiculous.* [...] *Well, why don't I try maximizing how much good I can do for mankind?* I have no idea where that came from. Pretty big thoughts".[27]

Engelbart himself is not entirely correct about his biography in this quote, since there is indeed a specific source where these *pretty big thoughts* came from: an essay named "As We May Think", published in July 1945 in the Atlantic magazine.[28] Written by engineer Vannevar Bush, who was the *Director of the Office of Scientific Research and Development* in the USA during World War II, the article asks about the future of science when weapons finally remain silent. Right at the dusk of war, Bush's answer concludes that the power of one's mind rather than the pursuit for physical power should be the focus of new inventions. Bush sketches the concept of a *universal knowledge machine* which is

26 This is well illustrated by the statement made by Bob Taylor, founder of Xerox PARC's iconic laboratory that will be the subject of interest in the course of this chapter. Regarding Engelbart and his text, Taylor stated: "There was this proposal called 'Augmenting the Human Intellect' [...], whom I had never heard of. I loved the ideas in this proposal. The thing that I was most attracted to was the fact that he was going to use computers in a way that people had not: to, as he put it, 'augment human intellect'. That's about as distinct a phrase as I can think of to describe it". Bill Paxton, computer scientist and co-founder of Adobe Systems underlines the importance on the future development of the Silicon Valley by adding: "There were a few people like Bob Taylor who picked up on the idea. And it eventually fed out into Xerox PARC and then Apple to take over the world. But, at the time, Doug was a voice crying into the wilderness". Cf. Fisher, *Valley of Genius*, "The Big Bang" section, para. 2.

27 Fisher, *Valley of Genius*, "Cast of Characters" section.

28 The complete text is archived online and can be retrieved under: Vannevar Bush, "As We May Think," *The Atlantic*, [accessed 26th April, 2019], https://www.theatlantic.com/magazine/archive/1945/07/as-we-may-think/303881/.

considered a precursor of the modern PC. Just as Engelbart did decades later, Bush provides a detailed description of how he envisions the way *we may think*: "One can now picture a future investigator in his laboratory. His hands are free, and he is not anchored. As he moves about and observes, he photographs and comments".[29] Similarities to Doug Engelbart's description of his *working machine* in action are quite noticeable in both style and content. Moreover, it is worth noting that Bush also explicitly addresses creativity by pointing out that "creative thought and essentially repetitive thought are very different things".[30] According to Bush, there are already "powerful mechanical aids" for the latter, but "every time one combines and records facts in accordance with established logical processes, the creative aspect of thinking is concerned only with the selection of the data".[31] This is where his idea of a new device fits in, "a device in which an individual stores all his books, records, and communications, and which is mechanized so that it may be consulted with exceeding speed and flexibility. It is an enlarged intimate supplement to his memory".[32] Hence, a creative human capacity can be seen as an essential stimulus towards the development of such a machine in this 1945 true blueprint for the development of the later PC and template for Engelbart's visionary text. And again, it seems not to be far-fetched to make a link between both texts in general and Bush's *intimate supplement* of one's memory and Engelbart's approach to *augment human intellect* in particular. The aim here already is to recognise and develop potentials in already given texts or artefacts. The new (i.e., the creativity) here is the continuation of something already known, an innovative process that is more than pure recombination. This form of imaginative anticipation, of adapting and rethinking already available knowledge becomes a common phenomenon within Silicon Valley and will be addressed later anew.

But even beyond that, Engelbart shaped the Silicon Valley prototype when he gave *the mother of all demos* in December 1968 at the national computer conference in San Francisco to show what his computer (that had a keyboard, a mouse, and early programs similar to Skype and e-mail) is capable off. Fisher describes the situation as follows: "To modern eyes, Engelbart's computer system looks pretty familiar, but to an audience used to punch cards and print-

29 Ibid.

30 Ibid.

31 Ibid.

32 Vannevar Bush, "As We May Think", [accessed 26th April, 2019], https://www.theatlantic.com/magazine/archive/1945/07/as-we-may-think/303881/.

outs it was a revelation. The computer could be more than a number cruncher; it could be a communications and information-retrieval tool".[33] Andries van Dam, professor of computer science at Brown University attended this *mother of all demos* and remembers this experience as follows: "I was blown away to see this professional system with this unbelievable richness and complexity. It was an otherworldly experience, and in fact, I couldn't quite bring myself to believe that it was all for real".[34]

And although being funded by the *Defense Advanced Research Projects Agency* (DARPA) and therefore the US Department of Defense, Engelbart is said to have detached computer technology from its war-driven origin,[35] therefore making it accessible to a different type of people that would predominate Silicon Valley's habitus for the years to come. In Adam Fisher's words, Engelbart "shattered the military-industrial computing paradigm, and gave the hippies and freethinkers and radicals who were already gathering in Silicon Valley a vision of the future that would drive the culture of technology for the next several decades".[36] As early as the 1960s it was already valid what Silicon Valley in general and Steve Jobs with Apple in particular continued to cultivate over time: it is not enough to have a good idea (or to be more precise: to recognise and adapt a good idea),[37] one must also be able to market it.

The terms *hippies*, *freethinkers* and *radicals* are semantically fuzzy and difficult to sum up in one common understanding. Either single or various of these movements are reflected in various individual concepts, which range from Touraine's *post-industrial society* and *economy*,[38] to Levy's *hacker culture*[39] and later includes notions such as *programmed society* or Castells' *network society*,[40] to mention only a few. Though several parallel movements are implied, they are discursively jointly connected with the concept of creativity via the pop cultural narrative of *counterculture* in a broader sense, in which creativity

33 Fisher, *Valley of Genius*, "The Big Bang" section, para. 3.

34 Ibid.

35 Cf. Fisher, *Valley of Genius*, "The Big Bang" section, para. 1.

36 Fisher, *Valley of Genius*, "The Big Bang" section, para. 5.

37 Cf. chapter 5.1.5.

38 Cf. Alain Touraine, *Die postindustrielle Gesellschaft*. (Frankfurt am Main: Suhrkamp, 1969).

39 Cf. Levy, *Hackers* (Sebastopol: O'Reilly, 2010).

40 Cf. Manuel Castells, *Das Informationszeitalter. Band 1: Der Aufstieg der Netzwerkgesellschaft*. (Leverkusen: Leske und Budrich Verlag, 2004).

is seen as a means of deviance, with attributions such as freedom or authenticity.[41]

Those *hippies, freethinkers* and *radicals* have decisively shaped the notion of creativity in IT with their way of thinking and acting when they became the dominant social power in Silicon Valley.[42] In order to outline this, one aspect that seems indispensable for a better understanding of the connection between hippies, technology and creativity must first be addressed: the constitutive role of the military for early Silicon Valley companies.

5.1.3 *"DIE LUFT DER FREIHEIT WEHT"* - THE STANFORD UNIVERSITY AND THE MILITARY

As being stated above, Engelbart is said to have detached electronics and computer technology from its military origin, allowing alternative lifestyles mostly based on the 1960s counterculture to approach this field in a different manner. At this point, it seems worth considering the military heritage of Silicon Valley. On the one hand, the apparent contrast between the military and the hippie clichés mentioned above seems paradoxical and difficult to resolve without further explanation. On the other hand, the entanglements with the US military also influenced the further evolution of the locally coined concept of creativity to a great extent.

In 1885, Jane Stanford and her husband, the tycoon and politician Leland Stanford decided to found a university named after their deceased and

41 The concept of counterculture here refers to the specific counterculture of the 1960s, which is dealt with more closely in chapter 5.2.2. The connection between counterculture and creativity is part of numerous publications. Cf. only: Paul Perry, *On the bus: the complete guide to the legendary trip of Ken Kesey and the Merry Pranksters and the birth of the counterculture* (New York: Thunder's Mouth Press, 1990); Richard Candida Smith, *Utopia and dissent: art, poetry and politics in California* (Berkeley: University of California Press, 1995).

42 One typical example for this is the book "How the Hippies Saved Physics: Science, Counterculture, and the Quantum Revival", in which the hippies as part of counterculture are identified as the driving force behind the changes in (Californian) science during the 1970s. Thanks to them and their endless curiosity, the author says, stagnation and conformity have been overcome in favour of creativity and a rather speculative approach to physics – also thanks to the help of Eastern-mythicist literature or drugs like LSD. Cf. David Kaiser, *How the Hippies Saved Physics: Science, Counterculture, and the Quantum Revival* (New York: W.W. Norton & Company, 2011).

only son to do something for "other people's" [children]".[43] After six years of planning, the Leland Stanford Junior University opened its coeducational and nondenominational doors for the first 555 – female and male – students in 1891. This at the time progressive orientation of the university was further promoted by a linkage to the concept of freedom. More precisely, the term freedom referred to here derives from the German 19th century Wilhelm von Humboldt's university model of *freedom of teaching* and *freedom of learning* that both encouraged and promoted research.[44] The first president of Stanford University, David Starr Jordan, introduced the university's motto, written in German and still valid today: *Die Luft der Freiheit weht* (The air of freedom blows).[45] The exact reasons for choosing this motto and its language have not yet been fully researched. What is certain, however, is that Jordan was influenced and deeply impressed by the German humanist Ulrich von Hutten and the freedom aspirations of the Reformation.[46] While still at Indiana University, Jordan in his inaugural address as president of this university stresses the essential character of freedom for both scholarship and mankind, adding that "The ideas of 'Lehrfreiheit' and 'Lernfreiheit,' – freedom of teaching and freedom of learning, – on which the German university is based, will become a central feature of the American college system".[47]

From the very beginning, the University has been committed to not only educating students for themselves, but to contribute to the greater good through each individual's education. Considering the constituent document,

43 Stanford University, "The Founding of the University", *Stanford University*, last modified 15th February, 2019, https://facts.stanford.edu/about/.

44 The internal Faculty Handbook literally states: "Stanford University was in the vanguard of American universities patterned on the German model, which stressed research and the freedom to learn and teach". Cf. Stanford University, "Stanford. Faculty Handbook", *Stanford University*, last modified 1st September, 2017, https://facultyhandbook.stanford.edu/1-university#1.1.

45 Gerhard Casper, "Die Luft der Freiheit weht - On and Off: On the Origins and History of the Stanford Motto on October 5, 1995", *Stanford University. Office of the President*, [accessed 22nd April, 2019], https://web.stanford.edu/dept/pres-provost/president/speeches/951005dieluft.html.

46 However, Jordan did not study primary sources from von Hutten, but texts from German theological critic David Friedrich Strauss, most notably Strauss' biography of von Hutten.

47 Gerhard Casper, "Die Luft der Freiheit - On and Off", Stanford University Office of the president, [accessed on 1st May, 2019], https://web.stanford.edu/dept/pres-provost/president/speeches/951005dieluft.html.

known as the Founding Grant, the following section emphasises this attitude right at the beginning of the first section on nature, scope and purpose of the newly founded university: "Its object, to qualify its students for personal success, and direct usefulness in life; And its purposes, to promote the public welfare by exercising an influence in behalf of humanity and civilisation".[48] Hence, since its foundation, the university in the heart of what later became Silicon Valley has been committed to changing the world for the better. Examining the style of the Founding Grant more closely, the texts by Bush (*As We May Think*) and Engelbart (*Augmenting the Human Intellect*) appear to be in the tradition of a self-image, as was already expressed during the founding of Stanford University. All three (Stanford's, Bush's and Engelbart's) approaches do not aim at the personal and individual pursuit of happiness but have the fortune of the whole (at least American) world in mind. To formulate such a claim presupposes to assume that one is able to understand what the fortune of the whole might be and then to do this.

One of the first to encourage students to find out if they are able to put new ideas into practice was professor Frederick Terman, who is widely regarded as a "father of Silicon Valley".[49] Being an undergraduate student at Stanford himself, went off to MIT for a PhD in electrical engineering (were Vannevar Bush, author of *As We May Think*, was his doctoral advisor),[50] before returning as dean to Stanford's School of Engineering in 1925 where he "promptly launched an aggressive, commercially oriented program in radio electronics".[51] Terman, in particular, seems to have pursued the idea that this *promotion of the public welfare by exercising an influence in behalf of humanity and civilization* stated in the Founding Grant can best be achieved through innovative entrepreneurship. He encouraged his students not to leave it at ideas, but to create something new in the form of locally founded start-ups, where

48 Stanford University, "The Founding Grant with Amendments, Legislation, and Court Decrees", *Stanford University*, last modified 1987, https://wasc.stanford.edu/sites/g/files/sbiybj10311/f/foundinggrant.pdf, p. 4.

49 Cf. Matt Bowling, "Stanford Research Park: The Engine of Silicon Valley", *The Palo Alto History Project*, [accessed on 19th March, 2019], https://web.archive.org/web/20100116012546/http://www.paloaltohistory.com/stanfordresearchpark.html.

50 Cf. C. Stewart*Gillmor, Fred Terman at Stanford. Building a Discipline, a University, and Silicon Valley* (Stanford: Stanford University Press, 2004).

51 Stuart W. Leslie, "The Biggest 'Angel' of Them All: The Military and the Making of Silicon Valley", in *Understanding Silicon Valley: The Anatomy of an Entrepreneurial Region*, ed. Martin Kenney (Stanford: Stanford University Press, 2000), p.51.

he would personally invest to keep them in the area. In 1939, Bill Hewlett and David Packard put an idea into practice they had from Terman and founded Hewlett-Packard (HP)[52] – the electronics company that for many is the epitome of the first Silicon Valley start-up. Next to HP, whose founding myth and its effect on the concept of creativity will be discussed in more detail later, many other spin-offs of Stanford University were created on the initiative of professor Terman and others. Nevertheless, companies associated with Stanford remained comparatively small in the pre-war period, mostly exploiting technical niches by developing new products or improving existing ones, as Stuart Leslie points out in his study *The biggest „Angel" of Them All: The Military and the Making of Silicon Valley*.[53] This changed generally with the outbreak of the Second World War in 1939 and especially from December 1941 onwards when the USA actively entered the war against Japan and Germany. The military became increasingly interested in the innovative strength of the area resulting in numerous lucrative contracts with the government: "East Coast giants won the lion's share of the defense electronics contracts, but even relatively small orders could make a big difference for the West Coast start-ups" [54] Leslie continues, revealing an early rivalry with enterprises located at the American East Coast and whose successful economic system served as an antagonist for the blueprint of Silicon Valley, as will be discussed later. HP, for example, "jumped from nine employees and $37,000 in sales in 1940 to one hundred employees and $1 million in sales just three years later".[55] But the end of World War II sees a shift in paradigms, that Terman and others were quick to encounter, though:

> "Yet Terman and his colleagues recognized that the war had advanced more than hopes. [The war] had revolutionized electronics. And since most of that new knowledge had been created under government sponsorship, and would therefore be available to anyone, the East Coast industry would no longer be able to control the field through patents as it had done before the war. More than ever, they all realized, in the postwar world the secret of success was going to be research".[56]

52 Leslie, "The Biggest 'Angel' of Them All: The Military and the Making of Silicon Valley", p. 51f.

53 Ibid., p. 52.

54 Ibid., p. 52f.

55 Ibid., p. 77.

56 Ibid., p. 54.

The high-tech companies had to continue developing new ideas and products in order to stay one step ahead of their competitors from other regions. And with Terman, who spent the war-time as the director of Harvard's Radio Research Laboratory and returned to Stanford with numerous other military contracts and contacts as well as engineers, the path was prepared to intensify the ties with the U.S. military for which the start-ups created new and innovative products. Accordingly, the focus was not on preserving what was already there, but on further research that comes with appreciating innovations. Abandoning the principle of protection by patents and the corresponding *leading by research* doctrine follows the tradition of rejecting the *covenant not to compete* around three-quarters of a century before. Both concepts abandon the protection of intellectual property in favour of a flexible, but also highly competitive innovation power. From 1870 onwards employees could profit by acting promptly and transforming ideas into new companies (and then, as companies themselves, run the risk of being cheated because of their own employees). And from 1945 onwards, it was the incentives from Stanford University (hence: Frederick Terman) that enabled the companies themselves to act swiftly, recognize the signs of time and escape stagnation by not resting on pre-war patents. Companies affiliated with Stanford grew steady. Nevertheless, this still did not imply a rejection of contracts with the military. The opposite is rather the case, as can be shown by the following example of Varian.

Founded in 1948, Varian is a classic early example of a start-up made by faculty members of Stanford University.[57] Varian's first board meeting took place on campus and several university members were part of Varian's board of directors. In consequence, the company's first commercially successful product, a component for guided missiles is based on the design of a Stanford University consultant.[58] With the Korean War on the horizon, Varian and other electronic companies become "big business".[59] The increasing number

57 Much information in this paragraph is described by Stuart W. Leslie, professor at the department of *History of Science and Technology* at Johns Hopkins University, in his study of the connection between the military and early Silicon Valley. Cf. Leslie, "The Biggest 'Angel' of Them All: The Military and the Making of Silicon Valley".

58 Ibid., p. 55.

59 Ibid. So does the whole area. As Leslie points out, "California's share of prime military contracts doubled during the course of the war, from 13.2 percent to 26 percent. From 1951 to 1953 California received some thirteen billion dollars in prime contracts, overtaking longtime defense contract leader New York State". Cf. Ibid.

of research and development contracts from the government (thanks to Terman's approach described above) and the ahead coming production contracts show the success of both "of California aerospace and electronics companies in anticipating and cultivating the military market".[60] Varian expanded its range of products with "all but a tiny fraction destined for the defense industry" and "strengthened its ongoing ties to the university by signing on as the first tenant of the Stanford Industrial Park".[61] Varian's products in the 1950s and beyond were nearly exclusively made for the military – and so were research and products of many other already established companies and newly founded spinoffs emerging out of Stanford.[62]

Although Leland Stanford's and Vannevar Bush's goal of working towards a better world of understanding and knowledge continued to survive in the background, the aim to go for profits in dependencies with the military prevailed. Creativity, at this first cold-war episode, is a means to an end. It was used to be one step ahead of competitors in the bid for contracts from the military through new or innovative ideas – purposefully focused on producing a final value. Here, too, a seemingly paradoxical mix of rather idealistic world-improving ideas on the one hand and a competitive purpose-oriented business logic on the other hand was created; a combination that continues to this very day, as will be analysed later on.

5.1.4 A DIFFERENT PLACE – INNOVATING BY BEING DIFFERENT

The above discussed very early historical preconditions laid the foundation for a creativity narrative on which to further build. However, they are not yet an expression of the Silicon Valley's own awareness regarding an indistinctive and genuine notion of creativity. Up to this point, creativity operated more in the background, at the interconnections of tacit structures such

60 Ibid.

61 Leslie, "The Biggest 'Angel' of Them All: The Military and the Making of Silicon Valley", p. 55f.

62 Ibid., p. 56. Varian still exists as a company today, and its headquarter is still in Palo Alto, hence, in the Silicon Valley. However, it is not easy today to draw conclusions about the company's military past. In 1999, the company split into three independent divisions: Varian, Inc., Varian Semiconductor and Varian Medical Systems. The latter is still at home in Palo Alto; the website *www.varion.com* leads to the medically oriented part of the conglomerate. On the website itself there is as well nothing about the past with the military. Neither do the other two companies say or publish.

as the *nonenforceable covenant not to compete*, while companies (predominantly from the semiconductor industry) emerged in the foreground seeking large contracts with the government – all compliant with given rules and manners. This changed with the ideas and ideals of Counterculture in the 1960s, which opened a new way for some members of IT to understand and develop technology – as it will be analysed in chapter 5.2. In the course of these changes, the external expression and with it the self-image of some entrepreneurs in Silicon Valley also changed, which helped the place to become the geographical and idealistic centre of a symbiosis between counter- and hacker culture. This self-conception was nourished by the demarcation to other, long-established institutions, in particular via "a keen awareness of the region as existing largely outside the purview of the large, ponderous, bureaucratic electronics firms and financial institutions of the East Coast".[63] Hence, self-awareness succeeded through opposition to the existing. In the process of becoming, attempts are made to do everything in exactly the opposite way so as to create the greatest possible dissociation from the established – no longer only in an intrinsic respect, but also in an expressive way.

This is represented by the archetypal co-founder of the games company Atari, the iconic enterprise whose founders and employees "invented a culture and paved the way for today's tech moguls":[64] Nolan Bushnell, the "first t-shirt tycoon" who "also wrote what has become the quintessential Silicon Valley script", [65] as Fisher describes it. He characterises this script as follows: "Young kid with radical idea hacks together something cool, builds a wild freewheeling company around it, and becomes rich and famous in the process".[66] When Bushnell co-founded Atari in 1972, he and his company were different in many ways. Atari is producing consumer electronics instead of "heavy-duty hardware"[67] with which he corresponds to the new dogma of Counterculture: to regard technology as something rather small, individual and interesting; a personal tool and toy that is.[68]

---

63 Sturgeon, "How Silicon Valley Came to Be", p. 16f.

64 Chris Stokel-Walker, "Atari Teenage Riot: The Inside Story Of Pong And The Video Game Industry's Big Bang, *BuzzFeed*, last modified 29th November, 2012, https://www.buzzfeed.com/chrisstokelwalker/atari-teenage-riot-the-inside-story-of-pong-and-t.

65 Fisher, *Valley of Genius*, "Ready Player One" section, para. 1.

66 Ibid.

67 Ibid., para 2.

68 Cf. see chapter 5.2.2.

Furthermore, Bushnell has a main influence on the attire of engineers and computer specialists working in IT. Clothing for employees working with mainframe computers before the 1970s were formal and strict. The dominant culture back then, which embodies a rigid and bureaucratic understanding of technology, is represented by the numerous semiconductor companies based in Silicon Valley but most and foremost by an omnipotent but "flawed"[69] IBM. With its market power and influence, IBM was chosen as an ideal opponent by all those technology-affine movements, communities and individuals that could identify with the Counterculture in one way or another. This eventually led to Stewart Brand, editor of the Whole Earth Catalog,[70] saying in a now-famous 1972 *Rolling Stone* article: "In every computer-business story I've ever heard, IBM invariably plays the heavy".[71] But the general public was also aware of the importance of the company. This was, for example, due to the moon landing in 1969, when numerous IBMers (as the company's employees call themselves), recognizable by the embroidered initials "IBM" on the back of their shirts, were part of the staff team in NASA's *Apollo Control Center*[72] as Figure 1 reveals rather strongly:

69 George DeMet, "The Search for Meaning in 2001", *The 2001 Archive*, [accessed 22nd June, 2019], https://2001archive.org/resources/the-search-for-meaning-in-2001/.

70 Cf. Fisher, *Valley of Genius*, "The Time Machine" section, para. 3.

71 Stewart Brand, "Spacewar: Fanatic Life and Symbolic Death Among the Computer Bums", *Spacewar*, [accessed 22nd June, 2019], http://www.wheels.org/spacewar/stone/rolling_stone.html.

72 Cf. Sam Gordy, "IBM & NASA: Working Side-by-Side to Land on the Moon", *IBM*, last modified 19th July, 2019, https://www.ibm.com/blogs/think/2019/07/ibm-nasa-working-side-by-side-to-land-on-the-moon/.

Fig. 1: NASA & IBM, the official subtitles are: "IBM engineers monitor data from a Saturn Instrument Unit during an Apollo launch, at Cape Kennedy, Florida. Throughout the manned space program, IBM and NASA personnel worked side-by-side.

(Photo: IBM)", https://www.ibm.com/blogs/think/2019/07/ibm-nasa-working-side-by-side-to-land-on-the-moon/.

In the black and white image, which is not exactly dated, but which, based on the historical background knowledge, can be roughly attributed to the year of the moon landing, 1969, numerous (exclusively male) people can be seen behind contemporary electronic devices, partly operating them and partly engaged in conversation with each other. The equipment is arranged in rows causing the people to stand and act in a certain row as well, albeit casually scattered. At least 80 people can be recognised. The whole scene looks lively and busy. Most men are dressed in white long-sleeved shirts, a few have kept their jackets on, and even fewer are wearing short-sleeved shirts (such as the man prominently positioned in the centre-right of the picture). Of a great many of the people pictured, the back view is visible – including two people positioned almost exactly in the centre of the photograph. On their white shirts, the initials "IBM" are clearly visible in large black letters on the back of their shirts. A little to the right of the two men and in the same row is another man with "IBM" initials on his back. He appears to be involved in a discussion with at least two other men who stand in a small circle for this purpose. A fourth individual gives the impression as though he is listening and possibly also taking part in the discussion. Three rows in front of this small group, and thus further away and more difficult for the observer to recognise, are at least two, but probably three, other people with the "IBM" logo on their shirts. Whether there are other people with "IBM" logo in the room is not evident due to the picture's quality and the arrangement of the people, but it can by no means be ruled out.

The picture has been published on the official IBM website for the purpose of the 50th anniversary of the moon landing and is intended to remind viewers of the close cooperation between IBM and NASA. This is certainly conveyed in the picture, although it only represents a single moment in time (which again is the very nature of any photograph). Indeed, it is not only the presence of no small number of IBM employees at the epicentre of the lunar landing, but especially their incorporation and self-evident presence that emphasise the private company's close collaboration with the US public space agency.

This led to the emergence of some pop cultural references reminiscent of a certain unease against the dominance of the company which are widely recognised and iconised by this day.[73] In reflecting the role of *hackers* for the

73 This sentence is referring specifically to the urban myth surrounding the fictious friendly and polite, but ultimately murderous artificial intelligence system called *HAL* in Stanley Kubrick's film "2001: A Space Odyssey" from 1968.The name of this AI, and thus the AI itself, appears to be an innuendo of IBM: If one takes the following letter in the alphabet for each letter in HAL, one arrives at IBM. However, both director Kubrick as well as the film's co-writer Arthur C. Clarke contradicted the assumption that this was intentional. Rather, according to them, it was a coincidence. Clarke actually denounced the fact that they were asked almost every week about the possible connection between HAL and IBM, which both would be very annoyed about in his book *The Lost Words of 2001*. In addition, IBM was involved in the making of the movie and the final play should contain product placements of IBM, but when the company learned that a murderous computer is part of the cast, they made sure

computer revolution, book author Steven Levy noted in 1984: "All you had to do was look at someone in the IBM world and note the button-down white shirt, the neatly pinned black tie, the hair carefully held in place, and the tray of punch cards in hand".[74] By the early 1970s, IBM was part of the US public scientific establishment – and looked like it, too.

The following visual example (Figure 2) illustrates this more precisely:

Fig. 2: IBM's System/360.

https://www.ibm.com/ibm/history/ibm100/us/en/icons/system360/.

their trademark is in no relation to HAL whatsoever. Cf. DeMet, "The Search for Meaning in 2001," [accessed 21st June, 2019], https://2001archive.org/resources/the-search-for-meaning-in-2001/; Aisha Harris, "Is HAL Really IBM?" *Slate*, last modified 7th January, 2013, https://slate.com/culture/2013/01/hal-9000-ibm-theory-stanley-kubrick-letters-shed-new-light-on-old-debate.html; Arthur C. Clarke, *The Lost Worlds of 2001* (1971).

74 Steven Levy, *Hackers* (Sebastopol: O'Reilly, 2010), p. 30.

The colour photo from the mid-1960s shows a large room with several computers and cabinets. The floor is tiled, and flat lamps are set into the ceiling, immersing the room in a rather cool light. The mainframe computer is a System 360 from IBM, as can be seen from the inscribed sign above the front calculator cabinet. In the foreground, directly in front of the IBM System 360 branding sign, there is a small, narrow desk at which a man in a black suit sits. The face is not recognisable, it is turned away from the observer. The man's hairstyle looks accurately trimmed; he wears glasses. In his hands he holds a sheet of paper, presented to him by a second man standing to his right. The man standing points out something on the paper to the man sitting. This man also wears a suit and a neat short hairstyle. His face is also turned away, only a part of the profile is visible.

The picture is part of a series on IBM's achievements on the occasion of their 100th anniversary in 2011. The accompanying text highlights the importance of the portrayed System 360 computer, which, according to IBM, generated 20 years of (economic and cultural) dominance in the computer industry for the company from the mid-1960s onwards.[75]

The men seem to be talking about what is written on the sheet of paper. Their posture seems strict and controlled, they seem impersonal by turning their faces away. The whole atmosphere looks very tidy, very clean, almost clinical or even sterile, but also firm and stable, yet inflexible and not very agile due to the apparent massiveness of the mainframe computer and the uniformity of the two faceless (supposed) employees. It becomes noticeable: the picture is about the mainframe computer in the room, the human being is subordinated to it here and only plays a serving role.

The already mentioned cliché of uniform men in black suits representing the dominant power seems to be confirmed in these two images. In response, Nolan Bushnell put on a wardrobe showing to the outside which new spirit prevails at Atari and where this influence came from. In his own words he recalls on this account: "As an engineer I wore a coat and tie to work every day; however, we all had our hippie costumes and we would go to San Francisco and pretend we were flower children. The ultimate posers, we were! The hippie culture was fascinating to us".[76]

---

75 Cf. w. A., "System 360 From Computers to Computer Systems", [accessed 20th March, 2020], https://www.ibm.com/ibm/history/ibm100/us/en/icons/system360/.

76 Fisher, *Valley of Genius*, "Ready Player One" section, para. 2.

In contrast to other influential developments, this like no other before shows a very pronounced awareness of a Silicon Valley-specific *otherness* and the desire to embody and show it externally. References to the difference in clothing and its significance for the overall self-perception of IT appear repeatedly in those pop cultural sources known to be in close relation to the communal spirit of IT or are mouthpieces of the tech world. One example is a detailed story about the emergence of Atari and its first well-known arcade game called *Pong* on the website of the media and technology company *BuzzFeed*, stating both: "*Pong* took video games out of windowless computer labs full of buttoned-up coders and brought it to the masses", and: "the men who created and crafted *Pong* embodied the bootstrap start-up culture that typifies the most exciting edges of today's tech landscape. They were knocked back by old men in drab suits who said games weren't going to be big business".[77] For author David Kushner, the Silicon Valley changed from "essentially men in suits" to "smelly hippies in jeans smoking weed"[78] because of Atari and its new established casual culture: "Atari was the counterculture come to Silicon Valley" ,[79] Kushner says, with which he especially deals with the expression and staging of hippieism and does not further question the possible connection between Counterculture and Silicon Valley.[80]

Not only in terms of workwear Atari pioneered a new work environment, which became progressively shaped by the notion of creativity and initially spread to clusters of the emerging *creative class*,[81] but eventually to almost all areas of western working life. According to the chief designer of Atari and

---

77 Stokel-Walker, "Atari Teenage Riot: The Inside Story of Pong and The Video Game Industry's Big Bang". The reference to *old men in grey suits* and thus to a stereotyped *old system* is reminiscent of Michael Ende's book "Momo" – the publication of which coincides roughly with the time of Atari's foundation, namely 1974 – and the tale's antagonists, the "grey men", with whom Ende is said to have criticised the existing financial system and the *aging money*, a dictum of Rudolf Steiner. Cf. Michael Ende in Werner Onken, „Die ökonomische Botschaft von Michael Endes 'Momo'. Mit einem Brief von Michael Ende an Werner Onken vom 3. September 1986", *Sozialökonomie.info*, [accessed 23rd June, 2019], https://www.sozialoekonomie.info/Weiterf%C3%BChrendes/weiterfuehrendes-3-werner-onken-die-oekonomische-botschaft-von-michael-endes-momo.html.

78 Ibid.

79 Fisher, *Valley of Genius*, "Breakout" section, para. 4.

80 The specific influences and connections of 1960s counterculture on IT will be discussed in particular in chapter 5.2.2 (The Improbable Affinity of Hippies and Hackers with Technology).

81 Cf. Florida, *The Rise of the Creative Class, Revisited*.

creator of *Pong*, Allan Alcorn, it was due to the founder's young age and their inexperience the founders did not set up any rules in the first time with Atari. For example, employees did not have to arrive on time for work.

What mattered was whether the work was done or not: "Punching a time clock wasn't the point, it was getting the job done. If you could do it without showing up, so be it!".[82] In direct comparison, the next image (Figure 3) represents a sharp contrast to what is shown in the previous image:

Fig. 3: The PARC Computer Science Laboratory (CSL).

https://www.computerhistory.org/revolution/input-output/14/348/1868.

The photograph from around 1970 shows a scene insight the "beanbag" conference room at Xerox PARC, where laboratory director Bob Taylor held informal meetings for employees to present their new ideas, as stated in the official description of the image. Six people are recognizable who, sitting on beanbags, have formed an almost closed circle and seem to be engaged in

82 Fisher, *Valley of Genius*, "Ready Player One" section, para. 9.

a discussion among themselves. The are located in a relatively large room which, as far as is recognisable from the detail of the picture, is enclosed to the right by many floor-to-ceiling windows. The back wall of the room is mostly white, though it appears that it has been extensively marked and painted by notes at various spots. Many more beanbags and some cushions can be seen in the room, which are spread all over the floor. Apart from a small wall clock at the back left there is no other visible interior. No other furniture is apparent. All persons suggest a relaxed impression, one laughs, one smokes. One person wears a T-shirt, another a turtleneck sweater. Only one person wears a tie. One person is holding a sheet of paper and studying it.

The presented scene is meaningful for the creativity narrative in IT because of several different aspects. The most obvious are the beanbags as office furniture, which today can also be seen as an exhibit at the Computer History Museum in Silicon Valley. As a limitation, it must be mentioned that Figure 2 obviously portrays a mainframe computer workstation and Figure 3 a meeting room especially designed for informal meetings. However, the architecture of the room itself is the next peculiarity, as the walls can be written on. The room itself is included in the creative process of exchanging ideas – a concept that continues to enjoy great popularity in places of knowledge production today. Finally, by comparing the outfits of the employees present in Figure 2 and 3, the differences in work and corporate culture described above are revealed.

Bushnell himself, in addition, also contributed to the emergence of a Silicon Valley prototype. His "personality established an important paradigm for Silicon Valley entrepreneurs: willful, daring, imaginative, hypercompetitive, [...] It's difficult to imagine Steve Jobs without Bushnell before him".[83] Thanks to the success of Pong, Atari made a lot of money and Bushnell developed a very expressive lifestyle, which he exhibited to the outside world. Retrospectively at the end of the 1990s, he gained the attribution of "a myth-feeding embodiment of a flashy entrepreneurial lifestyle that inspired a generation to forgo ties, quit day jobs and change the world".[84]

---

83 Henry Lowood in Stokel-Walker, "Atari Teenage Riot: The Inside Story of Pong and The Video Game Industry's Big Bang".

84 Dan Pulcrano, "Back to the Garage", *Metro*, 16th-22nd September, 1999, http://www.metroactive.com/papers/metro/09.16.99/cover/bushnell1-9937.html. This lifestyle was portrayed in detail by the media: Bushnell gave an interview to Playboy, Time magazine had a cover story about him, and Fortune magazine took pictures from him sitting in a hot tub next to a "lady friend". Bushnell owned expensive cars and boats as well. But the new luxury was also recognizable within the company: allegedly the company jet

This lifestyle, as well as the rejection of formal clothing as an expression of the opposition to the established and the resonant, new own *otherness*, collided with their equivalents in a single moment when Bushnell decided to hire an external manager as CEO, who came from the fashion company Ralph Lauren.[85] Ray Kassar, the manager's name, remembers: "When I arrived there on the first day I was dressed in a business suit and tie and I met Nolan Bushnell. He had a T-shirt on with the printed inscription "I LOVE TO FUCK". That was my introduction to Atari".[86]

Due to the discrepancy between alien management and local employees, Atari was quickly confronted with a clash of cultures. Al Alcorn empathises that Ray Kassar indeed was a businessman. But he has never visited the West Coast before, and therefore could not understand electronic products. Alcorn goes on to say:

> "Ray had an executive parking spot for his chauffeur-driven Rolls-Royce. He had a helicopter landing pad. He had an executive dining room so the executives did not have to rub shoulders with the unwashed. It was a term they liked to use: "the great unwashed." He was really tone-deaf to what was going on around him".[87]

This quote shows the persistent rejection of an established and conservative type of entrepreneur from the East Coast. By contrast, there is the notion of creativity personified in the ordinary Atari employees and their founders. This creativity is also literally brought to the fore against the supremacy of managers in one's own company, as the following short anecdote from programmer and later co-founder of several video game companies, Alan Miller, testifies:

> "I was at one of the very first meetings that Ray had with the entire group. There were probably eighty to a hundred technologists in the room and somebody asked him, 'Well, what kind of experience do you have dealing

---

was used to fly in fresh shrimps, the size of which showed how well Atari was doing. This was made possible by the extraordinary and rapid growth of the company. To put this into perspective, as early as 1981 Atari was making 3.2 billion dollars gross, more money than all of Hollywood at that time. Cf. Ibid.; Fisher, *Valley of Genius*, "3P1C F41L" section, para. 2.

85 Fisher, *Valley of Genius*, "Towel Designers" section, para. 4.

86 Ibid.

87 Fisher, *Valley of Genius*, "Towel Designers" section, para. 4.

> with creative people?' Because, you know, we were creating entertainment. And he said, 'Oh, I've had a lot of experience dealing with creative people. I've worked with towel designers my entire career.' And I don't know about the other people, but I was just flabbergasted when he said that, because it showed he was entirely clueless about the industry and what we were doing".[88]

These sentences show a new self-confidence of the programmers who now start to take pride in their own creativity. They see themselves as smarter than the managers who did neither understand nor seem to be prepared to take on such employees. Programmers saw more in the games they developed and granted them the ability to address geopolitical fears (such as a potential thermonuclear war or the fear that the "society was robotizing)[89] and reflect them in gameplay. Like books or music before, some programmers saw games as a means of expressing these subtle fears: "Games were responding to these floating senses of technological threat that were in the air. There is really something dreamlike about them. They were the poetry of the age".[90] It was also an early celebration of IT's self-proclaiming exceptionism, which is displayed here (especially in the example above by Nolan Bushnell). Alcorn, Bushnell and other members of Atari not only saw themselves as different, but they were also convinced they were better at what they did. And this was made possible by their own *creative ability*, which they not only believed they possessed, but could now also express through the new and informal patterns at Atari and which others from outside their world simply could not understand. The misunderstanding between external managers who take over leadership responsibility within the company and the so far developed inward logic of the creativity narrative was not only about the method of running a company and the underlying differences in culture, though. It could also be found in the discrepancies between a parent company and a subsidiary or branch located in Silicon Valley. Alcorn, in particular, emphasised this opposition consistently. Hence, when Atari was taken over by Warner Communications in 1976 and

---

88 Ibid.

89 Ibid.

90 Ibid. Stanford's Henry Lowood adds on this point: "The main impact of Pong on contemporary culture is that it had an impact on contemporary culture [...]. Before this, connecting games and culture wasn't even a question on anyone's mind". Lowood in Stokel-Walker, "Atari Teenage Riot: The Inside Story of Pong and The Video Game Industry's Big Bang".

Bushnell left the company in 1978, many were waiting for the next groundbreaking game console. But this never happened. For Alcorn, this was again due to different types of management culture: "You know in Silicon Valley if you don't obsolete yourself somebody else will, right? The Warner guys didn't really understand that. They were from an East Coast company and thought that they had an evergreen kind of product".[91]

However, while Atari's parent company did not understand how to revive local innovation, other companies did not realize their subsidiary's potential in Silicon Valley even when it was fully developed and ready for rollout. The best-known and most important example of this is the case of Xerox PARC, which impressively demonstrates the discrepancy between the existing visionary ideas on the one hand and the lack to fully grasp and appreciate them on the other hand.

Xerox was founded in 1906 in Rochester, New York, and by the 1960s it became the dominant company in the photocopying industry. But competitors were catching up: In April 1970, IBM presented its first copier for office use, "marking the end of Xerox's historic monopoly and introducing a period of painful retrenchment at Xerox". [92] Concerned about losing market power, Xerox opened the Xerox Palo Alto Research Center, Xerox PARC for short, in July of the same year with "one of the most exceptional teams of inventing talent ever assembled in one place".[93] As early as 1972, it was possible to learn about the excellence of the researchers and at the same time about the advanced office equipment (here: a bean-bag chair) of Xerox PARC at *Rolling Stone*:

> "[Distinguished researcher] Ian Kay, 32, child prodigy (National Quiz Kid at ten), former musician and artist [...]. Alan shifts comfortably in his office bean-bag chair and appraises his colleagues. 'This is really a frightening group, by far the best I know of as far as talent and creativity. The people here all have track records and are used to dealing lightning with both hands.'"[94]

---

91 Fisher, *Valley of Genius*, "Towel Designers" section, para. 8.

92 Michael Hiltzik, *Dealers of Lightning: Xerox PARC and the Dawn of the Computer Age* (New York: HarperCollins Publishers Inc., 1999), p. x.

93 Ibid., p.xx.

94 Stewart Brand, "Spacewar: Fanatic Life and Symbolic Death Among the Computer Bums".

In the coming years, several of the most important inventions and developments that form the foundation for the later PC revolution and establish Silicon Valley as the world's leading innovation area for technology were to be developed at PARC. Among other major technological milestones, the first laser printer, Ethernet, the first graphical user interface (GUI) and the concept of the laptop were invented and developed in the premises of this research centre. However, Xerox's management was so focused on the copying industry that, except for the laser printer, they were unable to successfully bring these inventions to market:

> "The scientists' unfettered creativity, not to mention their alien habits of mind and behavior, fomented unrelenting conflict with their stolid parent company. [...] Xerox management regarded PARC's achievements first with bemusement, then uneasiness, and finally hostility. Because Xerox never fully understood the potential value of PARC's technology, it stood frozen on the threshold of new markets while its rivals—including big, lumbering IBM—shot past into the computer age."[95]

This 1999 quotation addresses several key elements introduced in this subchapter that have been critical in developing the creativity narrative in IT and which is now represented by the author. It first demonstrates the change in work climate and the ascription of creativity as a decisive distinctive factor, which is also apparent at the Atari example, but which in this quote is not explicitly communicated by means of an informal approach to clothing but is generally described as *unfettered*. In retrospect, the author of the quote also takes a very clear stance against the parent company and evidently advocates the narrative of creativity outlined so far – a narrative that is affirmative of IT but condemns the perspective of the corporate world beyond Silicon Valley in terms of *stolid* or *lumbering*. The author of the quote also takes a very clear stance against the parent company in retrospect, and obviously represents the narrative of creativity that has been sketched so far: in hindsight, the author – like most Silicon Valley chroniclers – refuses to treat the lack of recognising the numerous potentials in Silicon Valley (and here in Xerox PARC) in a neutral way. Rather, he shows no sympathy for those who neither recognised nor promoted creativity before it became a compulsory exercise, as can be seen from the choice of words and the tendentious description.

---

95 Hiltzik, *Dealers of Lightning*, p. xxii.

It is significant to note that the innovations came out of Xerox PARC, even though the research laboratory was newly founded by Xerox in Silicon Valley instead of them buying up an existing institute with an already established certain and typical work mentality. Hence, the place's inherent attraction and influence (and thus the kind of people it tempted) was considerably greater than that of the parent company far away in the state of New York.

5.1.5 NO NEED TO INVENT SOMETHING NEW, JUST LOOK AROUND

The geographic presence and close interaction between individual actors[96] in Silicon Valley are another formative influence on the creativity narrative developed in the Silicon Valley. Actors here are not only humans, but also include material things (here especially the agglomeration of tech companies, the corresponding technical infrastructure, the presence of latest technical achievements and the infrastructure to quickly set up new businesses) and semiotic concepts (here especially the political-ideological foundations that frame the logic of a local creativity narrative, the ability to identify new ideas and their connectivity to resulting visions, as well as the opposition to the established East-Coast economy and the awareness of a genuine and general *otherness*).

96 The use of the term "actor" prompts a connection with the actor-network theory (ANT) (Latour 2013). Indeed, there is relevant literature dealing with the question of whether Foucault's concept of a dispositif might have anticipated the basic idea of ANT. After all, according to philologist and communication scholar Simon Ganahl (2016), the dispositif is a network that links discursive and material elements, i.e., it also opens up to the objective world and does not remain in the theoretical – similar to the ANT developed years later. Dutch sociologist and expert on ANT Annemarie Mol quotes Michael Callon (1999), who emphasised that the actor-network theory is actually not a theory (Mol 2010, p. 253) – because just like Foucault's original thoughts on discourse analysis ANT "offers no causal explanations and no consistent method. It rather takes the form of a repertoire" (Ibid., p. 261). Ganahl sees the fundamental difference between the two approaches less in specific differences in content than in the typological quality of an analysis: unlike ANT, a dispositif is always also a political intervention. For this reason alone, a reference to ANT will not be pursued further here. However, for reasons of clarity, some of the terminology (e.g. "network") will be adopted and indicated where appropriate. Cf. Simon Ganahl, „Ist Foucaults dispositif ein Akteur-Netzwerk?" *foucaultblog*, 2016; Annemarie Mol, „Actor-Network Theory: sensitive terms and enduring tensions", *Kölner Zeitschrift für Soziologie und Sozialpsychologie* Sonderheft, no. 50 (2010), pp. 253-269; Bruno Latour, "Reassembling the social. An introduction to actor-network-theory", *Journal of Economic Sociology* (2013), p. 73-87.

By connecting, hence *enacting, enabling and adapting*[97] with each other, people, things and concepts collectively form *networks* known as Silicon Valley using the site as a metonym that can be further legitimised as such, since it also functions as an superordinate entity, when referring to *the* Silicon Valley (or even just the *Valley*), which *acts* or *thinks* on behalf of (and through) the connected (human and nonhuman) actors.[98] Grammatically speaking, this is a metonymy. It underlines the assumption that a singular predominant reading of creativity exists, since it is not differentiated whether Facebook, or Apple, etc. does or say something when talking about Silicon Valley as a metonym.

In addition, it is important to note that the term *network* is not only meant in a figurative or at least subtle sense, but that it is physically very easily accessible and literally real for insiders – which is why this aspect of IT's creativity narrative is situated in the chapter on its geosocial setting. The former CEO of Yahoo and early employee at Google Marissa Mayer describes this as follows: "I've heard both the founding stories of Google and Yahoo, and for both those companies, the founders didn't even have to get into a car. They could literally go to the law office, the venture capitalists, the bank... on a bike. It's all that close together." [99] Already Doug Engelbart benefited from the presence of all the important elements needed to make his *Mother of all Demos* a success. And Stewart Brand's[100] office when he was publishing the Whole Earth Catalog was "located right across the street"[101] from Doug Engelbart's office, so Brand recalls: "I remember walking over there thinking, *This could be interesting and maybe even important*".[102] For computer engineer and pioneer Lee Felsenstein "the story of Silicon Valley is the story of networks".[103] He continues to say: "There was never any centralized place. They were all what they call local maxima, little mounds of people here and there, and people move between

97 These terms are borrowed from ANT terminology (see note above). Cf. Annemarie Mol, "Actor-Network Theory: sensitive terms and enduring tensions", p. 260.

98 For example, article headlines on the topic of how Silicon Valley *wants* to abolish dying: John Naughton, "Why Silicon Valley wants to thwart the grim reaper", *The Guardian*, last modified 9th April, 2017, https://www.theguardian.com/commentisfree/2017/apr/09/silicon-valley-wants-to-cheat-grim-reaper-google.

99 Fisher, *Valley of Genius*, "Silicon Valley, Explained" section, para. 2.

100 Ibid., "The Big Bang" section, para. 2.

101 Fisher, *Valley of Genius*, "Silicon Valley, Explained" section, para. 2.

102 Ibid. [emph. in original].

103 Ibid.

them, that's the important thing. So it's a decentralized set of networks with mobility among them".[104]

Silicon Valley as a whole is not a relatively volatile network – just as it did not suddenly emerge overnight, as the previous subsections of this chapter have already shown. Rather, Felsenstein's mobile *decentralised set of networks* proves to be extremely open to disruption (which again is due to the aspects outlined in previous and upcoming subchapters), so that, although it persists in the external structures, it constantly redeveloped internally[105] and with increasing speed.[106]

The latter has mainly been possible due to a certain type of funding, whose influence on the creativity narrative in IT has steadily increased: the so-called venture capital (VC).[107] The policy framework for this was established in 1953, when the Small Business Administration was established to support small and medium-sized enterprises and granted tax breaks for investments in such enterprises. This led to the emergence of small investment firms that co-financed up-and-coming start-ups. Very early on, Silicon Valley became the focus of investment firms. Fairchild Semiconductor, Intel and Xerox were among the first companies to be (partially) financed in this way.[108] Especially for the risk-hungry engineers, computer scientists and hobbyists in Silicon

104 Ibid.

105 While Silicon Valley has changed fundamentally over time, it has continued to extract the core aspects of today's creativity narrative in IT by introducing additional aspects that have further shaped the narrative. For example, the peak of the video game consoles under Atari's dominance up until the video game crash in 1983 has been referred to as the "first magical wave of Silicon Valley". Cf. Fisher, *Valley of Genius*, "Silicon Valley, Explained" section, para. 2.

106 In this sense, it is again in line with ANT's assumption that networks would quickly emerge and disappear, as the *network of networks* (by means of a structure for Felsenstein's *set of* networks) outlasts the individual decentralized networks in contrast.

107 Venture capital is defined as a financial intermediary. It invests capital of an investor in private companies that are part of a VC's portfolio and then takes on an active role by both monitoring and helping portfolio start-ups with the goal to generate a maximum profit from the initial investment. Cf. Andrew Metrick and Ayako Yasuda, Venture Capital and the Finance of Innovation (September 2010). Venture Capital and the Finance of Innovation, 2nd Edition, Andrew Metrick and Ayako Yasuda, eds., John Wiley and Sons, Inc., 2010. Available at SSRN: https://ssrn.com/abstract=929145.

108 Judy Radler Cohen, "A Brief History of Venture Capital", *Financial Poise*, last modified 21st November, 2018, https://www.financialpoise.com/a-brief-history-of-venture-capital/.

Valley, who were surrounded by potential innovations, this created a possibility to put an idea into practice: "There were bankers who could loan you money, but they wanted guarantees that could get it back. Venture capitalists expect failure. They discovered that they could gamble big with maybe ten firms..."[109] says Alvy Ray Smith, co-founder of Pixar. With massive growth of technical innovations in the areas of computers and electronics, VC investments in the Silicon Valley also grew rapidly in the 1960s and 1970s. That happened to the extent that the VC method soon became the standard for early financing of new tech start-ups.[110] With further legislative changes in favour of VC firms in the late 1970s, investment rose from $100-200 million in the 1970s to over $4 billion in the late 1980s.[111] The next few years saw a further steady increase in investments, and more and more potential founders were trying to raise venture capital funds – and an increasing number of VCs were trying to find and finance good ideas, bringing in more and more money.

This follows the concept of contingency. In this context, the term contingency is understood in the way that Baraldi presents it in relation to the field of logic: Contingency is the simultaneous exclusion of necessity and impossibility.[112] The concept of contingency refers to the actual matter that what currently is (and thus is not impossible) could also be possible (and thus is not necessary) in a different way. Contingency is the possibility that something might be different than what it actually is.[113] Possibilities can be realised in a way different than expected. Contingency therefore implies the possibility of disappointment and the necessity to take risks.[114]

For the creativity narrative in IT, this is a significant transition as the logic of the place with its vicinity and reciprocal connections is supplemented by a further aspect. With the appearance of venture capital in full force as an additional actor since the 1980s, the Silicon Valley network changes and a new mentality is introduced, as the companies also settled locally and looked for

---

109 Fisher, *Valley of Genius*, "Silicon Valley, Explained" section, para. 2.

110 Ibid.

111 Cf. Paul A. Gompers, "Optimal Investment, Monitoring, and the Staging of Venture Capital", *The Journal of Finance*, no. 50 (1995): 1461-1489, doi:10.1111/j.1540-6261.1995.tb05185.x.

112 Cf. Claudio Baraldi, „Doppelte Kontingenz", in *GLU. Glossar zu Niklas Luhmanns Theorie sozialer Systeme* (Frankfurt am Main: Suhrkamp, 2015), p. 37-39.

113 Cf. Ibid., p. 37.

114 See chapter 6.2.2 for a detailed consideration of contingency and VC.

new investment opportunities on-site, as the following quote of Chris Caen, manager at Atari demonstrates:

> "So imagine there is more money than God, and it has no place to go, but there are a lot of cocktail napkins with things scribbled on them, and those are what are called start-ups. [...] The joke used to be at the time, this being '97 through 2000 — the golden era — was basically all you had to do was stand at the corner with a cocktail napkin, and VCs would throw money at you from a passing car. I loved it".[115]

The mentioned *golden era* falls in the period before the so-called dotcom bubble, when funds were invested not primarily in technical product developments, but in Internet start-ups that wanted to offer and sell existing products on their websites. Two aspects are of particular significance for the creativity narrative's development. First, there are immaterial services that are to be created and no longer products with a physical presence such as new software, hardware or the like.[116] In order to receive funding from venture capitalists, the presentation and the presenter's power of persuasion must be sufficient – not necessarily the idea itself. Hence, a rather transformative idea ahead of its time might be impossible to grasp and to explain and would not receive any funding. Second, these marketplaces (because dotcom companies often were the digital illustration of an analogue sales business) are purely virtual in nature, but without a digital yet new product. In essence, the idea is just another (albeit non-physical) distribution channel that transfers services (such as buying animal feed)[117] from analogue to digital.

115 Fisher, *Valley of Genius*, "The Dot Bomb" section, para. 2.

116 Even though the software is not physical in this sense it must be stored; so the data carrier became the physical representation of the software, i.e. the product, and with the purchase of software one could hold a real product - namely the data carrier - in one's hands.

117 One of the most spectacular collapses of the dot-com bubble was the company "Pets.com", which ran a commercial at the Superbowl for $1.2 million even before its bankruptcy in 2000. In 1999, the revenues of $619,000 were offset by advertising expenditures of $11.8 million. It also remained uncertain whether there was a market for the brand known through the advertising campaign, so that it collapsed in the course of the dot-com crash. Cf. Kirk Cheyfitz, *Thinking Inside the Box: The 12 Timeless Rules for Managing a Successful Business* (New York: Simon and Schuster, 2003).

This was known to go wrong.[118] What lasted in the medium and long term was an even greater focus on the place itself and even more venture capital, since after the dot-com crash, more risk diversification was pursued. Start-ups were less and less publicly traded but became privately-owned. For the Harvard Business Review, this was a "silent, seismic shift [that] has dramatically altered corporate ownership and business governance globally. From 1996 to 2015, the number of publicly traded companies in the United States alone dropped nearly 50%".[119] As a result, the pace picked up further: either it worked, or it failed. And more often than not it failed. For founders, the definition of success shifts towards the front: it is no longer the success of the idea on the market that is decisive, but already the sum of investments achieved by VC upstream.

5.2 THE SELF IMAGE OF THE IT INDUSTRY

5.2.1. THE QUANTIFIABILITY OF CREATIVITY

Both Engelbart's text *Augmenting the Human Intellect* and his *Mother of All Demos* fits into a time in which a scientific examination of the concept of creativity has become increasingly popular. A research using Google Scholar, currently the largest online search engine for scientific texts,[120] indicates a general quantitative conjuncture for creativity at this time and beyond. The search engine indexes most scientific documents, whereby it is assumed that Google

118 Already in 1996, Federal Reserve's chairman Alan Greenspan gave a speech in which he used the term *irrational exuberance* (originally coined by Robert J. Shiller), meaning an exaggerated and incomprehensible behaviour with regard to the vast amounts of money invested in dot-com companies. With hindsight this speech was understood as an early warning of the bursting of an exaggerated inflation and the term became an iconic stylistic idiom in the aftermath of the dot-com crash of 2000-2004. Cf. Alan Greenspan, "The Challenge of Central Banking in a Democratic Society", *The Federal Reserve Board*, last modified 6th December, 1996, https://www.federalreserve.gov/boardocs/speeches/1996/19961205.htm.

119 Dave Ulrich and Justin Allen, "Private Equity's New Phase", *Harvard Business Review*, last modified 9th August, 2016, https://hbr.org/2016/08/private-equitys-new-phase.

120 Michael Gusenbauer, „Google Scholar to overshadow them all? Comparing the sizes of 12 academic search engines and bibliographic databases", *Scientometrics* 118, no. 1 (2019): 177-214, doi: https://doi.org/10.1007/s11192-018-2958-5.

Scholar has indexed about 80 to 90 percent of all documents published in English.[121] Accordingly, the following figures of documents dealing with creativity indicate an increased popularity of creativity in this time. The number of scientific contributions with "creativity" in the title more than quadrupled in the 1950s: while Google Scholar reports 1930 results for the 1940s[122] (after 829 recorded scientific contributions for the 1930s, which already translates into a doubling in the 1940s), the 1950s now see 8810 scientific contributions.[123] Measured in terms of quantity, it was not a short-term trend since the number of scientific contributions regarding creativity not only maintained the record high, but continued to grow. In the next two decades the number will continue to grow and each double – but not quadruple like in the 1950s – in percentage terms, leading to an overall of 19800 contributions in the 1960s[124] and 47800 published documents during the 1970s.[125] Hence, a minimum of 79169 publications with a material reference to creativity has been published in the time between 1930 and 1979 (considering that Google Scholar indexes about 80-90% of all scientific documents, the actual total number ranges from 87966 (with an estimated 90% coverage by Google Scholar) to 98961 (with an estimated 80%). Thus, of the rounded 80000 results, only a little more than one percent falls into the 1930s, just under two and a half percent into the 1940s, but then already a little more than eleven percent into the 1950s, 25 percent into the 1960s, and finally more than 60 percent into the 1970s.

---

121 Madian Khabsa and C. Lee Giles, "The Number of Scholarly Documents on the Public Web", *PLOS ONE*, [accessed 9th May, 2014], https://doi.org/10.1371/journal.pone.0093949.

122 Google Scholar, "1940-1950", [accessed 4th April, 2019], https://scholar.google.de/scholar?q=creativity&hl=de&as_sdt=0%2C5&as_ylo=1940&as_yhi=1950.

123 Ibid., "1950-1960", [accessed 4th April, 2019], https://scholar.google.de/scholar?q=creativity&hl=de&as_sdt=0%2C5&as_ylo=1950&as_yhi=1960.

124 Ibid., "1960-1970", [accessed 4th April, 2019], https://scholar.google.de/scholar?q=creativity&hl=de&as_sdt=0%2C5&as_ylo=1960&as_yhi=1970.

125 Ibid., "1970-1980", [accessed 4th April, 2019], https://scholar.google.de/scholar?q=creativity&hl=de&as_sdt=0%2C5&as_ylo=1970&as_yhi=1980.
In no other decade could a higher percentage increase be achieved than in the 1950s. On the contrary, the number of published articles on creativity decreased for the first time since the 2010s – although the decade has not yet fully passed. However, it has to be remarked that these figures – as mentioned – only refer to the percentage change. A certain saturation is not considered, nor is the ratio to the total number of published scientific documents, which continues to increase over the years.

The increase in the 1950s and beyond has largely been driven by the American psychologist, intelligence researcher and president of the American Psychological Association (APA) Joy Paul Guilford. In 1950, he published a "landmark address"[126] with only one word as title: "Creativity".[127] In it, he addresses the concern that the subject of creativity has so far been appallingly neglected by his peers.[128] Thanks to this (and thanks to the influence of Guilford as a person), creativity research as a scientific field quickly enjoyed great popularity. However, the propositions outlined by Guilford in this text were only accepted with some reservations by his peers. Though Guilford emphasizes the role of cognitive and social processes in creativity research, "the field stayed rather narrow for many years",[129] Harvard-based researcher on social psychology of creativity Teresa M. Amabile concludes. After exploring the state of research on creativity in the late 1970s, she described her impression about this *narrowness* in the 1950s to the mid-1970s as follows:

> "creativity is a quality of the person; most people lack that quality; people who possess the quality – geniuses – are different from everyone else, in talent and personality; we must identify, nurture, appreciate, and protect the creatives among us – but, aside from that, there isn't much we can do".[130]

Consequently, and in order to locate and compare those individuals having that *creative quality*, the longing for quantifiable creativity arose, which in parts is still valid today and became the predominant notion during the first decades of the 20th century's second half. [131] Nevertheless, other currents existed in parallel, which doubted the binary conception of people that are either creative or not but considered creativity as a skill that can be learned, taught, improved, hence trained if a sufficient training program would be

126 Teresa M. Amabile and Julianna Pillemer, "Perspectives on the social psychology of creativity", *The Journal of Creative Behavior* 46.1 (2012): 3.

127 Joy P. Guilford, "Creativity", *American Psychologist* 5, no. 9 (1950): 444–454, doi: 10.1037/h0063487.

128 Ibid., p. 445.

129 Amabile and Pillemer, "Perspectives on the social psychology of creativity, p. 3.

130 Ibid. In her capacity as an American psychologist, Amabile does not necessarily use the term "genius" to refer to the European-philosophically influenced idea of genius.

131 As an example, Amabile cites the Torrance Tests of Creative Thinking (TTCT), which E. Paul Torrance created and established in 1966 as a standard instrument for the aim of detecting numerous creative abilities and personality structures in individuals. Cf. Ibid., p. 3f.

available. Plenty of approaches emerged in this time, of which *brainstorming* is one (and arguably the best known and most durable of all programs). [132] First mentioned by advertiser Alex Osborn as early as ca. 1942,[133] brainstorming is based on clear sets of rules, which have been constantly evolved and led to new approaches – for both individuals and groups. By 1958, the brainstorming process had already been applied at eight out of the ten largest American corporations.[134]

For former Apple employee Alan Cannistraro "many of history's best ideas were generated from a process of brainstorming, experimentation, and iteration. This is one of the most important things I took away from my time at Apple".[135] In a blog article for the magazine *Medium* he describes the use of a technique frequently used at Apple named *Random Entry* with the help of which he claims to have filed twelve patents at least: "The goal is to free associate. While brainstorming these ideas, don't even consider which ideas are the most practical or feasible. That step will come later. Just write down what

---

132 Amabile distinguishes a total of five *hints*, all underlining – in her opinion – that creativity is not a special quality of only a few persons. Brainstorming and other currents is only one of these hints. Others include journals and autobiographies of allegedly creative persons showing that these people have very *uncreative* days as well; or research on the incoherency of conformity and creativity. Cf. Ibid.; R. S. Crutchfield, "Conformity and creative thinking", in *The Atherton Press behavioral science series. Contemporary approaches to creative thinking: A symposium held at the University of Colorado*, eds. H. E. Gruber, G. Terrell, & M. Wertheimer (New York: Atherton Press, 1962), 120-140.

133 There are several references to the first mention of brainstorming by Osborn, as he first presented and introduced the concept in his advertising company BBDO. First reference figures therefore vary between the years 1938 and 1953, as some figures are based on the official mention in Osborn's publications. The given year 1942 refers to the publication of Osborn's book "How to Think Up", which, however, is not commercially available. Cf. mindq, "What is Brainstorming and how is it helpful?" *Mindq*, [accessed on 4th April, 2019], https://www.imindq.com/uses/brainstorming; Knut Holt, "Brainstorming – From Classics to Electronics", *Journal of Engineering Design* 7, no. 1 (1996): 77-82, doi: 10.1080/09544829608907928; John R. Rossiter and Gary L. Lilien, "New 'Brainstorming' Principles", *Australian Journal of Management* 19, no. 1 (1994): 61–72, doi:10.1177/031289629401900104.

134 Hanisha Besant, "The Journey of Brainstorming Regent University School of Business & Leadership", *Journal of Transformational Innovation* 2, no. 1 (2016), pp. 1-7; p. 3.

135 Alan Cannistraro, "Generating Ideas at Apple", *Medium*, last modified 25th January, 2016, https://medium.com/self-starter/generating-ideas-at-apple-71e575a1e2e3. More about these terms and in particular about the concept of iteration, see chapter 6.2.2.

comes to mind".[136] However, when Steve Jobs was leading a brainstorming session, it made sense to think first and then speak:

An article describes how Steve Jobs and Bill Gates use the brainstorming process in their respective ways, showing rather different approaches. Bill Gates at Microsoft used the brainstorming process according to elements of the Yale School of Thought. He used a suggestion box to collect thoughts and suggestions from employees and then withdrew twice a year in his so-called "think week" to create his own ideas from these templates in isolation. He would spend these weeks "alone in deep thought in the confines of an isolated cottage where he would not be disturbed. He was occasionally visited by a caretaker who dropped off prepared meals for him".[137] On the other hand, there was the rather mixed approach by Steve Jobs, as recorded by employees at NeXT in 1987. Jobs' employees were informally sitting in the room using flipchart and notepads while Jobs explained an issue. Then the knowledgeable employees began to present "ideas from their knowledge based on past experiences and understanding of the issue at hand".[138] The session considered to be intense: "Steve Jobs was known to break the traditional rules of Osborn's no criticism approach where he quickly turned down topics that he thought were not relevant to the problem at hand in order to stay focused".[139] Whereas Gates first of all considered all thoughts, Jobs demanded quality from the outset and would accept that interesting ideas might slip by the table. However, following the collection, Gates dealt with the proposals on his own, without being accompanied by an alternative point of view.

5.2.2 THE IMPROBABLE AFFINITY OF HIPPIES AND HACKERS WITH TECHNOLOGY

Technology in general and large-scale information technology in particular appeared frigid and as the epitome of the *military-industrial complex* with its

---

136 Ibid. Cannistraro describes the technique as follows: "Here's how it works: You start with a well-defined problem statement. Then, choose a random word [...]. Then spend the next three minutes coming up with as many ideas as possible that associate that word with the problem statement. Discuss the ideas amongst your team, building on them where they stimulate deeper discussion. Rinse and repeat". Cf. ibid. 260 261 262

137 Cannistraro, "Generating Ideas at Apple", p. 4.

138 Ibid., p.5.

139 Ibid.

cold war bureaucracy,[140] causing an increasingly reluctant stance inside the counterculture communities. Fred Turner provides the 1964 *Free Speech Movement* (FSM) as example, when students at Berkeley University "feared that America's political leaders were treating them as if they were bits of abstract data". [141] Accordingly, Turner concludes that for the students, "computers loomed as technologies of dehumanization, of centralized bureaucracy and the rationalization of social life, and, ultimately, of the Vietnam War".[142] In a famous speech, Mario Savio, the informal student leader of the FSM, articulated the uneasiness of the students who, in his opinion, started to feel like raw materials in a firm rather than human beings in a university. The last part of his speech emphasises the hostility towards the economic involvement and orientation of the university and the underlying desire for freedom among the students:

> "There's a time when the operation of the machine becomes so odious, makes you so sick at heart, that you can't take part! You can't even passively take part! And you've got to put your bodies upon the gears and upon the wheels [...] And you've got to indicate to the people who run it, to the people who own it, that unless you're free, the machine will be prevented from working at all!"[143]

With that, Savio ultimately demands something close to what the Stanford family already envisioned for their newly founded university some decades earlier – as it is imprinted in the university's *Die Luft der Freiheit weht* motto. But as already mentioned, however, it is particularly the former Stanford University spin-offs that became long-established companies in the 1960s, and in which the university holds numerous shares. Yet, despite the FSM is seen as a key protest leading to the 1960s counterculture and their state of clear rejection of large-scale technology, "as [members of this counterculture] played

140 Cf. Fred Turner, *From Counterculture to Cyberculture: Stewart Brand, the Whole Earth Network, and the Rise of Digital Utopianism* (Chicago: The University of Chicago Press, 2006), p. 1 and 4.

141 Ibid., p.1.

142 Ibid., p.2.

143 Mario Savio,*Sproul Hall Steps*, 2nd December, 1964, [accessed 11th April, 2019], http://www.fsm-a.org/stacks/mario/mario_speech.html. In the further course of the speech, students were arrested on a massive scale. About 800 professors from Berkeley University then showed solidarity with the protesters and paid the necessary bail so that the students were released again.

their stereos and dropped LSD many came to believe that small-scale technologies could help bring about an alternative to that world".[144] Hence, technology became embraced and decisively determined by the counterculture of the 1960s – that subculture, which became one of the predominant social structures from the late 1960s onwards and that significantly promoted the prominence of creativity in the tech scene. For this reason, it is relevant to trace the apparent contradiction between rejection and enthusiasm of technology inside the counterculture.[145] This apparent contradiction was already addressed in the first landmark work of counterculture: The "Whole Earth Catalog", a compendium of product reviews, essays and lifestyle info – all for the purpose of living and surviving beyond an adapted and standardised society. First published in 1968 by Stewart Brand (born 1938),[146] who himself became a protagonist of both counterculture and Silicon Valley, the *catalog* provided the (both spiritual and life-practical) manual for a subculture and quickly became the "bible of the hippie movement".[147] Already in the first edition Brand addressed and overcame the apparent contradiction between the idea of a life close to nature on the one side and technology on the other. Now Brand was apparently very aware of this aversion to technology, so he claims: "Amongst the general flow of hippie romanticism, there was an opposition to technology and, by implication, an opposition to science. And I thought that was dreadful".[148] Consequently, the range of products and ideas discussed in the *catalog* is very wide, ranging from fishing equipment to guides such as "Fundamentals of Yoga" to a state-of-the-art Hewlett-Packard programmable calculator for $4,900.[149] Technology became embedded and fertile for a new

144 Fred Turner, "Where the Counterculture Met the New Economy: The WELL and the Origins of Virtual Community", *Technology and Culture* 46, no. 3 (2005): 488, [accessed 22nd August, 2019], https://muse.jhu.edu/.

145 If *counterculture* is mentioned in the following, the term is always limited to the specific counterculture of the 1960s, unless otherwise stated.

146 For publishing the first edition, Brand chooses the Portola Institute in Menlo Park, an area nearby Palo Alto and Stanford University and amidst today's Silicon Valley.

147 Fisher, *Valley of Genius*, "Cast of Characters" section, para. 1.

148 Ibid., "The Time Machine" section, para. 4.

149 Anna Wiener, "The Complicated Legacy of Stewart Brand's 'Whole Earth Catalog'", The New Yorker, last modified 16th November, 2018, https://www.newyorker.com/news/letter-from-silicon-valley/the-complicated-legacy-of-stewart-brands-whole-earth-catalog. It is interesting to note that the Whole Earth Catalog did not distribute the products itself and did not earn money from them. First of all, Turner admits, it seems strange that a community based on anti-commercial principles sees itself de-

way of life. Computer engineer Lee Felsenstein, who played a decisive role in the development of the PC and is said to have designed the first portable computer[150] said on this account: "You could say you were a hippie and didn't like technology, but what *Whole Earth* was telling us all and we all believed was that you are going to be using technology if you are a human".[151] And despite the *Catalog's* first edition bearing the simple but concise subheading "Access to Tools", Brand is rather concerned with the theoretical mediation of a certain way of life and with that a "vision for a new social order – one that eschewed institutions in favour of individual empowerment, achieved through the acquisition of skills and tools",[152] as *The New Yorker* retrospectively puts it in 2018. The first chapter of the *Catalog* is accordingly called "Understanding Whole Systems" and starts with a review on four books written by

---

picted in a catalogue. According to Turner, however, it would be premature to cite the *Catalog* as proof of an early commercialization of counterculture. Rather, the catalog "functioned as a pointer. At the bottom of each listing, after a brief review, usually written by Stewart Brand or a reader, the Catalog listed the item's price and gave information on where and how to acquire it". Cf. Fred Turner, "Where the Counterculture Met the New Economy: The WELL and the Origins of Virtual Community", 485. For Turner, the *Catalog* is rather about expanding an idea, marketing the "core readership's collective worldview to outsiders". Because: "When readers reviewed products in the pages of the Catalog they introduced other readers not only to new goods but also to ways of thinking and speaking-about technology, commerce, information, and community in particular" (cf. Ibid., p. 492). Further, the *Catalog* "marketed not so much goods as a way of looking at how life ought to be lived" (Ibid.). The Whole Earth Catalog thus anticipated an essential feature of the platform economy in an analogous form, in that it did not sell anything itself, but established contacts between buyers or interested parties and sellers.

150 The portable computer in question is the "Osborne 1" from 1981. Though it is not yet equivalent to a modern laptop, its relevance lies in its transformative train of thought to regard a computer not only as a huge stationary mainframe computer but something to carry and use at different places. It is another type of technology with literally more freedom of movement. Hence, it separates itself from the huge mainframes used in enterprises and the military so that it can function as an unbiased and unencumbered concept of a computer. Cf. w.a. "Computers: Carry Along, Punch In, Read Out", *Time Magazine*, 21st June, 1982, ://content.time.com/time/magazine/article/0,9171,925484,00.html.

151 Fisher, *Valley of Genius*, "The Whole Earth ´Lectronic Link" section, para. 2.

152 Anna Wiener, "The Complicated Legacy of Stewart Brand's 'Whole Earth Catalog", *The New Yorker*, last modified 16th November, 2018, https://www.newyorker.com/news/letter-from-silicon-valley/the-complicated-legacy-of-stewart-brands-whole-earth-catalog. These tools include digital technologies. Cf. Ibid.

Buckminster Fuller (1895-1983) – whose insights are, as it is stated in the very beginning of the reviews – "what initiated this catalog".[153] Fuller, for his part, maintained a Silicon Valley tradition by following in the footsteps of Leland Stanford, Vannevar Bush and Doug Engelbart. What they all have in common is their desire to contribute to the *good in the world* and to make the most of what they themselves can achieve while pursuing this goal. For Fuller, this means to be "determined to make his life 'an experiment to find what a single individual can contribute to changing the world and benefiting all humanity'".[154] It is the renewed return of a philanthropic and generalized ambition to better the world, which has literally at least been in use since Vannevar Bush's essay *As We May Think*. But through Buckminster Fuller as a new role model, Brand succeeds in making this romanticised claim accessible to counterculture and its ideas: "The counterculture movement idolized the Whole Earth Catalog, which symbolized this kind of holistic view of the world".[155] But the *Catalog* is not only a guidance for a person already associated with the counterculture, its *back-to-the-land* movement and a respectively broad interest in various topics instead of a narrow-minded thinking. Rather, it simultaneously provides the needed foundation to become such an open-minded person in the first place. In contemplating on the impact of selected books

153 Stewart Brand, Whole Earth Catalog, p. 3. Before Brand published the catalog, he wrote to Fuller to ask him for help with his project "Why haven't we seen an image of the whole earth yet?" (the question came up when Brand took LSD and he "came to the notion that seeing an image of the Earth from space would change a lot of things" – the request was addressed to NASA and ultimately led to the first image of Earth taken from space, to the cover of the catalog and to its name). Fuller's answer to Brand was rather short. He wrote: "Dear boy, it's a charming notion but you must realize you can never see more than half the earth from any particular point in space." However, Fuller agreed at a meeting to help Brand with his campaign to show that there are only limited resources and no backup for Earth. Cf. Jennifer Leonard, "Stewart Brand on the long view", Jennifer Leonard, [accessed 28th April, 2019], https://web.archive.org/web/20071212213039/http://www.renegademedia.info/books/stewart-brand.html.

154 Cf. Phil Patton, "A 3-Wheel Dream That Died at Takeoff", The New York Times, last modified 15th June, 2018, [accessed 5th May, 2019], https://www.nytimes.com/2008/06/15/automobiles/collectibles/15BUCKY.html?mtrref=en.wikipedia.org&gwh=81F084FFB2375D70DBEF22E236401615&gwt=pay.

155 Fisher, *Valley of Genius*, "The Whole Earth ´Lectronic Link" section, para. 2.

and magazines on his thinking "about the creative process",[156] science fiction writer and prospective biographer of Buckminster Fuller's life and work Alec Nevala-Lee retrospectively states that the *Catalog*

> "naturally emphasizes the connections between disciplines, [...] founded on an awareness of how systems evolve and how individuals fit within the overall picture. Its intended readers, both then and now, are resistant to specialization; interested in technology as a means of enabling human freedom".[157]

Combining a pragmatic gateway to tools with "a running commentary that articulated an entire theory of civilization",[158] the *Catalog* and its readers "helped to synthesize a vision of technology as a countercultural force that would shape public understandings of computing and other machines long after the social movements of the 1960s had faded from view".[159]

It is the combination of this long-lasting influence and the inherent ideas towards a new way of consciousness, which makes the *Catalog* remarkable regarding creativity in IT.

"We are as gods and might as well get used to it"[160] is the first sentence of the *Catalog's* first edition. Within the classical creativity theories, which primarily refer to the theological doctrines of God's creativeness, the concept of the ability to be creative was retained by these extra-worldly gods, as is commonly known from research.[161] It was not until the genius era that people were granted the privilege of being creative and creating something new themselves (cf. chapter 4.1). Brand, however, has no intention of staying with this detour, but elevates humankind[162] to a godlike being (who now only *has to get used to it*).

156 Cf. Navalalee, "My ten creative books #3: The Whole Earth Catalog", *Alex Nevala-Lee* (blog), last modified 1st August, 2018, https://nevalalee.wordpress.com/2018/08/01/my-ten-creative-books-3-the-wholeearth-catalog/.

157 Ibid.

158 Ibid.

159 Fred Turner, *From counterculture to cyberculture*, p. 6.

160 Stewart Brand, *Whole Earth Catalog* (Menlo Park: Portola Institute, 1968), p. 2.

161 Cf. Boris Groys, *Über das Neue* (Frankfurt am Main: Fischer, 2002), p. 66.

162 Who exactly is meant by Brand's "we are" cannot be answered here. Therefore, the term *humankind* may be too generalizing, but against better knowledge it is used here as interpretation approach.

The divine myth of creation is credited with the ability to produce the new *out of nothing*. Even if this *nothing* is not understood as the creation of entirely new things, it is often regarded as the origin of absolute freedom of choice in an existentialistic sense, from which every time a new meaning is given, as Groys points out, stating that it was the most radical (and atheistic) programs of the European avant-garde that gladly granted the artist this prerogative of divine creativity out of nothing.[163]

Brand might not be aware of this affiliation with the European avant-garde, but its heritage fits in with the counterculture's self-image to realise itself in opposition to the existing system, therefore not to build on what already exists but to create something radical new – albeit with known means: The worldly gods still need instructions and suitable tools – hence the subtitle: "access to tools". For gods are not subjected, not even to the influential technology of a military-bureaucratic complex, as outlined above and formulated, for example, in Savio's speech at the University of Berkeley. Rather, gods subdue things. If the individual technical knowledge worker is still there to support and operate huge computer and large-scale technology itself, the new gods enthroned by Brand are given the possibilities of small-scale technology, which can help them to realize their own ideas, ideals and conceptions. Technology is seen as a creative tool to promote one's own personal power. For Brand and like-minded people, first and foremost the hackers of the Silicon Valley, technology shall augment the human mind, not the other way round. After all, this form of technology is flexible, handy and personal. [164] Steve Jobs, who later described the Whole Earth Catalog as "Google in book form"[165] and who often mentioned the strong influence of the *Catalog* on his thinking echoes this thought, saying: "We humans are tool builders. We can fashion tools that amplify these inherent abilities that we have to spectacular magnitudes. And so for me, a computer has always been a bicycle of the mind".[166] The *Catalog* was the missing link between the counterculture and the techculture, between technology, economy and "alternative forms of community that

163 Cf. Ibid., p. 66f.

164 Technically, it may still be a long way from here to the PC – the personal computer, which brings with it a liberating feeling of equality and development – but conceptually it has already been walked on.

165 Nevalalee, "My ten creative books #3: The Whole Earth Catalog", last modified 1st August, 2018, https://nevalalee.wordpress.com/2018/08/01/my-ten-creative-books-3-the-whole-earth-catalog/.

166 Fisher, *Valley of Genius*, "The Big Bang" section, para. 6.

would outlast the counterculture itself and become a key feature of the digital world".[167]

Also thanks to the preparatory groundwork of the other reasons for the origin of the creativity concept in IT – the special policy regulations, the pursuit for a higher purpose by single inventors and entrepreneurs, the aim to quantify creativity, the rise of Stanford University, the role of the military and the reluctance of large-scale technology by a majority of the rising counterculture – Brand creates a blueprint with his now regularly published *Catalog*: the result is a place and an idea in which creativity becomes both a driving force and a legitimation for demarcation. Silicon Valley, a stronghold of successful companies commissioned by the government, becomes a subversive, playful-creative *otherness*.

5.2.3 THE COMPUTER REVOLUTION - TOOLS FOR CREATIVE PEOPLE

If in chapter 5.1 Silicon Valley was used to describe a place that provided the soil for the evolution of a particular creativity narrative in IT, and in the previous parts of chapter 5.2 the inner conception of this narrative continued to develop, the following section now demonstrates how the personal computer as an expression of human creation is the most striking outcome of previous evolutionary steps. The PC could not only be imagined and designed thanks to IT's creativity narrative. Over and above, it is the physical representation of this narrative in the early years of the computer revolution, which in turn further (re)shapes and continues to develop the unique narrative of creativity. Or, to put it metaphorically: first, the seed was sown, then it grew into a plant and blossomed, and now the result of the harvest is considered in this paragraph. [168]

---

167 Fred Turner, „Where the Counterculture Met the New Economy: The WELL and the Origins of Virtual Community", p. 488.

168 In principle, the development of the personal computer and the related history of the (micro-, or personal-) computer revolution is of great importance for the creativity narrative in IT's development. However, since a complete account of both aspects would require a very comprehensive consideration and since the literature has already covered them in rich detail, this section is limited to some of the key information necessary for the relationship between them and the creativity narrative. For a profound account of events and developments on the creation of the personal computer and the computer revolution, see esp.: Michael Swaine and Paul Freiberger, Fire in the Valley. The

A connection between PC and creativity already existed before the actual and not only theoretical advent of personal computers (made possible by the development of computer chips and microprocessors in the early 1970s, in particular by Intel). Already at the beginning of this diachronic analysis it was pointed out briefly that both Vannevar Bush's and Doug Engelbart's outlines of their respective ideas of a *universal knowledge machine* and a *working machine* include the use of computer power for the augmentation of one's own creativity.[169] This was not a matter of course. Even in 1970, computers were regarded as being the very opposite: "They [the computers] were exasperatingly difficult to use, the tools of a cult of professional engineers and designers who seemed to take a perverse pride in making them as obscure and intimidating as the oracles of ancient Greece",[170] as it reads in a 1999 book on the development of the Xerox PARC. This obscure-mythic reference also appears elsewhere, where the term "mainframe priesthood"[171] is used to paraphrase those people working with large mainframe computers. Scientists at PARC, then, were among the first to seek a renewed connection to Bush's and Engelbart's visions of an augmentative machine, thereby requiring that a computer must: "serve the user rather than the other way around. That it must be easy and intuitive to operate. That it must communicate with the user in human terms and on a human scale, even if at supernatural speeds".[172] The PARC engineers therefore not only granted the future users of PCs a somewhat creative capacity, PCs were also especially designed for people attempting to break out of the blunt understanding of technology as the *mainframe priesthood* propagates: "And that is the general bent of research at Xerox, soft, away from hugeness and centrality, toward the small and the personal, toward putting maximum computer power in the hands of every individual who wants it".[173] Hence, PCs were not just smaller and therefore accessible to single users, they also served a completely different purpose than their huge mainframe relatives.

Birth and Death of the Personal Computer (Dallas/Raleigh: The Pragmatic Bookshelf, 2014).

169 Cf. chapter 5.1.

170 Hiltzik, *Dealers of Lightning*, p. xx.

171 John J. Anderson, "Dave tells Ahl - the history of Creative Computing", *Creative Computing* 10, no. 11 (1984): 66, https://www.atarimagazines.com/creative/v10n11/66_Dave_tells_Ahl__the_hist.php.

172 Ibid.

173 Brand, "Spacewar".

This is also shown by one, if not the first computer journal dedicated to the emerging personal computer revolution that is accordingly called *Creative Computing*. First published in 1974, the journal believed and argued "the idea that computers should be fun".[174] The environment at *Creative Computing* has been described as "intellectually playful"[175], which, from the magazine's point of view, is "the essence of a truly creative environment"[176] and the reason its founder chose this title. When Steve Jobs needed money to fund a trip to India in early 1974, he searched for a possibility to earn money in newspaper announcements and found an advertisement by Atari, which, according to Jobs, read: "Have fun and make money".[177]

The same is true for a well-known regular meeting of technology enthusiasts, developers, hackers and computer scientists, the so-called Homebrew Computer Club. Some of the most known IT actors that later made it to fame started to unfold their interest in PCs at this club, describes as "a remarkable anarchist assembly of engineers, hackers, and fellow travelers [sic!] that began as a genuine counterculture and ended by changing the world".[178]

At the dawn of the personal computer revolution, a PC is hence seen as a (free) tool for hackers, influenced by ideals and ideas of the counterculture. Internally, there were debates about how and whether it would be morally justified to make money with one's own ideas. This is particularly apparent from an event at the first *Hackers conference*, which was actually a book party, but then became a seminal meeting of the IT scene of the 1980s. Here for the first time a real sense of community was conveyed, and ideas were exchanged on a grand scale. The term "Hackers" was already coined before the Hackers conference, when Steven Levy, renowned journalist for technology, published the book *Hackers: Heroes of the Computer Revolution* in 1984, in which a coherent *hacker ethic* (a neologism of Levy, too) was formulated at first.[179] The confer-

174 Anderson, "Dave tells Ahl - the history of Creative Computing", p. 66. There is a general view that *Creative Computing* was one of the pioneering magazines for personal computers, with the journal itself claiming to be the industry's first. Cf. Ibid.

175 Paul Freiberger and Michael Swaine, *Fire in the Valley. The Birth and Death of the Personal Computer*, (Dalles, Texas: The Pragmatic Programmers, LLC, 2012).

176 Ibid.

177 Fisher, *Valley of Genius*, "Breakout" section, para. 4.

178 Freiberger and Swaine, *Fire in the Valley*, p. xviii.

179 The term "hack" in turn was coined by a group of young people at MIT who tried something new with electronic parts from the garbage dump and thereby developed their own jargon: "munged", for example meant "a piece of equipment was ruined"- and "a

ence "really was a gathering of the illuminati. The important thing was that all the illuminati had never before gotten in a room at the same time"[180] – therefore it became known as "the Woodstock of the computer elite".[181]

A new self-confidence arose, which, in addition to technical aspects, also led to much discussion of issues such as the question of authorship and recognition.

Steve Wozniak on this issue: "Hackers frequently want to look at code, like operating systems, listings, and the like, to learn how it was done before them. Source should be made available reasonably to that sort of people. [...] Information should be free – but your time should not".[182] Stewart Brand slightly changed the meaning of Wozniak's statement by saying that information *wants* to be free, "giving information its own desires" as he puts it.[183] A fine line was drawn between economy and freedom, which deal with the moral difficulties of not exploiting the desire for creativity and continuing to offer codes free of charge – but not what is produced by them. A distinction is made between intellectual property (which may be or even wants to be available for free) and craftsmanship, the finished product for which money can be demanded.

This idea lasted quite a while and was used by Steve Jobs, for example, in a marketing speech as a final argument: "A lot of times people think they're crazy. But in that craziness we see genius. And those are the people we're making tools for".[184] On the other hand, for Steve Wozniak, the focus remained on the idea of free distribution of ideas and tools. revealing the conflicting characters of the two Steves: Because Wozniak's "commitment was to the computer rather than to the company. To Woz, the Apple was a brilliant hack, not an investment. It was his art, not his business".[185]

---

project undertaken or a product built not solely to fulfill some constructive goal, but with some wild pleasure taken in mere involvement, was called a 'hack'." However, to hack also meant to respect the hacked object. In contrast to more recent approaches, the hackers of the first hour did not want to cause chaos or destroy anything, but primarily change and redesign. Cf. Levy, *Hackers*, p. 9f.

180 Fisher, *Valley of Genius*, "What Information Wants" section, para. 2.

181 Ibid.

182 Fisher, *Valley of Genius*, "What Information Wants" section, para. 2.

183 Ibid.

184 Steve Jobs at *Macworld 1997-Full Version*, YouTube, posted by JoshuaG, March 6, 2006, [accessed 2nd August, 2019], https://www.youtube.com/watch?v=PEHNrqPkefI. [308]

185 Levy, *Hackers*, p. 264.

5.2.4 THE UNEQUAL YET CONGENIAL PARTNERSHIP

During the computer revolution and the discussion about free information and tools, more and more unequal couples within the computer community arose, which subsequently had a great influence on the creativity narrative in IT. Whether William Hewlett and David Packard (HP), Sergey Brin and Larry Page (Google) or Steve Jobs and Steve Wozniak (Apple): it was often several people who founded one of today's well-known IT companies. Often it was a very unequal couple. One had the role of the hardworking and basically amicable developer. The other knew how to innovatively evolve and market the developments made. This dynamic is evident in the Apple founders Jobs and Wozniak very early on, long before they founded the computer company, as can be seen from their behaviour in the so-called sale of Blueboxes.

Blueboxing was developed by a group led by John T. Draper. Draper is better known by his nickname "Captain Crunch". He adapted the name from a cornflakes package of the Cap'n Crunch brand, which had a small whistle with it. This whistle generated a frequency of 2600 Hertz – the exact frequency that interrupted a telephone connection, as was discovered by a blind man with perfect pitch called Joybubbles in 1957.[186] It was precisely the sound of 2600 Hertz that made it possible to make free calls by apparently ending a free call and then dialling a new number at the old (free) rate. This special kind of hacking has been called "phreaking" since Joybubbles. Draper (Captain Crunch) recorded the sound on tape, thus the Blueboxes were created, whose sale was obviously illegal.[187]

---

186 Born as Josef Carl Engressia, he legally changed his name in 1991 after deciding to be only five years old of age from then on forever. Before that, Joybubbles became widely known for his ability to place free phone calls and was featured in a now iconic 1971 article in Esquire Magazine called "Secrets of the Little Blue Box" – the article claims to have inspired Steve Jobs to sell Blue Boxes as well. Cf. Ron Rosenbaum, "'Secrets of the Little Blue Box': The 1971 article about phone hacking that inspired Steve Jobs", *Slate*, last modified October 7, 2011, http://www.slate.com/articles/technology/the_spectator/2011/10/the_article_that_inspired_steve_jobs_secrets_of_the_little_blue_.html.

187 For the subversive Counterculture this was not always easily compatible with its moral concept. To justify this, it was often argued that the telephone fraud actively supported the anti-war efforts, as a special tax on making telephone calls to finance the Vietnam War was imposed. Thus, illegal phreaking could be understood as civil disobedience in opposition to the war. Cf. w.a. "History of the Telephone Tax and Campaigns", *National War Tax Resistance Coordinating Committee*, [accessed 14th May, 2019], https://nwtrcc.org/programs-events/hang-up-on-war/history-of-the-telephone-tax-and-campaigns/.

Unimpressed by this, the later founders of Apple Steve Jobs and Steve Wozniak nevertheless sold Blueboxes to earn money. In terms of unequal but congenial partnership, the difference was in the division of roles and the respective perception of these roles and their effects. While Wozniak's perspective is as follows: "So I designed this little box and Steve said, 'Oh, let's sell it'", Jobs said: "We built the best blue box in the world! It was all digital".[188] The division of the partnership is already evident here in a condensed form: One partner (Wozniak) is more interested in the idea and the development process itself, whereas the other partner (Jobs) exploits the idea and markets it commercially – but not without attributing a large part of the development process to him- or herself and praising the idea as excellent. The inequality in the partnership became even more apparent when Jobs started working for Atari, presenting a console developed by Wozniak on this occasion there and claiming to have developed it together with him.[189]

Jobs ignores teamplay and the role of Steve Wozniak, who actually did most of the technical work. Even after Apple was founded and although Wozniak was considered a cofounder inside and beyond the tech scene, Jobs promoted the image of the holistic person who both thinks and creates, once again supporting his argument by creating an analogy to a well-known artist:

> "The people who really create things that change this industry are both the thinker and the doer in one person. The doers are the major thinkers. Did Leonardo have a guy off to the side that was thinking five years out about the future? About what he would paint or the technology he would use to paint it? Of course not. Leonardo was the artist – but he also mixed all his own paints. He also was a fairly good chemist. He knew about pigments, knew about human anatomy. And combining all those skills together – the art and the science, the thinking and the doing – was what resulted in the exceptional result".[190]

5.2.5 "GOOD ARTISTS COPY; GREAT ARTISTS STEAL"

Another aspect of the creativity narrative of IT that evolved from previous developments, is the ability to recognize and market the potential of new ideas.

188 Fisher, *Valley of Genius*, "Breakout" section, para. 2.

189 Wozniak had made a replica of *Pong* because he had the technical know-how to do so. Cf. Fisher, *Valley of Genius*, "Breakout" section, para. 4.

190 Fisher, *Valley of Genius*, "Silicon Valley, Explained" section, para. 2.

The cases already presented can be used to distinguish two fundamentally different types of individuals and collectives (hence companies) in the process of creating something new. On the one hand, there are those people and institutions who came up with and nurture rather genuinely new and innovative ideas[191] but either do not bring new technologies to market maturity, do not recognize their full potential, keep it to a theoretical thought, or do not sufficiently market their idea or product. On the other hand, there are those who do not directly come up with new ideas but are able to see *more* in the already existing ones. In an iconic 1996 interview with Wired magazine, Steve Jobs described such a "sort of apocalyptic"[192] encounter with a novel product as follows:

> "When I went to Xerox PARC in 1979, I saw a very rudimentary graphical user interface. It wasn't complete. It wasn't quite right. But within 10 minutes, it was obvious that every computer in the world would work this way someday. And you could argue about the number of years it would take, and you could argue about who would be the winners and the losers, but I don't think you could argue that every computer in the world wouldn't eventually work this way".[193]

Hence, this type of people (of which Jobs can be considered a role model) adopt, combine and further develop ideas, thoughts and already given products with a certain vision until these (physical or theoretical) things evolve into something mature – and successful because of the ability to market it and generate a need. In the logic of Silicon Valley, this type of person deserves the greater attention and the attribute of *being creative*. Of these, there are quite a few and, above all, very successful ones: as outlined before, Doug Engelbart gets his idea of *working machines* from Vannevar Bush's *Memex* and rethinks the visions inside Bush's work *As we may think* as presented in his work *Augmenting Human Intellect*. William R. Hewlett and David Packard build their

191 This means neither the emergence of an idea ex nihilo, nor a mere innovation, but something new with a transformative quality. The concept of transformative creativity goes back to Margaret Boden, whose concept of distinguishing creative efforts is examined in more detail in chapter 6.2.3.

192 Fisher, *Valley of Genius*, "PARC Opens the Kimono" section, para. 4.

193 Gary Wolf, "Steve Jobs: The next insanely great thing", *Wired*, last modified 1st January, 1996, https://www.wired.com/1996/02/jobs-2/.

resistance-tuned oscillators after "an idea they'd heard about from [Frederick] Terman".[194] Steve Wozniak and Steve Jobs transform the subversive and initially anti-commercial notion of phreaking by selling blue boxes for money to enable free long-distance calls for their customers. And there is the well-known above-mentioned case of the Apple management, who visited the Xerox PARC institute where they first saw a demonstration of how a computer mouse is used on a graphical user interface (GUI) – both are concepts that he later adopted and marketed himself (Xerox PARC researcher's in turn did not came up with a concept of a computer mouse themselves either but adopted the idea from Engelbart's prototype of a mouse at the *Mother of all Demos* – Jobs was too young to have seen this demo back in 1968, so he first came into contact with the concept of a mouse with Xerox).[195] Jobs asked a design studio to design him a mouse, who, after admitting that they "had no idea what a mouse was",[196] in turn looked around to find out "and see what ideas we could steal, which is how engineers work – why reinvent the wheel?",[197] as one designer remembers the situation, while one of the founders of the design company expresses how he thinks something new is created – namely not from scratch. Rather: "you take a good idea and run with it and improve it. It's very rare that a lightning bolt strikes and you come up with something that's never been thought of before. It's a lot more taking from this, taking from that, and trying to make something work, and going for it".[198]

In 1972, the "gaming-industry forefather"[199] Ralph Baer designed and demonstrated the first home console based on a television, and one of the games created for the console named *Magnavox Odyssey* was a simple form of tennis. When Bushnell could keep an eye on the game, he was intrigued. Because Atari still needed to develop two more games in order to fulfil a contract, he figured to adapt the tennis game for a stand-alone gaming machine (known as arcade machines). Not personally, though: "He had a plan: Dabney would handle the creation of the pinball machine [...]; Alcorn

194 Leslie, "The biggest 'Angel' of Them All: The Military and the Making of Silicon Valley", p. 51f.

195 Cf. Fisher, *Valley of Genius*, "PARC Opens the Kimono" section, para. 1.

196 Ibid., para. 4.

197 Fisher, *Valley of Genius*, "PARC Opens the Kimono" section, para. 1.

198 Ibid.

199 Cf. Stokel-Walker, "Atari Teenage Riot: The Inside Story of Pong and The Video Game Industry's Big Bang".

would re-create the tennis game for arcades".[200] And so *Pong* was born – and Atari and Bushnell became famous. This example particularly illustrates the mechanisms of creativity narrative because Baer – the true inventor behind Pong – managed to come to terms with this mental theft and tries to put things in perspective: "'Mr. B. didn't 'invent' anything, [...] but he started a whole industry, the arcade video game industry. Give the man credit for that achievement. He just simply didn't invent anything'".[201]

This would not have been possible without the specific geosocial effects described in the previous sub-chapter. It took these developments, such as the rejection of the *covenant not to compete* or the tradition of Stanford as an incubator with their associated economic competition, to not only make such *adaptations* legal and socially acceptable, but to regard them as exemplary and aspiring. Again, it is Steve Jobs who come up with a popular quotation (again from the 1996 interview with Wired) that summarizes and ennobles the aspect presented here at the same time. For him "creativity is just connecting things".[202] The quote goes on as follows: "When you ask creative people how they did something, they feel a little guilty because they didn't really do it, they just saw something. It seemed obvious to them after a while".[203] With attributing this approach to a notion of creativity, he also reshapes the meaning of such creativity. Being creative in this sense means recognizing possibilities. With this, both a self-attribution and generalization takes place, as Jobs is indirectly referring to himself as *creative people* while he does not further define or differentiate these *creative people*. Instead, he implies that all people of this type would act like this, albeit feeling *a little guilty*.

In addition, there is another quotation from Jobs which in this context draws closer to an understanding of the creative narrative in IT outlined in this section, while indirectly focusing on the account of guilt. As already briefly mentioned above, this narrative does not necessarily pay the most attention to the actual authors and designers of an inventive idea. This means that creative empowerment is not primarily synonymous with the process of designing or developing something new and unique. Rather, those individuals are esteemed to be creative who have the foresight and vision to put the theoretical potential of an idea into practice by first recognizing

200 Ibid.

201 Ibid.

202 Gary Wolf, "Steve Jobs: The next insanely great thing".

203 Ibid.

it, then further developing or adapting it and finally marketing and selling it. Steve Jobs' well-known quote "good artists copy, great artists steal",[204] which he ascribes somewhat inaccurately to Pablo Picasso, seems to further prove this attitude in a self-confident manner. In fact, there have been many discussions about the actual meaning of Jobs' 1996 quote. It was presumably originally intended exactly the other way around, meaning that copying was good while *stealing and spoiling* was unworthy of an artist.[205] However, Jobs was not the first to this quote in this manner, though, as others used the phrase in a similar way, like T.S. Eliot in 1920[206] yet it is widely attributed to Jobs. As a possible explanation, Apple's Phil Schiller, who goes with the title *Senior Vice President of Worldwide Marketing*, recalls a conversation with Jobs in which the latter is supposed to have said that copying means *doing the same thing*, while *steal* stands for the ability to "learn, as artists have, from past masters; you figure out what you like about it and what you want to incorporate into your idea, and you take it further and do something new with it".[207] Accordingly, it is no longer be necessary to keep a vacancy for a concept of guilt, as *to steal* stands for *to learn*.

In Steve Jobs' storytelling and legacy, however, Schiller's *something new* is by no means just a mere further development or an innovating process. In an interview in 2000, former Apple CEO John Sculley recalled a joint visit with Jobs to Polaroid co-founder Edwin H. Land, where both allegedly agreed that products need to be discovered and not invented:

> "Dr Land was saying: 'I could see what the Polaroid camera should be. It was just as real to me as if it was sitting in front of me before I had ever built one.' And Steve said: 'Yeah, that's exactly the way I saw the Macintosh.' He said if I asked someone who had only used a personal calculator what

---

204 Ibid.

205 Cf. W. H. Davenport Adams, "Imitators and Plagiarists (Part 2 of 2)", *The Gentleman's Magazine* 272, June (1892): pp. 627-628.

206 T. S. Eliot, *The Sacred Wood: Essays on Poetry and Criticism* (London: Methuen & Company Ltd., 1920), p. 114.

207 Dan Farber, "What Steve Jobs really meant when he said 'Good artists copy; great artists steal'", *cnet*, last modified 28th January, 2014, https://www.cnet.com/news/what-steve-jobs-really-meant-when-he-said-good-artists-copy-great-artists-steal. Additionally worth noting about this statement is Jobs' (or Schiller's) reference to an artist that, like Jobs' reference to Picasso (and thus a generally known and renowned artist), aims to situate the behaviour of Jobs and Apple in the context of art and its related artistic practices. This aspect will be discussed in chapter 5.2.6.

> a Macintosh should be like they couldn't have told me. [...] I had to go and create it and then show it to people and say now what do you think?"[208]

Thus, in this reading *something new* (and not just a further development) emerges through an imaginative anticipation of a not yet existing thing or idea. Creative development is hence not based on a process of tabula rasa but requires precise knowledge of current developments in order to recognise and further exploit their potentialities (which includes the economic point of view). Nonetheless, Jobs' statement concerning the Macintosh is obviously falsified, because his template for the Macintosh was not only a *personal calculator*, but numerous ground-breaking inventions at Xerox PARC.[209]

This case is therefore an example that the creativity narrative in IT is not limited in appreciating *stealing* more than *inventing*. It also represents an artificial increase in one's own appreciation through one' s creative ability to be visionary in perceiving and connecting more things and ideas than others. This also happens, as shown, through conscious exaggeration or distortion of facts. Steve Jobs embodied this role like no other – a role that continues to be further cultivated and exploited by third parties. This is happening to an extent that tech insiders started to claim: "It's cliche [sic!] to look to Steve Jobs for inspiration in the tech and investing worlds. This inspiration typically shows up in turtleneck-rich wardrobes, unconfirmed fealty to design, and, way too often, being cruel to subordinates".[210] Yet this role attribution still exists and continues to nourish the creativity narrative of IT.

A certain staged role emerges that is not limited to what is but exaggerates the creativity narrative in order to exploit it for itself. Jobs, and with him Apple, adopts a more and more Machiavellian approach, ignoring some unwritten and previously pointed out basic rules of IT. Apple started to *think*

---

208 Leander Kahney, "John Sculley On Steve Jobs, The Full Interview Transcript", *Cult of Mac*, last modified 14th October, 2010, https://www.cultofmac.com/63295/john-sculley-on-steve-jobs-the-full-interview-transcript/63295/.

209 Cf. chapter 5.1.2. Since the quote originates from Sculley and not directly from Jobs, it cannot be checked whether Jobs actually said this to Land (nor whether Land said anything similar to Polaroid) or not. Certain doubts are justified, as Sculley talks benevolently and almost submissively about jobs throughout the interview and considers all the mistakes that led to Apple's near-death experience to be his mistakes, presented in the style of a *mea culpa*.

210 Pete Mortensen, "What Matters Next: Creativity is Just Connecting Things", *Medium*, last modified 31st March, 2016. https://medium.com/matter-driven-narrative/what-matters-next-creativity-is-just-connecting-things-ebd5f24fb0fd.

different – the staging superimposed authenticity and storytelling took precedence over the Silicon Valley legacy: in 1988, Apple sued Microsoft for copying the *look and feel* of the Macintosh's graphical user interface in their newly created *Windows* operating system. But when Jobs accused Bill Gates of stealing, Gates argues that both enterprises had stolen from Xerox,[211] responding: "Well, Steve, I think there's more than one way of looking at it. I think it's more like we both had this rich neighbor named Xerox and I broke into his house to steal the TV set and found out that you had already stolen it".[212] In 2017, Gates added on reddit (in an *ask-me-anything*-session): "The main 'copying' that went on relative to Steve and me is that we both benefited from the work that Xerox Parc did in creating graphical interface – it wasn't just them but they did the best work."[213]

Even though Apple lost the litigation, it shows a fundamental change in the development of the creativity narrative in IT.

5.2.6 THE AFFINITY OF IT TO ART AND THE ARTISTS

Within the framework of the creativity narrative of IT, the reference to art seems both mystified and romanticised. [214] Steve Jobs used various options to associate the achievements of IT (and Apple in particular) with an art narrative. The notion of art is strongly connected to the history of the Silicon Valley and here in particular to Apple, being propagated by its people through clichés of art.

---

211 Hiltzik, *Dealers of Lightning*, p. xxi.

212 Walter Isaacson, *Steve Jobs* (London: Abacus, 2015) p. 212.

213 Thisisbillgates, "I'm Bill Gates, co-chair of the Bill& Melinda Gates Foundation. Ask Me Anything", reddit, last modified 27th February, 2017, https://www.reddit.com/r/IAmA/comments/5whpqs/im_bill_gates_cochair_of_the_bill_melinda_gates/dea731b/. In addition, Xerox sued Apple in the course of the case for the same reason Apple sued Microsoft but lost due to a number of legal reasons applied in California and therefore also in Silicon Valley. Cf. Lawrence M. Fisher, "COMPANY NEWS; Xerox Sues Apple Computer over Macintosh Copyright", *The New York Times*, 15th December, 1989, https://www.nytimes.com/1989/12/15/business/company-news-xerox-sues-apple-computer-over-macintosh-copyright.html?scp=3&sq=apple+xerox&st=nyt.

214 The following deals with the contribution of the concept of art to the creativity narrative in IT. Here, adjoining discourses are inevitably excluded, which are nonetheless of great importance for the understanding of the connection between art or artists and IT or economy. Cf. only: Boltanski and Chiapello, *The New Spirit of Capitalism*.

Jobs often uses certain clichés of art and artists and selects especially well-known but noncontemporary artists for his analogies. His dialectic refers to art as something worth striving for. From his point of view, it is worth highlighting the fact someone is doing some kind of art:

> "In the seventies and the eighties the best people in computers would have normally been poets and writers and musicians. Almost all of them were musicians. A lot of them were poets on the side. And they went into computers, because it was so compelling, because it was fresh and new. It was a new medium of expression".[215]

In addition, the *fresh and new* enhances IT, or rather the development of the PC, by constituting it as a medium of expression and integrating the computer into the exquisite circle of utensils and instruments that represent the artists' tools.

But while in this example Steve Jobs still locates the programmers' credentials as artists in their artistic skills beyond their profession, other scene protagonists no longer distinguish between art on this side and beyond IT. For example, motivation is most important for the renowned computer scientist Andy Hertzfeld, who worked at both Apple and Google in key development teams. "That seeps into the product at every level".[216] He asks why a product exists as a research project in the first place and finds the answer in the existence of basic human values, which "are essentially the architecture of the project".[217] Hertzfeld distinguishes three different sets of values. The first two are rather common and are either money-oriented or of technical interest. He then continues:

> "But then there is a third set of values that are much less common: and they are the values essentially of the art world or the artist. And artistic values are when you want to create something new under the sun. If you want to contribute to art, your technique isn't what matters. What matters is originality. It's an emotional value".[218]

At this point, at the latest, the creativity narrative in IT literally ties in with a discourse on originality. Yet, Hertzfeld remains uncertain as to what exactly,

215 Fisher, *Valley of Genius* "Silicon Valley, Explained" section, para. 2.

216 Ibid.

217 Ibid.

218 Ibid.

in his opinion, is in fact the *something new* and *originality*. In his approximation, traditional or almost romantically transfigured ideas of art and artists resonate. Instead of conceptual clarity he rather attributes this *set of artistic values* to himself and his fellow programmer, Apple's cofounder Steve Wozniak:

> "Woz might not say that he is driven by artistic values, but if you look at the work—that's what it is. All that crazy creativity in the Apple II was art. Steve was fundamentally motivated by artistic values. I had artistic values. The artist wants to spiritually elevate the planet".[219]

The final sentence of this quote dissolves the exclusively personal component and merges the – in his opinion – artistic values with principles of the Counterculture.[220] Regardless of the actual connection between Counterculture and artists, the artist has no choice here, she involuntarily becomes part of this culture. Above all, however, Hertzfeld's quoted sentence fulfils an aspiration that is deeply rooted in the logic of Silicon Valley, as has already been shown: the artists (and among them now also the programmers and hackers) elevate not only themselves with their art. The focus is not just on the pursuit for personal fulfilment and success, but on the big picture or, with Stewart Brand, on the *whole world*.

For Atari game programmer and founder of Atari's competing game company *Activision*, Al Miller[221] describes this holistic stance towards a notion of art as follows: "we were doing creative efforts much like book authors. In that era it was single-person work. We did all the music. We did all the art. We did all the programming. We did virtually all of the conceptual design as well".[222]

A link to art also takes place in a rather superficial and obvious manner. An example of this is the explanation of how important creativity is for IT, using coders as an example: the website *TechRepublic* agrees that creativity is important for the career success of a skilled worker in IT and metaphorically

219 Ibid.

220 This particularly applies to the relationship between counterculture and the political and social context. It was external grievances such as the escalating Vietnam War that gave rise to the movement. Accordingly, the ethical motive for resolving these grievances through cultural opposition is constitutive for the Counterculture movement of the 1960s. Cf. Miller, Timothy S. *The Hippies and American Values* (Knoxville: University of Tennessee Press, 2011), p. 87ff.

221 Cf. Fisher, *Valley of Genius* "Cast of character's" section, para. 1.

222 Fisher, *Valley of Genius* "Towel Designers" section, para. 3.

describes that "[it is] like they all have the same 'palette,' but each coder has the opportunity to use the 'colors' in a different way. If you have the talent to recognize and implement this, then you are going to be more successful".[223]

These compact examples show the ambivalent connection between art and IT. In both connections, the creative narrative experiences a positive charge through the concept of art. On the one hand, however, it is understood as a *quasi-origin* and intrinsic motivation to act (Miller, Wozniak), but also as an additionally amplified kitsch momentum, through which the creations of IT experience a boost that is consistent with both market-economic and countercultural values, as Jobs exemplarily illustrates in the above quotation. The second connection is based on the first understanding, making it all the more difficult to expose the exaggeration as marketing on account of the creativity narrative's roots in the hippie and hacker scene.

5.3 A BRIEF ACCOUNT ON THE CONNECTION BETWEEN ARTIFICIAL INTELLIGENCE AND CREATIVITY

The notion of artificial creativity is another aspect important for the development of the creativity narrative in IT. *Artificial creativity* here is meant as a discourse that incorporates both thought experiments and attempts of practical implementation. Hence, it is not limited to the alleged *dawn of creative machines*, as presented in chapter 4.4, but instead draws on the role of the concept of creativity within the conceptual development of an AI as well: both the IT narrative and computational creativity affect and influence each other in the course of their respective developments, as will be analysed below, so that a diachronic view of the creativity narrative in IT would remain incomplete without this perspective.

Since its inception in 1956, AI as a scientific field of research (whose development in relation to creativity in IT is presented below) is considered to be an interdisciplinary subject, whereby IT has been and continues to be a decisive factor in questions of technical feasibility from a developmental point of view. For this, it is of paramount importance that large IT companies such

223 Toni Bowers, "The short answer to the question posed in that title is yes", last modified 18th December, 2011, https://www.techrepublic.com/blog/career-management/is-there-a-place-for-creativity-in-it/.

as Google, Facebook, Amazon or Twitter have entered the race for the development of artificial intelligence in recent years or have at least increased their investments in this area.[224] This also includes the attempt to develop autonomous systems with the ability to be creative. The discourse about artificial creativity complements the creativity narrative of IT with an independent and quasi-inverted logic: the fundamental difference lies in the fact that so far, the creativity narrative in IT claims to enable innovative *things* (by means of products, services and ideas) to emerge through creativity. In contrast, artificial creativity is about using these innovative *things* to create creativity itself. In the course of this, parts of IT have come to realize that an understanding of artificial creativity can only be created through a comparative approach to natural creativity, namely human creativity. Those IT enterprises who have already implemented this mindset are now not only confronted with a terminological understanding of the concept of creativity and questions regarding development and implementation, but also with ontological issues regarding the potential of an artificial consciousness, or the exploration of differentiating factors between humans and machines.

As Chapter 4.4 has demonstrated before, this mutual relationship leads to a current climax of the narrative, which now has to consider the ontological query about the meaning of creativity for human self-awareness and identity. Thereby, the term creativity evolved not only into a field of scientific research, but also into a concept of a unique human characteristic that aims to distinguish humans from intelligent machines and systems in the light of the latter's approaches to emulate human abilities: to this day, the concept of creativity is used as a means of defense against the possibility that machines and artificial systems can think independently or even develop a state of consciousness – and the further the technical development progresses, the more attention will be paid to a notion of creativity in the field of artificial intelligence. The concept of artificial creativity therefore appears to be intrinsically and undetachable linked to the exploration of artificial intelligence (AI).[225]

---

224 Cf. w.a. "The Race For AI: Google, Intel, Apple In A Rush To Grab Artificial Intelligence Startups, *CBInsights*, last modified 27th February, 2018, https://www.cbinsights.com/research/top-acquirers-ai-startupsma-timeline/.

225 The idea of an artificially created intelligence somehow is as old as mankind itself. Throughout history, people came up with AI-related ideas and concepts of both philosophical and technical nature – long time before technological advancements could realize a physical or digital, non-human entity or system that somehow could be called *intelligent*. The history of AI is hence not only influenced by scientific achievements but

This results in the phenomenon of computational creativity being closely tied to the special discourse of scientific AI research as well as the superordinate interdiscourse on AI.

This is by no means self-evident: 30 years before the concept of artificial intelligence has been scientifically introduced, the term *robot* was developed by Czech novelist Karel

Capek, who coined it in his 1920[226] iconic play "R.U.R." (an acronym for *Rossum's Universal Robots*, a fictitious company).[227] Robots displace older human-like AI descriptions such as Automatons[228] and became a colloquial term for an AI with a physical presence, mostly in the shape of a human being. Notably, the term derives from the Czech word *robota*, meaning as much as *unfree* or *exploited labour* or *hard work*. Precisely because the robots in R.U.R. revolt and ultimately destroy humanity, the famous science fiction author Isaac Asimov designed his "Three Laws of Robotics" in his 1942 short story *Runaround* to fictitiously prevent such a dystopic scenario and to leave robots (which are aware of their existence in his short stories and are therefore not just a mechanical shell) in the Czech literal sense of the word *unfree*. Long before an AI self-awareness could be a reality in a foreseeable future, related moral and ethical problems become unresolved issues in semi-scientific literature. *Runaround* and other stories by Asimov became a major pop-cultural impact for society but also for engineers and scientists in their teen years. A whole "generation of scientists [...] were tremendously influenced by his writing".[229] Hence, on the eve of the introduction to artificial intelligence

moreover by socio-cultural conditions at a certain time. Pamela McCorduck points out that origins of AI can already be found in antiquity where it is considered as an ancient dream to recreate gods. Cf. Pamela McCorduck, *Machines Who Think. A Personal Inquiry into the History and Prospects of Artificial Intelligence* (Natick: A K Peters, 2004), p. 4). The idea of an AI has therefore always been related to the etymology of the concept of creativity.

226 Capek wrote the play in 1920, but it was not played before 1923.

227 Cf. Karel Capek, *R.U.R. Rossum's universal robots* (University of Toronto Library, 1920). Capek points out that his brother Josef strikes on the idea of calling the book's mechanical entities *robots* – so technically, he coined the word.

228 The term *automaton* derived from Greek, meaning *acting of one's own will*. It is first used in Homer's *Iliad* to describe an automated door opener.

229 This is how science journalist John Markoff writes in an obituary to Asimov in the New York Times. Among others, the AI pioneer Marvin Minsky has his say on Asimov's influence on him: "I was just beginning my teens and he was only in his early 30's, yet he seemed centuries ahead. I was entranced by his stories about space and time, but

and creativity research as independent scientific fields, Capek and Asimov in particular set the course for a bipolarity of discomfort and confidence towards AI.

Five years after the psychologist Guilford directed the focus of his scientific field to creativity research, four scientists, with one from IBM among them,[230] created a proposal to conduct an extended conference on AI that should be held in 1956 at Dartmouth College, coining the term *Artificial Intelligence*. The proposal and its related conferences in the course of the summer of 1956 are considered to be the foundation for the scientific consideration of AI development. Within the initial proposal McCarthy et al. defined the essential issues of the upcoming AI research while completely underestimating the needed effort in doing so. Because in the proposal they conjectured:

> "that every aspect of learning or any other feature of intelligence can in principle be so precisely described that a machine can be made to simulate it. An attempt will be made to find how to make machines use language, form abstractions and concepts, solve kinds of problems now reserved for humans, and improve themselves. We think that a significant advance can be made in one or more of these problems if a carefully selected group of scientists work on it together for a summer".[231]

The variety of aspects and its holistic view presented in this excerpt emphasises the meaning of this proposal as a foundation for AI development in the second half of the 20thcentury.[232] The proposal then continues to formulate "some aspects of the artificial intelligence problem", that should be considered during the summer study, thereby addressing the above points – among

---

the ideas about robots affected me most". Cf. John Markoff, "A Celebration of Isaac Asimov", last modified 12th April, 1992, https://www.nytimes.com/1992/04/12/business/technology-a-celebration-of-isaac-asimov.html?pagewanted=all&src=pm.

230 The scientists are: McCarthy from Dartmouth College; Minsky from Harvard University; Rochester from IBM and Shannon from Bell Telephone Laboratories. Cf. John McCarthy, Marvin L. Minsky, N. Rochester and C.E. Shannon, "A Proposal for the Dartmouth Summer Research Project on Artificial Intelligence", last modified 31st August, 1955, http://www-formal.stanford.edu/jmc/history/dartmouth/dartmouth.html.

231 Ibid.

232 Single aspects already farsightedly describe the complexity and difficulties of future AI developments, like the following excerpt: "The speeds and memory capacities of present computers may be insufficient to simulate many of the higher functions of the human brain, but the major obstacle is not lack of machine capacity, but our inability to write programs taking full advantage of what we have". Cf. ibid.

them, as the last aspect out of seven is *Randomness and Creativity*.[233] Thus, since the inception of scientific AI research, the concept of creativity has been literally taken into account. It does not have a subtle or metaphorical significance only but is an integral part of a total of seven constitutively aspects for the origin of scientific AI research.

With the term *randomness*, the direction in which the concept of creativity is understood in this aspect becomes more obvious. This understanding is made even sharper considering the brief description of *Randomness and Creativity*:

> "A fairly attractive and yet clearly incomplete conjecture is that the difference between creative thinking and unimaginative competent thinking lies in the injection of a [sic!] some randomness. The randomness must be guided by intuition to be efficient. In other words, the educated guess or the hunch include controlled randomness in otherwise orderly thinking".[234]

What is presented here is that the initiators of the Dartmouth Conferences understand randomness to be tamed in order to make it feasible (or efficient in their own words). Creativity is therefore purposeful and orderly, as it can only be distinguished from orderly thinking by complementary randomness. Randomness – according to the quote's tenor – can be controlled to a certain extent.

With the hype around the Dartmouth Conferences and subsequent promising developments, scientists were eager to outbid themselves in predicting the pace in which further developments will occur. The general believe was that in a few years, research would have solved the issue of creating an AI.[235]

It is well known that nothing came of it for the time being. The expectations were far too high. In particular, there was a lack of computer power to process the increasingly demanding calculations. As a consequence, funding for AI research was greatly reduced. This was all the more remarkable since a large US military fund was at the free disposal of the researchers and was not tied to a specific project or purpose. However, the researcher's financial freedom did not seem to be profitable for the military. What follows

233 Ibid.

234 Ibid.

235 Marvin L. Minsky, *Computation: Finite and Infinite Machines* (Englewood Cliffs, N.J.: Prentice-Hall, 1967).

was the first so-called major AI *winter*.[236] In the 1980s, the idea of an artificial intelligence that would be on a par with, or even superior to, humans in all respects was abandoned for the time being. [237] Instead, research focused on so-called *expert systems*, i.e. systems that can support people in solving more complex problems like an expert by deducing recommendations from a knowledge base.

In 1982, Japan's Ministry of International Trade and Industry launched the "Fifth Generation Computer Systems project (FGCS)" with the goal of building a computer with unprecedented performance that would suffice to create artificial intelligence: "They're going to give the world the next generation – Fifth Generation – of computers, and those machines are going to be intelligent".[238] A new enthusiasm for AI and a new *summer* for research arose – but now with a focus on expert systems, also known as the concept of *Nouvelle AI*. [239]

One of most famous examples of such an expert system is IBM's 1996 *Deep Blue* chess playing computer that defeated chess grandmaster Garry Kasparov in 1997. Successes in AI development remain connected to well-known social games in a media-effective way: in 2011 the Watson system (again from IBM) beats the world's best *Jeopardy!* players in a live show. And in 2016, Google DeepMind's AlphaGo computer program beat the world champion Lee Sedol in the game of Go. The increasing complexity of the selected games shows the evolution of the development of artificial intelligence: Chess has clear, firm rules, Jeopardy! requires a corner-thinking, and Go is "a game that is exponentially more complex than chess and requires, at least among the top

236 The term first appeared in 1984 as the topic of a public debate at the annual meeting of AAAI (then called the "American Association of Artificial Intelligence").

237 This form of AI is also known as strong AI or general AI. The term strong AI was first coined by John Searle in 1980. Cf. Ben Goertzel and Cassio Pennachin, eds., *Artificial General Intelligence*. Berlin/Heidelberg: Springer, 2007; John Preston and Mark Bishop, *Views into the Chinese Room: New Essays on Searle and Artificial Intelligence* (Oxford: Clarendon Press, 2002).

238 Edward Feigenbaum and Pamela McCorduck, "The fifth generation: Japan's computer challenge to the world", [accessed August 19, 2019], http://www.atarimagazines.com/creative/v10n8/103_The_fifth_generation_Jap.php.

239 Cf. Jack Copeland, "What is Artificial Intelligence?", [accessed 19th August, 2019], http://www.alanturing.net/turing_archive/pages/reference%20articles/what_is_AI/What%20is%20AI11.html.

humans, a certain degree of intuition".[240] In addition, AlphaGo is capable of improving autonomously.[241]

As impressive as the victories of artificial systems over human beings were, they must still be regarded as restrictive. This form of AI always refers to a very limited area only, as e.g. Deep Blue is *only* capable of playing chess. Kasparov, although being defeated in this special domain where a system excels, unites in himself various social practices (his personality is not limited to be a chess player). However, for some years now there have been so-called smart speakers and other speech recognition software, i.e., systems such as Amazon Echo or Apple's Siri. Certainly, they are far off from the diversity of the social practice of individuals. However, they do not exist as many individual systems, but as cloud-based algorithms that conduct millions of parallel conversations and continuously learn from human input and answers.[242] People, on the other hand, remain in the singular experience (maybe omitting certain multitasking abilities)[243] and are physically confined to themselves (even though the digital world brings about a certain resolution).

240 Cade Metz, "Google's AI Wins First Game in Historic Match With Go Champion", last modified 3rd September, 2016, https://www.wired.com/2016/03/googles-ai-wins-first-game-historic-match-gochampion/.

241 Ibid.

242 Matthew B. Hoy, "Alexa, Siri, Cortana, and More: An Introduction to Voice Assistants", *Medical Reference Services Quarterly* 37, no. 1 (2018): 81-88, doi: 10.1080/02763869.2018.1404391.

243 Dario D. Salvucci and Niels A. Taatgen, *The multitasking Mind* (New York: Oxford University Press, 2010).

6 OBSERVATIONS – MATERIAL SEMANTICS OF REALIZING CREATIVITY

The following chapter complements the diachronic analysis of the creativity narrative in IT and focuses on the present. Building on the analysis of the historically constituted creativity narrative in IT, this chapter outlines how the meaning of this narrative and its immanent logics perform and present themselves today.

For this, I first examine *how* and by what means creativity is *expressed*. For this, I compare the propagated representation of creativity with the actual events and effects of this narrative before I continue to analyse the underlying organisation of the narrative's performative portrayal.

6.1 HABITAT AND HABITUS: EXPLICIT AND IMPLICIT CODES, METHODS AND PATTERNS OF EXPRESSION

I would like to proceed by exploring the idea of a performative portrayal of IT (in the form of its various human and nonhuman actors). It focuses on the representation of working methods with creativity as a characteristic and special feature. It is thus about a specific translation and representation of creativity inherent and intrinsic to the tech world. This *how* implies both habitus and habitat of this creative realisation. Here, an autoethnographic addition enhances the existing material with my *situated knowledge*[1], i.e., my observations, glimpses and sentiments originating from a particular site of the tech world for the purpose of revealing specific micro-sociological practices and idiosyncrasies. To contextualise, I briefly outline the factual and quantifiable

1 The use of the pair of terms "situated knowledge" is adapted from the American post-modernist and scholar in the field of technology and science Donna Haraway (1988).

framework of the enterprise, its research division and particular place where I have been present in order to then supplement autoethnographic additions.

6.1.1 AUTOETHNOGRAPHIC ACCOUNT

For this analysis, I draw on my accumulated experience gained by working in a think tank of IBM's largest European research centre for about four and a half years. I use these to broaden the scope of this thesis by adding an internal perspective. As the diachronic analysis has shown, IBM is not a typical representative of Silicon Valley. Rather, for a certain time, the company seemed to play the role of an anachronism, on which the young, up-and-coming companies could grind and set themselves apart, making IBM a constitutive element in shaping the Silicon Valley's meaning of creativity.

During my research on the creativity narrative in IT, I was regularly on site at the IBM research lab, and in some cases I even continued my own theoretical studies directly from there. The influence I was exposed to as a result is something I want to take into account here. It became increasingly obvious that although I was working in a long-established IT company that had played a decisive role in shaping the fate of technological development in the last century, I now increasingly had to see this very company in the role of the underdog, despite its heritage and experience, and that other IT companies had overtaken its rank in terms of name recognition and influence. This resulting ambivalent situation in my work environment, this mixture of having to prove oneself and being challenged at the same time has caused numerous irritations on my part, enhanced my sensibility for a need of differentiating IT's concepts of creativity and, not least, has had a constitutive influence on the research question of this thesis.

For a better understanding, a brief context overview of my working environment and my scope of work in the research laboratory will be provided first. Being "one of the most prolific research companies in existence",[2] IBM Research is the research and development division of the large-scale technology corporation IBM. With over 3000 researchers and engineers working in

2 Arne Holst, "IBM's expenditure on research, development and engineering from 2005 to 2018 (in billion U.S. dollars)", *statista*, last modified 9th August, 2019, https://www.statista.com/statistics/274821/ibms-expenditure-on-research-and-development-since-2005/.

twelve research laboratories in ten countries, it is the largest IT research organisation in the world. The budget in 2018 amounted to $5.38 billion.[3] IBM has been the top recipient of U.S. patents for 26 consecutive years. For 2018 this means a record of 9100 patent applications – followed by Samsung with a large gap and 5850 grants (in comparison, Apple, Google and Amazon as representatives of the comparatively young companies in Silicon Valley have all filed around 2000 patents).[4] A third of the more than 9000 IBM patents were filed in the areas of AI, cloud and quantum computing – thus areas that are currently identified by IT as the industry's main trends.[5]

Established in 1956, IBM Research – Zurich is the oldest IBM Research laboratory in Europe as well as the largest and most diverse one with scientists originally coming from over 45 different countries.[6] The institute's work led to ground-breaking inventions. Among the awards that scientists have received for their discoveries, developments and achievements at the Zurich laboratory over the years, the two Nobel Prizes in Physics for a total of four researchers are particularly noteworthy: in 1986, Heinrich Rohrer and Gerd K. Binnig received the Nobel Prize for the invention of the *scanning tunnelling microscope*; Karl Alexander Müller and Georg Bednorz received the Prize for the discovery of *high-temperature superconductivity* the following year.[7] In order to do justice to the importance of the location, the European Physical Society awarded the research centre the title "EPS Historic Site", making it one of 41 locations in Europe to date, including the Geneva CERN or the Paris Curie Institute to name but a few.[8]

---

3 Ibid.

4 Ifi Claims Patent Services, "2018 Top 50 US Patent Assignees", *Ifi Claims Patent Services*, last modified 2nd January, 2018, https://www.ificlaims.com/rankings-top-50-2018.htm . Apple takes 9th place, Google 11th and Amazon 12th. However, it should be recalled that these companies do not attach the same importance to patents than IBM due to their own logic, which is determined by the creativity narrative, as was shown in the introduction to chapter 6.

5 Arvind Krishna, "IBM Marks More Than a Quarter Century of Patent Leadership with Record Year" *IBM Research Center*, last modified 8th January, 2019, https://www.ibm.com/blogs/research/2019/01/2018-patent/.

6 IBM, "IBM Research – Zurich. Fact Sheet", *IBM*, [accessed 8th August, 2019], https://www.zurich.ibm.com/pdf/employment/ZRL_FactSheet.pdf.

7 Ibid.

8 Luisa Cifarelli, "The EPS Historic Sites", *EPS*, [accessed 8th August, 2019], http://epn.eps.org/historicsites-booklet#p=37.

In terms of mere and tangible figures, IBM Research – Zurich can therefore be perceived as a highly innovative place. To further exploit and build on this, the so-called THINKLab exists, which acts as an intermediate think tank between local research on the one hand and industry as well as society on the other hand. Being an intersection in between these two poles, it negotiates between them, researches and strives for synergy effects. In its own official words:

> "The THINKLab at IBM Research – Zurich is a unique place in Europe to gain insights from IBM researchers, industry and trend experts in order to meet today's and tomorrow's challenges. This think-tank [...] gives companies, academia and governments the opportunity to learn how IBM's R&D assets, trend research, advanced technologies and solutions can enhance their success. It is also the place where clients can get first-hand experience with innovative prototype solutions."[9]

In this environment I took on an intermediate role, with most of my colleagues having a scientific or technical background and are therefore closer related to the laboratory's scientific heritage. My own background in humanities initially made me both an insider (due to the corporate attempt of empowering the ambiguity tolerance and interdisciplinary orientation, my academic *deviation* was welcomed immediately) and an outsider (still, my background remained a distinction, albeit expressed in colleagues by enduring curiosity which in turn opened up a constant stream of fascinating discussions regarding different views on a certain issue). The latter changed noticeably within the first few months and after about a year I had the feeling that I started to understand the complex structure of this widely intertwined company and its specific nature. Especially in terms of outward appearance, I quickly adapted to the given status quo which advocates that clothing is of less importance and is not in favour of formal attire. Joining the lab, I first continued to wear a suit and tie, but abandoned this idea after a few days, as it seemed increasingly silly to myself. What I had intended as a small and harmless jibe against the *uniformity of the displayed non-uniformity* was not recognised as such in everyday life anyway, so that I received slightly irritated but also discreetly pitying looks when I walked down the corridors and in passing met work colleagues (still) unknown to me. Of course, there were people in classic business outfits,

9 IBM. "IBM Client Center THINKLab", *IBM*, [accessed 8th August, 2019], https://www.ibm.com/ibm/clientcenter/zurich/research/.

even those working for IBM Research; but somehow these people managed to camouflage themselves more effectively and remain more inconspicuous, blending in with the rest of the people. Quickly I disliked to be noticed this way and I changed my style of dressing. Nevertheless, the scientists' relation to clothing was generally determined by a lack of interest. If at all, clothing is simply not important enough to worry about, thus it may not have been my formal attire per se that irritated others but the fact that I consequently had to waste thoughts on it – for reasons unknown and incomprehensible to some of my colleagues and only to strive for an ideal that has no validity within the lab anyway. Of course, my assumption certainly does not apply to all employees, possibly not even to the majority. Clothing simply did not play a major role. Not only do I mention this as my initial practical joke failed so quickly, but also because both the impression of IBM's stiff business attitudes – which I had gained in advance through research – no longer existed, as well as no imminently visible new stylistic codes substituted for them. I had anticipated the usual clichés associated with the tech sector – i.e., intentionally casual clothing in form of hooded sweaters.

It was precisely this cliché of hoodie-wearing techies that I then encountered at an IT conference hosted by a major bank in Zurich. Two high-ranking Google managers were announced as speakers. One came from the recently built research centre in Zurich, another arrived from the USA where he held worldwide responsibility for Google's research on virtual reality. It was easy to recognize the two keynote speakers: both wore the iconic hoodies (in contrast to the vast majority of other participants and guests from the tech scene). More remarkable, however, was the fact that they smiled more or less constantly and without a break, demonstrating a permanent good mood and optimism during their presentations and beyond. Simultaneously, they struck me as strangely detached, very professional but not necessarily personal. As with few people, I was aware that I could not know anything about the private person behind the management role; nothing was disclosed by their outward appearance. Without being able to assign them to a company at first (we had no name tags or other identifying marks on us), both of them appeared to me as being smooth and especially concerned with standing out personally, knowing that they had the best to offer, letting people come to them without themselves taking too much interest in other participants or conversations. Like no other speakers that day they referred to their company, Google, numerous times, stressing out collective efforts and success, speaking about the "we" and "we, the Zooglers" (as Google employees in Zurich call themselves);

all at the expense of an "I". Also, I was surprised by their level of self-confidence. After all, both Google employees gave scientific lectures in front of a mostly skilled audience. I was used to IBM scientists having doubts and self-criticism, proactively pointing out possible research flaws or gaps. On several occasions, I watched and listened high-ranking IBM scientists being indulged in conversations about limits and overestimations of their own research with guests from other political, scientific or economic institutions, intrinsically concerned about others' opinion and evaluation on the respective topic in question. There was none of this in the Google talks. Admittedly, it was a very large audience – but even the next speaker, a philosopher of technology, came across as very self-doubting and far from being at peace with himself and his research compared to the two Google employees.

For local IBMers, as IBM employees tend to call themselves, it is especially true with regard to the rivalry with Google that competition does not only take place in the digital sphere, but also right on the spot in the very area. Just like IBM, Google's main European research lab is situated in Zurich as well, with only a few kilometres between both sites. When a "Google Streetview" car drove slowly past the IBM campus one day, it first slowed down and then stopped in front of the IBM compound for an extended period of time, provoking a confrontation with in-house security (when I saw the Google car slowly rolling by, I couldn't help but reminisce about an incident in the so-called "Little Italy" part of New York's Manhattan district, when a black limousine packed with grim-faced men rolled by in front of a local restaurant, who the bystanders assumed must have come from neighbouring Chinatown). In Zurich, what appears to be a show of force among hostile clans may have served the purpose of gathering as much data as possible from the research lab with the antennas and data collectors mounted on the car, as was quickly suspected). Although the little "incident" amused me and many colleagues for a short time, it did not leave a lasting impression that would have been discussed for a considerable time.

Whenever Google was mentioned in conversations, snippets of dialogue or brief interjections during our lunch together, for example, there was no pronounced feeling of *us versus them*. The location of Google Research in the immediate global neighbourhood was rather expressed in a certain uneasiness; a respectful caution towards the changed new, which the established place stag is now confronted with and, above all, the unpredictability, which Google brought with it through its geographical presence, so close to one's own place of research. At the same time, there was a certain feeling of appreciation of not having to work in an environment with constant hyper-competitiveness but here, on the *island* which is IBM Research's Zurich lab, as some put it figuratively. However, there is by no means any fear of comparison, but rather a sometimes-defiant conviction that one's own approach (which even includes the concept of a private life detached from IBM Research) is more effective, socially acceptable, and will prevail in the long run. As a tangible practice this opinion manifests itself in occasional and, if possible, extended lunch breaks in teams or in pairs, in order to exchange and evaluate both subject-related and non-subject-related news and topics. Time and again, I was impressed by the interdisciplinary curiosity and intrinsic breadth of interests that were evident in such discussions. Thus, when IBM launched an AI application able to create unique recipes, a heated discussion between the main course and coffee could ensue about the pros and cons of cooking; with advocates of cooking as an aesthetic practice on the one hand, and advocates of the interpretation of cooking designed for pragmatic food consumption in the sense of minimizing time waste on the other (the latter was represented by engineers in particular). A glance at the neighbouring tables in the spacious cafeteria told me that we were by no means the only ones who were engrossed in conversation as lunch drew to a close – and many a time we continued the discussions on the way back to the office without one party emerging as the winner of the playful dispute. By no means was this curiosity limited to singular snapshots or individual employees. On my way to the open-air cafeteria at lunchtime, I once recognised a group of perhaps a dozen colleagues standing together by the side of a path, gazing at a spot on the ground, seemingly discussing it. Only when I joined them with interest did I notice a caterpillar on the grass next to the gravel path that seemed to attract the common interest of all the bystanders. Passing by and listening with one ear, I overheard a solitary researcher, apparently well versed in the local flora and fauna, lecturing on this particular caterpillar specimen, remarking how rare and strange it was for this species, of all things, to be found in this place at this time. Without having even the slightest knowledge about caterpillars, it was easy for me to guess that the colleague in question had a profound knowledge about this subject – which was appreciated by the surrounding colleagues with further curious and interested questions. The gathering to admire this obviously peculiar caterpillar specimen was by no means short-lived or trivial but had the character of a practical seminar on the example of a living object in the wild when looking at it from the outside.

At first, I underestimated the sheer size of the company behind the research lab – meaning not only tangible figures such as IBM's headcount or turnover, but also its historicity and the resulting institutionalized sense of long-lasting existence beyond one's own career or life span. The place itself – and by this I indeed refer to the physical existence of the things present – emanated an effect of *relevance* and *significance* on me: for example, when I walked past the office of a Nobel Prize winner or found myself standing in a room prepared with enormous effort and expertise for highly sensitive nanometer-scale studies, which is almost completely silent, thus considered one of the quietest places in the world, and in which highly sensitive sensors could detect my presence long after I had left the room again so that experiments could be carried out only hours after a human being had acoustically contaminated the room. I catch myself in no small part crediting the fascination of this space to my inability of scientifically comprehending such processes. My technical incompetence fuelled the intensity of my perception, since it was not distracted or diluted by any rational logical understanding of how such silence is technologically feasible. In fact, this is precisely what happened again and again in this specific chamber: regardless of their academic background and potential subject matter knowledge, visitors were less fascinated by the very experiments and results than by the context of possibilities inherent in the infrastructural framework. The idea of being here in one of, or perhaps even the most tranquil place in the world aroused astonishment and created a sense of humility and exceptionality in many people – including myself (it is hardly surprising that this has been one of the highlights of every guided tour). Both examples – the office of a Nobel laureate and the quietest laboratory in the world – always were in a passive state when I have been there. The office because something relevant once happened there that still resonates today, the lab because something relevant will only happen when I, myself (or someone else) is not present in the immediate vicinity. The site itself, then, augurs a sense of opportunity, all through these shimmering narratives of accomplished past and potential future creative endeavours. The place bears history and strives to create more stories through cutting-edge techniques and developments. The work setting is based on this and, depending on the age of the building and wing, emphasises either what has already happened or what is still to come. The atmosphere, determined by laboratories, individual offices and small to medium-sized meeting rooms seems to me to be very much aligned with practicality and feasibility. The THINKLab in particular is characterised by an architecture rich in daylight and space and an interior that corresponds to the purpose of the THINKLab and is therefore also designed for representational purposes. This includes a demo area in which IBM's latest developments are exhibited for guests, or various types of versatile meeting rooms in which one side of the room is usually completely covered by whiteboards, while in one particular room an entire wall is covered with flat screens that enable interactive access to an IBM Research collaboration tool using complex gesture control, which was intended to ensure the global networking and showcasing of all research projects from all over the world. In practice, however, it quickly became apparent that the implementation did not always live up to its promise in one place or another. Accordingly, the system did not enjoy the greatest popularity, which in turn was made no secret of. Researchers were irritated by something that claimed to be greater than it really turned out to be – though the tool was far from being non-functional or a mere gimmick. It may, however, be representative of a fundamental unease in the research community about any form of pomposity or what is perceived by them as excessive marketing. To me, this felt completely different compared to e.g. the loudish, colourful, playful extroversion of a Google centre, or the monochrome, cool, tidy and to me almost clinical looking interior as demonstrated by Apple. The working environment at IBM did not seem to be one thing or the other. Similar to clothing, the environment first and foremost serves a purpose that is not, at its core, aimed at the external effect. The façade remained a façade and was not part of the content but rather negligible.

Nevertheless, or perhaps precisely because of this, many media and companies seemed to be clearly more oriented towards companies whose façade gleamed. Interestingly, my impression was that this was particularly due to taking recourse to the concepts of creativity and innovation, even though I also found these concepts applied here at IBM Research – the sheer number of patents cited at the beginning of this paragraph underlined my subjective perception (which was of course highly irrationally charged by my presence at IBM) in a rational, tangible way. This provided a major driving force for my further endeavour: how could it be that, for all the differences between Apple, Google, Facebook and co., they all nevertheless rely on the concept of creativity, which, on top of that, was used by them in rare unanimity in a similar style?

It was all the more irritating for me to move from one newer building to the next that happen to be there for decades. It felt like I was travelling back in time to another place. In particular, the older part of the building ensemble was characterised by an academic, inward-looking seriousness that to me did not fit in at all with the bright and extroverted THINKLab or the comparatively new Nanotech Centre. The campus is a tense simultaneity of what IBM used to be and what IBM is today. Both perceptions of this enterprise are merged on this site and alternate, building by building.

However, in both areas – the old and the new – there is an absence of overly hip lounge areas or leisure facilities. If anything, it is the old section that still houses a room dedicated to leisure (called the *Blue Lagoon*) featuring a piano, some older games consoles and the like. If you did not know about this place, you would not get there too quickly, as it does not seem to be a regular meeting place, nor to have been frequented too often (at least that was my perception, which is very limited, however, as I have only been there very rarely myself – but then never encountered anyone). Metaphorically speaking, I felt as though the *Blue Lagoon* was one of those hidden spaces that one stumbles upon by chance during an extended exploration into the uninhabited and unmapped areas of an old estate.

People from different age groups now work in this specific setting. Quite a few employees built decades-long careers in this one place, or at least within the IBM microcosm. These people experienced IBM at the beginning and, depending on their age, probably in the first third of their career as an immensely well-known, less volatile company; as a brand with economic supremacy and great influence also on culture and politics (here, the example of IBM's contribution to the moon landing as discussed in chapter 5.1.4 is just one more recollection).

Hence, for quite a few of my colleagues the research centre in Zurich is a place to stay – not a professional stopover or a steppingstone to a career outside IBM. Among some of the employees I was talking to and as quickly mentioned above, the IBM Research facility in Zurich is paraphrased and compared to the image of an island – in several respects: within the multi-layered corporate structures of its parent company IBM, the research division stands for a comparatively more tranquil economy, oriented less toward short-term success and more toward long-term sustainability. The lab and its employees appear to radiate a rather unagitated but keen mode of operation – of which its employees seem to be very well aware of.

6.1.2 NONVERBAL ASPECTS OF A DISCOURSE ON CREATIVITY

With the autoethnographic remarks on the spatial organisation of creativity at IBM in mind, I would like to contrast and analyse the localization of creativity in the IT world outside IBM.

For current research, places represent unique spaces[10] in which material objects are arranged and charged with meaning in such a way that they are experienced with a particularly composed spatial density.[11] These places have their own logic.[12] IT's atmospherically dense office landscapes are pioneers of this logic and, as is well known, export hits: on closer examination, it becomes evident that the specific creativity narrative of IT can be located particularly in the imitations of this logic, as it is exemplary to see on the concept of coworking spaces.

In fact, there are almost always references to a howsoever creative way of working in the description of coworking spaces. This not only happens emblematically in relation to the overall presentation, but also in a striking and literal sense, as the following example shows: the online magazine "Coworking Mag" lists twelve "awesome yet affordable coworking spaces in Palo Alto".[13] These are either "spots for people who require a creative space" (Sacred Space), workspaces "with energetic professionals who understand the importance of creative collaborations" (Enerspace) or straightforward "a creative coworking space" (BootUP Ventures), "housing a community of creative professionals and entrepreneurs" (Sandbox Suites).[14] While plenty of descriptions are literally referring to creativity, other coworking spaces presented by Coworking Mag are perfect for an "innovator who likes to experiment with new things" (HanaHaus), or generally for "innovative professionals who harbor big dreams and

---

10 Here, the concept of space is based on Martina Löw's concept of the constitution of space. The constitution of space is determined by goods and people. In addition, not only individual goods or people can be linked to form spaces, but also entire ensembles of buildings or single room units. Seen in this light, the individual employee in an office at Google is just as much *space* as the gigantic headquarters of Apple, the Infinity Loop. Cf. Martina Löw, *Raumsoziologie* (Frankfurt am Main: Suhrkamp, 2000), p. 157.

11 Reckwitz, *Die Gesellschaft der Singularitäten*, p, 60.

12 Ibid., p. 61.

13 Asma Hafiz, "12 Awesome Yet Affordable Coworking Spaces in Palo Alto (2019)", *Coworking Mag*, [accessed 8th August, 2019], https://coworkingmag.com/united-states/coworking-space-palo-alto/.

14 Hafiz, "12 Awesome Yet Affordable Coworking Spaces in Palo Alto (2019)".

aspirations just like you!" (Nordic Innovation House), supporting "the community of innovators" (OnePiece Work).[15] Others are perfect to "chance upon a new idea" (Pacific Workplaces) or, if that *Heureka!* moment already happened, a workspace "that will transform your dreams into reality!" (Alley Coworking). In its conclusion, Coworking Mag stresses out that the workspaces presented above "will give you a great coworking experience wherein you will learn the importance of creative collaboration [...]."[16]

While many coworking spaces – true to their name – rely on collaboration among each other and hope to stimulate *creative work*, some of them nevertheless offer quiet single cabins or small, isolated rooms. This alone would not be noticeable, but the firms also refer to the role model of creativity in IT in advertising these non-collaborative rooms.

HanaHaus, a coworking firm with workspaces in Newport Beach and Silicon Valley's Palo Alto has a "maker room" named "Silicon Valley" in their latter branch. Although quite small and almost constricting but "private", its description starts with the sentence: "This room can be as creative as you are".[17] In addition to a fancy ceiling lamp, this creativity seems to be expressed in bright wooden furniture, white chairs, at least one glass wall, a television, a mixer and / or a coffee machine as well as some pens for a whiteboard. This *Maker Room* is intended for up to eight people.

In this context (that happens to be in the tech-scene's epicentre, Palo Alto), the idea of Silicon Valley functions as an advertising medium on a small scale that is inherent in a culture of empowerment, which in turn emerged and is expressed through creativity.

However, this logic also operates on a grand scale, as can be seen not least from the phenomenon of creative cities.[18] Nowadays, an immense develop-

---

15 Ibid.

16 Ibid.

17 HanaHaus, "Workspace in Palo Alto", *HanaHaus*, [accessed 9th August, 2019], https://www.hanahaus.com/workspace-palo-alto#pal-private-seating. The Coworking space HanaHaus archetypically stands for the connection between collaborative work and creativity.

18 The term *creative city* is coined by Charles Landry, who researched urban creativity through his studies in Britain and Germany in 1990 and 1994. According to Landry, the notion has been preconfigured in a 1988 agenda by the former Australian Minister of Planning and Environment in Victoria, David Yencken, who suggested that a city "should be emotionally satisfying and stimulate creativity amongst its citizens". Moreover, "creative planning is based on the idea of cultural resources and

ment in the context of the spread and number of *creative cities* is observable that Charles Landry called a "rash" and a "mantra of our age"[19] already in 2005. As of 2019, the UNESCO (United Nations Educational, Scientific and Cultural Organization) homepage lists 180 creative cities from 72 countries as members of their UNESCO Creative Cities Network. One of the most impressive examples of the creativity narrative in IT's exportability with regard to the constitution of space is the so-called *Samsung Digital City* that resembles many aspects of the Silicon Valley space.[20]

The inherent logic of space in the sense of the creativity narrative in IT can be identified at various levels. While the above listed export examples were aimed at the big picture, the narrative can also be traced at an individual and personal level. Chapter 5.1.x change in work clothing towards a new but rather subtle uniformity, which is still valid today. Hence, the impression that formal clothing stands for restraint and narrowness is still present in IT today. When Steven Levy came to interview Mark Zuckerberg in Palo Alto for an afterword to a new edition of his influential book *Hackers: Heroes of the Computer Revolution*, he noticed:

> "Surprisingly, the CEO, best known for wearing North Face fleece, is sporting a tie. He explains that he is nearing the end of a year in which he promised his team that he would show up for work in neckwear every day. [...] 'Maybe it's a charm,' he says, of the attire. 'But I think it mostly just chokes me.'"[21]

---

the holistic notion that every problem is merely an opportunity in disguise; every weakness has a potential strength", thus showing many traces of the geosocial logic of the Silicon Valley, as it was examined in chapter 5.1. Cf. Charles Landry, "Lineages of the Creative City", *Creativity and the City Netherlands Architecture Institute* (2005), http://charleslandry.com/panel/wp-content/uploads/downloads/2013/03/Lineages-of-the-Creative-City.pdf#page=11&zoom=auto,-82,259.

19 Cf. Ibid., p. 1.

20 The Samsung Digital City inhabits around 35000 Samsung employees. They work in four *landmark office towers* and 131 smaller buildings. On their homepage, Samsung advertises its digital city with pictures of leisure aspects such as massage tables, swimming pools, or a 30 feet high rock-climbing wall, referred to as *wall of innovation*. In addition, Samsung mentions incentives such as free food, free healthcare, teachers for the 900 children of employees and a *work smart* concept that allows employees to choose their time of work. Cf. Samsung newsroom, "20 Things You Didn't Know about Samsung's Headquarters in Suwon", *Samsung Newsroom*, last modified 29th September, 2014, https://news.samsung.com/global/purposely-leaked-20-things-about-samsungs-digital-city. Since 1987, Samsung has a branch in Silicon Valley as well. Cf. Ibid.

21 Levy, *Hackers*, p. 475.

In contrast to earlier times, when IBMers in black suits and ties symbolized exactly this alleged narrowness, it is now natural in this IT company of the first hour to appear in informal clothing (at least this seems to apply to the microcosm of the IBM research laboratory; in other business divisions, a formal attire is still somewhat commonplace). Formal clothing is seen as atypical, something that does not fit into this world. The subtle, yet existing pressure not to correspond to a stereotype of uniformity ultimately results in the same thing: a uniform, albeit with opposite signs.

As it was my impression presented in the previous chapter regarding my autoethnographic account, the Google employees' (the *Zooglers*') habitus mirrored this kind of uniformity in the sense of their physical expressions of both their clothing and acting. I could not tell anything about their personalities despite them being Google employees.

The special constitution of space, as produced by IT as an expression of the narrative of creativity, is also reflected in the arrangement of an office atmosphere. It is a mixture of objects, architecture and people, which should convey a harmonious overall picture. With Italian sociologist Maurizio Lazzaratto in mind, this arrangement is immaterial work in a broader sense for Reckwitz. For although it deals with materials, it is still about the overall impression conveyed on the basis of narrative and aesthetic references.[22] How this arrangement can translate into physical existence is exemplified by two pictures showing office scenes at Google Research in Zurich.

Google's offices have a reputation for being special and enjoy great popularity on relevant specific websites.[23] Their distinctiveness becomes apparent with the examination of the two following pictures:

22 Reckwitz, *Die Gesellschaft der Singularitäten*, p. 69.

23 Cf. Tom Boredpanda staff. "The Best Place to Work: Google and their Office in Zurich", *Boredpanda*, [accessed 22nd August, 2019], https://www.boredpanda.com/the-best-place-to-work-google-and-their-office-in-zurich.

*Fig. 4: Evolution Design: Pendant, People, Phone / Study Booth from Office snapshots 2012.**

* Office Snapshots, "Awesome Previously Unpublished Photos of Google Zurich, *Office Snapshots*, [accessed 22nd August, 2019], https://officesnapshots.com/photos/8449/.

The photograph displays a bright room flooded by daylight with three different types of gondolas. The floor in the room is grey, with an almost room-filling cloud-shaped carpet with printed dots of clouds on it. The ceiling of the room consists of white panels with lampshades consisting of cloud-like structures. The back of the room is bordered by a window front. The right wall seems to be semi-transparent. Other exterior walls are not visible.

The three gondolas are placed next to each other with the middle of the gondolas being in the background. The most prominent gondola at the right side of the photograph consists of a basket of a hot-air balloon including a grey carrying frame, coloured balloon stripes and parts of something attending to be a burner. There are two men in the basket wearing black t-shirts, one shirt sporting the *YouTube* brand logo.

Another man is leaning against the scaffold from the outside, relaxed and smiling with his elbows placed on the railing of the basket. The second gondola on the left side of the picture appears to look like a cable car cabin, painted in red and yellow. Small rotor blades are on its roof, the doors are open. A man dressed in a suit is sitting inside, talking on the phone, holding a white note in his hand. The third gondola, placed in the background, is again a different type and appears to be empty. Yet, its doors are open. A plastic figure, which should represent an alien creature, is placed next to the grey gondola. In opposite to the other cabins, this one sports a pyramid-like roof. The scene appears to be staged, with all furniture and people being carefully arranged: despite the unusual furnishing, the picture conveys a working atmosphere, with the three men at the right cabin seem to be involved in a conversation while the businessman sitting in the left cabin works undisturbed for himself. Both groups appear to not noticing each other. They give the impression of being able to concentrate on their work – whether alone or in a group. The third gondola in the background is unoccupied, conveying the impression that this *office* is not working to full capacity.

Despite sitting in various types of gondolas surrounded by tinkered clouds, nobody gives the impression of being in a strange environment. The photo serves a stereotype of Switzerland by converting the means of transport known for this country into workplaces. Furthermore, according to Google, they "play the 'Heidi' song at 5 pm every Friday, where [they] have beer, snacks and fun themes".[24] The second selected picture, which will be briefly presented here, refers even more directly to the legacy of the creativity narrative in IT:

24 Google careers, "5 Surprises about Google Zurich", *Google careers*, [accessed 24th August, 2019], https://careers.google.com/stories/5-surprises-about-google-zurich/.

*Fig. 5: Brainstorm Room, People, Whiteboard from Office snapshots 2008.**

* Office Snapshots, "Google Zurich Offices, *Office Snapshots*, [accessed 22nd May, 2019], https://officesnapshots.com/photos/11833/.

This picture shows a narrow, elongated room. At the back of the area is a large window that lets daylight fall into the room. The right side is bordered by a glass front. A whiteboard on the left sidewall occupies half of this wall. The whiteboard is covered with formulas in red letters. In front of it stands a man, writing something on the whiteboard while apparently explaining something about it. Two other people in the room listen and watch to what he has to say and show. One of them, a man, sits on a beanbag in a sidetipped paddleboat, made of blue and white painted wood. Wearing a flower-dotted shirt, the man has an Apple laptop on his knees and looks interested towards the whiteboard. There's another, albeit unoccupied beanbag in the boat that could hold another person. A rope tied to the bow of the boat lies loosely on the ground. The other person, who is probably a woman (on account of her physique) is situated in the front left corner of the picture. She sits on another blue-coloured beanbag with her legs turned over. A blue and white striped carpet is on the ground between the boat and whiteboard. In the background, a pimple plant in a yellow-orange vase in front of a slightly different yellow-orange wall can be seen. A ceiling lamp and a small transparent table on the carpet complete the scenery.

The choice of colour has a very coordinated effect. The tilted boat, the sand-coloured bottom and the marine colours are reminiscent of a beach scene. In addition, people are not sitting on office chairs, but on loose, comfortable beanbags, also in matching colours. Again, the scene seems very posed. I chose the second picture because it is reminiscent of the working situation at Xerox PARC as it is shown in figure 3: From beanbags to whiteboards there are many identical details. The Google variant takes up the idea of casual, relaxed working and exaggerates it to the extreme. Nevertheless, it shows the evolution of the spatially expressed part of the creativity narrative in IT in a simple yet obvious way.

Both pictures emanate a pretended lightness, supposed to convey something playful and entertaining. Everything seems deliberately harmless, innocent and at the same time unagitated. In particular, the materials used in the first picture are reminiscent of a scene from kindergarten or primary school – exaggeratedly depicted. The very superficial and clichéd dealing with the subject of Switzerland serves this impression. The same is true for the second picture, where the marine scenery is depicted in an exaggerated way.

Apple, on the other hand, is known for its tidy, clean and rather monochrome workplaces[25], but at the same time is much more concerned with security. There are many myths surrounding the new "Apple Park" headquarters in Cupertino, California, with various websites taken on the task of (pseudo) investigatively compiling conjectures, facts and, above all, actual pictures.[26] But in fact, even after an extensive search, no current picture can be found that shows an interior area of the mega-building ensemble that is

25 Cf. Robin Parrish, "Inside Apple HQ", *AppleGazette*, last modified 5th April, 2012, https://www.applegazette.com/feature/inside-apple-hq/.

26 When the new Apple Campus was under construction, one website reads: "It's the chocolate factory for nerds. Search the web for 'Apple HQ,' and most of the results you get will be pictures of Apple's Cupertino headquarters – from the outside. [...] But what we really want to see is what's inside the ultra-top-secret place where all our favorite gizmos are dreamed up." Cf. Amy Senger and Steven Mandzik, "Photos from inside Apple Headquarters", *1x57*, last modified 11th April, 2012, http://1x57.com/b/photos-from-inside-apple-headquarters/.

only open to employees. As Apple officials say, the goal of the new headquarter is to "achieve the security and privacy required for the invention of new products by eliminating any public access through the site, and protecting the perimeters against trespassers".[27] The Los Angeles Times reports that this is taking some drastic measures: "[...] an Apple executive haggled over the location of a single tree. 'Also if we move the tree an additional five feet in, the tree becomes a security issue for us,' Apple executive Meg Thomas wrote. 'People will be able to potentially climb the tree and hop the fence'".[28]

6.1.3 THE FINE LINE BETWEEN INTERNAL AND EXTERNAL FAILURES

IT – and especially Silicon Valley – claims not only to tolerate mistakes, but to even *love* them and to regard them as a fundamentally important part of its self-image: "In the world of tech startups, messing up is practically a religion"[29] is the title of a Guardian article in this regard. However, the logic of the creativity narrative in IT propagates a very special kind of failure, which is strongly determined by social practices. It is clearly defined what such a *messing up* is for IT, what kind of failure to love and what kind to ignore and abandon. In an interview for German television, a Yahoo employee deals with the dissolution between leisure time and job. While guiding the television team around the Yahoo campus and showing them packed refrigerators and numerous recreational facilities, he mentions that a separation between work and life does not exist for him. There is no work-life balance in this sense here because it is all one. Everyone enjoys what they do, which is why they no longer want to distinguish between working and living.[30] Free drinks, snacks, meal, medical doctors and dentists, a gym, drugstore, and even a laundry service

27 Amy Moore, "Complete guide to Apple Park", *Macworld*, last modified 20th February, 2018, https://www.macworld.co.uk/feature/complete-guide-apple-park-3489704/#toc-3489704-4

28 Chris O'Brien, "At Apple Campus 2, security will be a priority", *Los Angeles Times*, last modified 1st October, 2013, https://www.latimes.com/business/la-xpm-2013-oct-01-la-fi-tn-security-will-be-priority-at-apple-campus-2-20130927-story.html.

29 Adrian Daub, "The undertakers of Silicon Valley: how failure became big business", *The Guardian*, last modified 21st August, 2018, https://www.theguardian.com/technology/2018/aug/21/the-undertakers-of-silicon-valley-how-failure-became-big-business.

30 Cf. Bayerischer Rundfunk, Silicon Valley | Faszination Wissen | Doku | BR, YouTube, w.d., 30th September, 2016, accessed 8th June, 2019, https://www.youtube.com/watch?v=mF8JkyQZUKU. In his native language, German, he states originally: „Eine Separation zwischen Arbeit und Leben gibt es nicht. WorkLife Balance in dem Sinne gibt es

– everything on site at the company's premises. According to the Yahoo employee it is okay if other employees play soccer for an hour at noon because they'll stay an hour longer.[31] For him it is basically no problem to stay longer, he is always there anyway, the employee continues. In any case, however, people are always available outside the office as well. Once again, it should be noted that he does not seem to regret this circumstance at all. He does not count whether he is in the office for 40 or 60 hours. He doesn't feel like Monday morning on a Monday morning because he's always in the flow anyway. He doesn't feel like he has to switch himself on. He is always on. After all, work is what he enjoys most.[32] Without exaggerating the employee's position, he seems to sketch a perfect working world – precisely because it no longer seems like a working world. Just like Google (see chapter 6.1), this Yahoo example shows an environment that cares about its employees and their well-being. One is not left alone, even with medical problems.

A few hundred kilometres further south, an ostensibly even more satisfying way of working is currently developing: at Silicon Beach in southern California, business is being done on the beach. People get to know each other while surfing and invest a large amount of money in the start-up of the surfer next to them.[33] At the same time, more than one in three schoolchildren in the Silicon Valley area was homeless at the end of 2016,[34] to provide only one example of the ongoing housing crisis in this area. This figure presents a strong gradient and an invisible wall between those *inside* and *outside* IT. But also, for those that participate in the social structures of IT it is not easy to keep

hier nicht, weil es ist alles eins. Wir haben alle Spaß dran was wir machen, wir wollen das gar nicht unterscheiden."

31 Ibid. In German, he states: „Wenn sie hier mittags 'ne Stunde Fußballspielen ist das okay, weil sie dann ne Stunde länger bleiben".

32 Ibid. In German, he states: "Es ist so, dass die Leute im aber auch außerhalb des Büros immer verfügbar sind. Ich zähle nicht ob ich jetzt hier 40, 50, 60 Stunden ransetze und ich fühl mich auch nicht montagmorgens oder Sonntagabend, dass ich irgendwie muss ich wieder auf Arbeit, sondern ich bin ja sowieso immer in dem Flow. Ich fühl mich nicht, als müsste ich anschalten. Ich bin immer an. Es ist ja auch das, was mir Spaß macht".

33 Cf. Jürgen Schmieder, "Unter der Sonne", *Sueddeutsche Zeitung*, last modified 25th June, 2019, https://www.sueddeutsche.de/wirtschaft/silicon-beach-unter-der-sonne-1.4498321.

34 Cf. Alastair Gee, "More than one-third of schoolchildren are homeless in shadow of Silicon Valley", *The Guardian*, last modified 28th December, 2016, https://www.theguardian.com/society/2016/dec/28/silicon-valley-homeless-east-palo-alto-california-schools.

pace. On the *Quora.com* website, which aims to be able to provide precise answers to questions and is known to repeatedly attract well-known IT actors such as Bill Gates for this purpose, the question was asked as to what a typical day in Silicon Valley would look like.[35] The respondents were not hesitant to point out the difference between presumed and experienced reality in a rather cynical way: a businesswoman living in the area since 1995 provides a detailed account of her day, which consists mainly of routine tasks (awakening children, walking dogs, etc.). Beforehand she sarcastically presents an ideal-typical day on which she gets up at 4.30 a.m. and drives to the chic and fancy gym, discussing world politics and investment ideas.[36] Other accounts are equally sarcastic in its basic tenor. With their sarcastic remarks they sketch the external expectations and the general impression of Silicon Valley's tech world that they believe there is.

Hence, people from within IT seem to be aware of the dichotomy between inside and outside, but not of the fact that it is possible to fail in a way that is unforgivable to the logic of IT. So, the following quote seems like proof of a double bottom. Because for Aaron Sittig, the inventor of Facebook's *like* button,[37] the Silicon Valley is everything but competitive:

> "The best way to think about Silicon Valley is as one large company, and what we think of as companies are actually just divisions. Sometimes divisions get shut down, but everyone who is capable gets put elsewhere in the company: Maybe at a new start-up, maybe at an existing division that's successful like Google, but everyone always just circulates. So you don't worry so much about failure. No one takes it personally, you just move on to something else. So that's the best way to think about the Valley. It's really engineered to absorb failure really naturally, make sure everyone is taken care of, and go on to something productive next. And there's no stigma around it."[38]

Nevertheless, there are unwritten laws and informal rules that must be obeyed. If one does not, no second chance is given, but one is consistently

35 Cf. Jessica Treat, "What is a typical day like in Silicon Valley?"*Quora* (blog), [accessed 22nd May, 2019], https://www.quora.com/What-is-a-typical-day-like-in-Silicon-Valley#MoreAnswers. 401 Cf. Ibid.

36 Cf. Ibid.

37 Cf. Fisher, "Cast of Character" section, para. 1.

38 Fisher, "Silicon Valley, explained" section, para. 2.

excluded. This can even be fatal, as the following example from the *Paris Innovation Review* shows: Glenn Mueller was a venture capitalist[39] who, contrary to the general rules, did not let the entrepreneur hold 30% of his start-up in shares, but only 2%. When the entrepreneur found out about this exploitation, he warned his network and coined the notion *vulture* capital.[40] Now, everybody knew about the disrespect of the *informal social norm*. Unpleasant consequences quickly followed for Glenn Mueller: "the deal flow stopped. Entrepreneurs stopped sending him their projects. [...] no one spoke to him when he went to fetch his children at school, he was no longer invited to weekend barbecues, nor to any other socializing activities. He was gradually excluded from all community networks".[41] When the cheated entrepreneur founded Netscape, he refused to do business with Glenn Mueller's company and chose another investor. "On that day, Glenn Mueller committed suicide. He was a multi-millionaire and nothing he had done was illegal. But he had violated an informal standard of Silicon Valley and was expelled from the network of his community".[42]

This anecdote shows the including and excluding logic, which ended here in an extreme conclusion. It also draws a deterministic-normative picture of the creativity narrative in IT, which offers freedom of movement only within its own limits. It also shows that IT hardly has an eye for the exterior, which is not inherent in its own logic.

6.2 THE SOCIAL ORGANISATION OF A PRODUCTIVE PRACTICE

6.2.1 INTRINSIC BASIC RESEARCH VS. APPLIED RESEARCH

IBM and companies such as Google, Yahoo, Apple or Amazon are active in two rather different business areas and are permeated by different logics, although these overlap on some occasions. As an example, and as described in Chapter 5.1, IBM as an alleged antagonist played an almost constitutive

39 More on the notion of venture capitalism and its connection to the creativity narrative in IT in chapter 6.2.2.

40 Michel Ferrey, "Silicon Valley: a cluster of venture capitalists?" Paris Innovation Review, last modified 21st September, 2017, http://parisinnovationreview.com/articles-en/silicon-valley-a-cluster-of-venture-capitalists.

41 Ibid.

42 Ibid.

role in the development of the concept of creativity in IT in the 1970s and 1980s. Today, however, many of the old signs have reversed. Whereas a few decades ago IBM was known to almost everyone, today it is the above-mentioned companies whose reputation and brand value are at the top of the list. To a not inconsiderable extent, this is due to the fact that IBM has increasingly concentrated on business customers in recent decades and offers neither services nor products to private end customers. Only recently has this changed again with the AI called IBM Watson, the development of cloud software and, in particular, the publicity-driven open access to prototype quantum processors that can be (restrictedly) used via a cloud based website.[43] The influence of Google[44] on the creativity narrative in IT is correspondingly high, which is why it also influences the practice at IBM.[45] Nevertheless, there are still fundamental differences, as the disparate significance of patent filings exemplifies. The way in which the intrinsic differences (with IBM on the one side and Google on the other side) and the creativity narrative interact can be well demonstrated by the different views on research and development. For IBM's senior vice president Arvind Krishna, the number of patents filed also has to do with endurance and, as he puts it, with research for the sake of research that does not relate to practical areas of application:

> "Our work in these areas, and others, began long before there were practical enterprise uses for the technology, and that spirit of research for the sake

43 This access to quantum computing is called *IBM Q Experience*. Cf. IBM, "IBM Q Experience is quantum on the cloud", *IBM Q*, [accessed 2nd August, YEAR], https://www.research.ibm.com/ibm-q/technology/experience/. The concept of a quantum computer has a certain mystic overlay: *The visual representation of the* quantum experience *is not particularly exciting in itself. Calculations can be made, which are graphically represented without much sensationalism. Nevertheless, this tool was often used by visitors to give them a foretaste of the computers of tomorrow. Interestingly enough, the statement indicating that these were actually calculations made by a quantum computer triggered great astonishment, curiosity and sometimes even a certain reverence for the incomprehensible technical innovation. The quantum computer spoke for itself and didn't have to (and couldn't) convince anyone otherwise.* Cf. Autoethnographic account.

44 ...and other companies mentioned above – for the sake of simplicity, only Google is mentioned hereafter, although the above-stated companies are meant here as well.

45 As outlined in chapter 6.1.

> of discovery is what has propelled us to lead the field in patent grants for more than a quarter of a century."[46]

With this statement Krishna advocates basic research. [47] Consequently, this type of research is also very much present in the Zurich research laboratory.

Large parts of the IT cosmos function according to a completely different logic. For companies like Google, it is common practice to not necessarily acquire and develop knowledge (e.g. new technologies) themselves, but to purchase this knowledge and to therefore close a gap to competitors or to build a competitive edge. Google, as an example, did not invent but acquire the technology for their mobile backbone structure *Android* by purchasing the eponymous start-up for an estimated $50 million in 2005, ensuring "the company's safe and profitable transition into the mobile era."[48] To lead the emerging race for supremacy in artificial intelligence research, Google bought the London-based start-up called *DeepMind* for an estimated $600 million in 2014.[49] DeepMind was only founded in 2010, made possible by the investment of venture capital. The AI developed by the company quickly made a name for itself so that not only Google but other companies such as Facebook showed interest in the young company as well.[50]

Overall, it has become part of the reporting that success of the *race for AI domination* – as it is called metaphorically-martially and with reference to the

46 Arvind Krishna, "IBM Marks More Than a Quarter Century of Patent Leadership with Record Year", *IBM Research Blog*, last modified 8th January, 2019, https://www.ibm.com/blogs/research/2019/01/2018-patent/.

47 Remarkably, it was Vannevar Bush who popularised the concept of basic research in the USA when he replied to a letter from President Roosevelt on the future of science after war, in which Bush emphasised the importance of basic research for the fundamental further evolution of research. Cf. Vannevar Bush, "Science: The Endless Frontier", *Transactions of the Kansas Academy of Science* (1903-) 48, no. 3 (1945).

48 Nitasha Tiku, "Three years of misery inside Google, the happiest company in tech", *Wired*, last modified 13th August, 2019, https://www.wired.com/story/inside-google-three-years-misery-happiest-company-tech/.

49 Sam Shead, "Google's 400 million acquisition of London AI startup DeepMind just got very interesting", *Business Insider*, https://www.businessinsider.de/googles-400-million-acquisition-of-deepmind-is-looking-good-2016-7?r=US&IR=T.

50 Cf. Amir Efrati, "Google Beat Facebook for DeepMind, Creates Ethics Board", *The Information*, last modified 26th January, 2014, https://www.theinformation.com/articles/Google-beat-Facebook-For-DeepMind-Creates-Ethics-Board. Apparently, DeepMind made it a condition of the acquisition to set up an ethics council so that the technology could not be abused under Google's aegis.

Space Race of the 1950s – is not primarily evaluated by a company's own research results, but by the acquisition of AI start-ups having the appropriate expertise. For example, a data journalist on the Statista website finds Google in the lead with eleven acquisitions between 2012 and March 2017, followed by Apple with seven and Facebook and Microsoft with five acquisitions of start-ups each.[51] Even though a title like *Google Leads the Race for AI Domination* might sound more appealing to potential readers than a rather direct statement that Google has taken over most AI start-ups, it is interesting to note that in the short accompanying text neither the quality of the takeovers nor the amount invested in the own AI research is being mentioned. Instead of R&D – research and development – the term A&D – acquisition and development – is more appropriate for companies like Google.

6.2.2 ITERATION AND CONTINGENCY – VENTURE CAPITAL IN FULL FORCE

When analysing the development of the creativity narrative in IT, it has already been argued that the logic of that narrative is strongly influenced by a state of contingency.[52] The following will demonstrate that organizing the financing of new ideas (which enables them to exist beyond their mere theoretical existence) has perfected the exploitation of the contingent state and is an essential driver of the logic of the creativity narrative.

In chapter 5.1.5 it was shown that all important actors needed to set up a new company are located within the Silicon Valley – from donors of ideas to financiers. Christopher Stone, co-founder of Twitter, describes the situation as follows: "The infrastructure is here: the real estate people, the legal people, the you-name-it people. They get start-ups, so it's easier: 'Oh, okay, you're a start-up. So, here you go.' It's just easier to do start-up stuff, because everyone in the whole ecosystem knows about start-ups".[53] Those who do know best about start-ups are the ones that finance them as *pre-businesses*, hence business plans that are hardly more than an idea: venture capital (VC) firms and so-called *angel* investors.[54] In fact, VC is the financial heart and accord-

51 Cf. Felix Richter, "Google Leads the Race for AI Domination", *statista*, last modified 17th May, 2017, https://www.statista.com/chart/9443/ai-acquisitions/.

52 Cf. chapter 5.1.5.

53 Fisher, *Valley of Genius*, "Silicon Valley, Explained" section, para. 2.

54 The difference between venture capital and an angel investor is that an angel is an individual while VCs are companies and funds. Accordingly, venture capital firms usually have more money to invest, but they are also more selective. Cf. Becca, "Startup

ingly the drive of IT's narrative of creativity; not only because it often provides the financial basis for start-ups in the first place, but also literally as many of the most important venture capital firms are located on a single street that passes Stanford University just a few hundred meters away and which has since become the most expensive in the world: Sand Hill Road.[55] The agglomeration of money willing to invest not far from one of the great incubators of the tech world has brought the street to some fame. Similar to Silicon Valley for tech giants, Sand Hill stands as a metonym for venture capital ("Sand Hill Road rules Silicon Valley")[56] – and is thus a network[57] within another, broader network, which further underscores its significance.

For the companies located there in particular as well as for venture capital in general, a special focus is on emerging high-technology companies with an insecure future that would otherwise not have been financed.[58] This includes research on AI, as "around 42% of the AI companies acquired since 2013 [until 2018] have had VC backing".[59] As already mentioned in Section 6.2.1, it is in particular the large tech companies that act as VC firms when it comes to acquire AI start-ups. The logic of VC is therefore not limited to classic venture capitalist firms, but describes the predominant type of financing in the outlined world of IT.

---

investment: What is a VC?" *twine* (blog), last modified 17th April, 2017, https://www.twine.fm/blog/vc-startup-investment/. For the sake of simplicity, however, the following only refers to venture capital, though this implies the investments of business angels, unless otherwise stated.

55 With $111 per square meter, renting office space in the USA is nowhere more expensive than here; even the famous Fifth Avenue in Manhattan is cheaper by $9 per square meter in direct comparison. These figures are from 2014. Cf. Bloomberg, "Venture Capital: Sand Hill Road Rules the Valley", *Bloomberg*, last modified 4th December, 2014, https://www.bloomberg.com/news/articles/2014-12-04/venture-capital-sandhill-road-rules-silicon-valley. [422] Ibid.

56 Ibid.

57 The use of the terms *actor* and *network* refer to the understanding related to the actor-network theory as described in chapter 5.1.x

58 Paul Gompers and Josh Lerner, "The Venture Capital Revolution", *Journal of Economic Perspectives* 15, no. 2 (2001): 145-168. doi: 10.1257/jep.15.2.145.

59 CBInsights, "The Race for AI", https://www.cbinsights.com/research/top-acquirers-ai-startups-ma-timeline/.

Besides money, an investment can contain strategic advice in order to increase the chance of a successful (financial) investment.[60] In return for their investments, VC firms receive shares or equity of a company and hence earn the (partial) ownership as well as the hope to be able to multiply their investment by a later sale of the then hopefully successful new company.[61] As stated in chapter 5 already, contingency implies the necessity to take risks and with that the potential of disappointment – after all, there are good reasons why start-ups take money from VC although they lose shares and therefore influence in their emerging company: the too high risk for *normal* banks is one of them (although not the only one, as will be shown later). The risk for VC can be minimized by risk diversification. This means that a VC company does not only rely on one potential start-up, but on many at the same time. If one is successful, it not only recoups the investments made in this business, but also subsidises the failures[62] of other company ideas that have failed.[63]

This is of great significance for the creativity narrative in IT if the underlying process is examined more closely and associated with the concept of *iteration* in a slightly, yet crucial modified form. This is due to the following. The term *iteration* originates from mathematics but is nowadays frequently used in various fields with similar, yet slightly iridescent meanings.[64] What

60 Stuart Logan, "What is a venture capitalist?" *Quora*, last modified 7th June, 2017, https://www.quora.com/What-is-a-venture-capitalist.

61 Becca, "Startup investment: What is a VC?", https://www.twine.fm/blog/vc-startup-investment/.

62 The notion of failure is related to the concept outlined in chapter 6.1.2.

63 Depending on the source, the failure rate of start-ups in the US is roughly between 50 and 90 percent within the first five years of their existence. However, the longer a company survives, the more it is likely to continue to exist. Cf. Failory, "The Ultimate Startup Failure RatevReport", *Failory*, last modified 2019, https://www.failory.com/blog/startup-failure-rate.

64 In philosophy, for example, Edmund Husserl uses the concept of iteration to describe the alteration of a conceptual meaning that is modified each time the concept is used. Each use of a concept irrevocably changes its meaning. Accordingly, there is no original, correct definition of a concept to which one could refer, but rather modifications which in turn refer to modifications and further develop a concept. Cf. Martin Heidegger, ed., *Edmund Husserls Vorlesungen zur Phänomenologie des inneren Zeitbewußtseins* (Halle: Max Niemeyer Verlag, 1928), p. 450ff. Within this thesis, however, the concept of iteration is not understood in Husserl's way, especially not with regard to the development of the concept of creativity in IT.

all understandings have in common, however, is the assumption that iteration describes a repetition that takes place step by step or repetitively, with the aim of approaching or achieving a certain objective or purpose. Translated into the logic of venture capital, this means that a repetition stands for an investment in a single new company with the goal being the successful growth of that company. Now, as many repetitions are made until a company is successful. The difference to a regular understanding of iteration (with all area-specific variations) lies in the meaning of repetition and in the correlation with contingency. Here, repetition does not mean a repetition over time, but a broad diversification in the awareness of the high probability of failure. Thus, the idea of investment is repeated by funding different start-ups simultaneously instead of chronologically. Instead of repetition, duplication appears to be a more suitable term.

The reference to contingency here is not only intriguing because of the iterative process' ability to reduce the prevailing risk in the face of the permanent uncertainty through duplication (formerly repetition). Usually, contingency is exposed by various approaches to the attempt to be overcome.[65] The iterative logic of venture capital[66] determines that many individual risks must be taken in order to minimize the overall risk. Despite a hard selection and preselection (so-called pitches), the failure rate shows that it is primarily about quantity instead of quality without exception. Not only does the logic of VC welcome contingency, it also needs it for its iterative process – a process in which there is no reduction but an increase in complexity.

In a certain contrast to the dotcom bubble period of the late 1990s,[67] potential start-ups are nonetheless dependent on presenting their ideas in a convincing way. Despite the logic of a contingent-iterative risk diversification, VC companies carefully select their protégés. In addition, from a start-up perspective it is not only relevant how much money one could raise for an

65 Niklas Luhmann, for example, attempts to overcome contingency through communication. The aim is to transfer the basic openness of human attitudes and actions through communication into a holistic, emergent order, which then leads to a reduction in complexity and a decrease in unpredictability. Luhmann refers to this emergent order as social systems. Cf. Niklas Luhmann, *Soziale Systeme. Grundriß einer allgemeinen Theorie* (Frankfurt am Main: Suhrkamp, 1987).

66 With reference to the significance of VC for the IT narrative of creativity this refers to the logic of IT as well.

67 Cf. chapter 5.1.5.

idea, but also who provided this money. Venerable VCs who can pride themselves on having already invested in companies such as Facebook and Google or Twitter and Skype and now reside on Sandhill Road[68] are considered by industry experts to be the *holy grail* of investment.[69] Receiving an investment from such companies – even if it is a significantly smaller fund than an alternative offered by a lesser-known venture capitalist – sends a signal to the entire ecosystem. As a result, there is a shift in defining *success* that in turn affects the creativity narrative.

For the financial backers, it is a matter of recognising potentials, thus following the tradition of IT's creativity narrative as it is outlined in the previous chapters. To be creative means to envision creativity. VC firms are successful if they are able to recognise and realise a presented potential (by funding it, not by producing or developing it). For prospective founders, the moment of success also shifts: success does not only occur when a service or a product can actually assert itself on the market, but already in advance, with the successful presentation of the non-existent service or product yet to exist. This can be summed up in the words of former Google product manager and founder of an early social network service Orkut Büyükkökten.[70] For him, the distinctive feature is not the amount of new ideas, but the ability to implement it, turning it from abstract to reality.[71]

First and foremost, however, it is a question of pretending. Often the narrative of known successes is adopted and reused without necessarily having the same great potential – as it was for example with Apple and other companies developing the personal computer. Thus, proposals for investments are often bursting with megalomaniac approaches. Everyone sets out to change the world following in the footsteps of digital models.[72] Even within IT, this tendency has not remained without criticism. On the contrary, many see the

---

68 The examples meant here are Kleiner Perkins Caufield & Byers and Andreesen Horowitz. Cf. Bloomberg, "Venture Capital: Sand Hill Road Rules the Valley", *Bloomberg*, last modified 4th December, 2014, https://www.bloomberg.com/news/articles/2014-12-04/venture-capital-sand-hill-road-rules-silicon-valley.

69 This has been told to me in a personal conversation by a tech manager and *angel investor* in 2015.

70 Cf. Jesse Lichtenstein, "The Real", *The New Yorker*, last modified 21st March, 2004, https://www.newyorker.com/magazine/2004/03/29/the-real.

71 Cf. Fisher, *Valley of Genius*, "Silicon Valley, Explained" section, para. 2.

72 In a more specific example, a teenager received a $100,000 scholarship from the Peter Thiel Foundation to mine asteroids for the idea of extracting all the rare minerals

motivation of the tech scene only in the accumulation of money. For some, this even sounds like a farewell to the *old days*. For Sean Parker, co-founder of Napster and former Facebook consultant, the logic of VC marks the entry into the "post-social media era",[73] in which it is not about the idea or the project, but quite simply about money:

> "It's all the people who would have become investment bankers who want to go start internet companies, and it's a purely commercial, purely transactional world. It's just become this transactional thing, and it's attracted the wrong type of people. It's become a very toxic environment. A lot of people have shown up believing, maybe correctly, that they can cash in. But that's Silicon Valley the ATM machine, not Silicon Valley the font of creativity and realization of your dreams".[74]

Creativity is (still) in demand. But the narrative has shifted and is now home to the hypothetical, speculative, purely virtual. The logic of venture capital promotes a general climate of opportunity and change, encouraging optimism and innovation – but also the constant danger of being *outsmarted* by someone who is faster, more innovative but most importantly the better persuader and pretender. As a consequence, the organisation of creativity has become hyper-competitive,[75], comparable (by means of its financial value) and can therefore be ranked and evaluated. This, too, is strongly criticized by members of the IT sector, as a further quote from Biz Stone demonstrates, who almost cynically describes what he considers to be the existing exaggerations of the VC logic presented here:

> "Only in Silicon Valley can you be like, 'Yeah, we would like $10 million and we'll sell you a percentage of our theoretical company that may one day have lots of profits and if we lose all the money we don't have to give it

---

found on them. After receiving the scholarship, however, his interest focused on other projects. Cf. Alexandra Wolfe, *Valley of the Gods* (New York: Simon & Schuster, 2017).

73 Fisher, *Valley of Genius*, "Silicon Valley, Explained" section, para. 2.

74 Ibid.

75 The concept of hypercompetitiveness is derived from Reckwitz, who states that markets live on attention and cultural valorisation. In addition, he concludes that there is a pronounced, unpredictable competition for attention and appreciation of uniqueness. Cf. Reckwitz, *Die Gesellschaft der Singularitäten*, p. 114. However, Reckwitz neither refers the unpredictability directly to the concept of contingency, nor does he describe venture capital as a decisive development or even as a usurper for this development.

> back to you. And maybe we'll start something else.' In what crazy world does something like that exist? [...] I mean it's just crazy. [...] Here's what some people do. They say, 'We need $25 million, but you know, just so we can stay focused my cofounder and I each need $3 million of that money in our bank accounts. Then we don't have to worry about bills so we can really focus. Okay?' And then they blow the money and they say, 'Oh, well, that didn't work out, but we're still keeping the $3 million each, so now we're rich.' What the hell? That is crazy. So, it's a crazy world. This is like some kind of nutty place where you can do that kind of stuff".[76]

At the same time, the narrative refers to all the past tales that have shaped the understanding of Silicon Valley (and that were examined in the previous subchapters for their influence on the creativity narrative in IT). The old stories retain their influence on the narrative, which of course does not completely reinvent itself. However, human actors are now very aware of the creative heritage of Silicon Valley and its specific *otherness*, which they use to promote one's own creative ability (and *otherness*) – hence, the creativity narrative in IT became a self-referential tool, used to keep the contingent iterative process running by means of an autopoietic manner.

6.2.3 ON THE ONTOLOGICAL NATURE OF COMPUTATIONAL CREATIVITY

Since its inception in 1956, AI as a scientific field of research[77] is considered to be an interdisciplinary subject, whereby IT has been and continues to be a decisive factor in questions of technical feasibility from a developmental point of view. For this, it is of paramount importance that large IT companies such as Google, Facebook and IBM have massively entered the race for the development of artificial intelligence in recent years or have at least increased their commitment.[78] This also includes the postulate to develop artificial intelligence systems with the ability to be somewhat creative. The discourse about artificial creativity complements the creativity narrative of IT with an independent and quasi-inverted logic: the fundamental difference lies in the fact that so far, the creativity narrative in IT claims to enable innovative *things* (by means of products, services and ideas) to emerge through creativity. In contrast, artificial creativity is about using these innovative things to *create*

76 Fisher, *Valley of Genius*, "Silicon Valley, Explained" section, para. 2.

77 ...whose development in relation to creativity in IT is presented in chapter 5.3.

78 Cf. chapter 6.2.2.

creativity itself. Therefore, it is the same people who *buy* or *sell* creativity – and thus add a quantifiable value – who also have the power of interpretation over artificial creativity. On the basis of the developments presented in Chapter 5.3, the following section will therefore outline and analyse how IT's view of the scientific field of research on artificial creativity is both influencing and influenced by the creativity narrative in IT.[79]

Despite its constitutive anchoring in the field of AI research, the study of artificial creativity "is a recent but burgeoning area of creativity research that brings together academics and practitioners from diverse disciplines, genres and modalities, to explore the potential of our machines to be creative in their own right".[80] In the course of this, parts of IT have come to realise that an understanding of artificial creativity can only be created through a comparative approach to natural creativity, namely human creativity.

Those IT enterprises who have already implemented the mindset to consider the concept of natural creativity are now not only confronted with a terminological understanding of the notion on creativity and questions regarding development and implementation, but also with ontological issues regarding the potential of an artificial consciousness and the resulting exploration of differentiating factors between humans and machines. Through the linkage to creativity research, the scientific part of research is of equal interest for artificial as well as natural creativity.[81] IT, on the other hand, takes a developmental engineering approach: as an engineering endeavour, it is claimed

79 By way of limitation, it may be noted that this subchapter certainly cannot claim to reflect all the major currents, actors, and developments in research into artificial creativity. This would not be possible in the context of this work from quantitative standpoints alone, since this young but broadly based area of research already has numerous and rather heterogeneous discursive strands from a broad range of special discourses.

80 Tony Veale, F. Amílcar Cardoso and Rafael Pérez y Pérez, "Systematizing Creativity: A Computational View", in *Computational Creativity. Computational Synthesis and Creative Systems*", eds. Tony Veale and F. Amílcar Cardoso (Cham: Springer, 2019), doi: https://doi.org/10.1007/978-3-319-43610-4_1, pp. 1-19. The recently published volume of editors from which this introductory quote is taken provides a comprehensive and broad overview of the subject area and related fields of interest and includes contributions from the leading experts in the field.

81 Ibid. However, and although the title of the article from which this quote derives from is *Computational Creativity. The Philosophy and Engineering of Autonomous Creative Systems*, the authors, who preface this as an introduction to a profoundly edited compendium on computational creativity, do not consider the *philosophy* to be an integral part of research on natural creativity, but rather scientific disciplines such as: "machine learning,

possible to construct autonomous systems that produce novel and useful outputs that deserve the label *to be creative*.[82] Here, too, the difficulty of defining creativity poses a challenge to the actors of this special discourse. In particular, institutions and associations that address the phenomenon of artificial creativity directly through research and development are trying to achieve a somewhat better understanding of the term. In this context, the former definition of artificial creativity provided by the Association for Computational Creativity [83] is of interest. Until 2013, this association suggested that "Computational Creativity is the study and simulation, by computational means, of behaviour, natural and artificial, which would, if observed in humans, be deemed creative".[84]

By adding the last few words, which reads *be deemed creative*, the above proposal for defining the creativity of AI systems points to the fact that creativity and *to be creative* are interpretative and evaluative ascriptions that require an evaluative capacity of interpretation that can differ – even if the conditions are objectively the same. It therefore takes human beings to evaluate and acknowledge and appreciate artificial creativity as such. Consequently, the updated definition approach adds the fact that it is the task of artificial creativity research to learn more about the phenomenon of human creativity and to develop systems that enhance human creativity – without necessarily having to be creative themselves.[85] Thus, the question of what it means to be creative seems to be equally valid for both artificial and human creativity research, notes the PROSECCO (Promoting the Scientific Exploration of Computational Creativity) research network.[86] In addition, these proposals

artificial intelligence, engineering, design, and experimental psychology". Cf. Ibid., p. ii.

82 Ibid.

83 The Association for Computational Creativity is an association on the subject of artificial creativity, which strives both for further development and the authority to interpret this field. Cf. Anna Jordanous, "What is Computational Creativity?" *The Creative Post*, last modified 10th April, 2014, http://www.creativitypost.com/science/what_is_computational_creativity/.

84 Anna Jordanous, "A Standardised Procedure for Evaluating Creative Systems: Computational Creativity Evaluation Based on What it is to be Creative", *Cognitive Computation* 4, no. 3 (2012): 246-279, p. 248.

85 Association for Computational Creativity, http://computationalcreativity.net/home/.

86 PROSECCO, "Introduction to Computational Creativity", *Promoting the Scientific Exploration of Computational Creativity*, [accessed 21st August, 2018], http://prosecco-network.eu/introduction-computational-creativity/.

for definition show evidence that there is a discourse strand, which considers the question of what artificial creativity is as ultimately not being effective. This led to diametrically opposed approaches in how to deal with the concept of creativity. The first approach does not give an assessment of creativity, as the following quote shows:

> "So creativity in the domain of sports [...] is clearly different from creativity in the arts domain [...], yet there are enough similarities for exemplary outcomes in each domain to be deserving of the same label, 'creative'. This heterogeneity makes creativity a notoriously difficult concept to pin down in formal terms, and definitions that favor one area of human activity (such as art) [sic!] are unlikely to do justice to other areas (such as science, engineering, or cooking) [sic!]."[87]

What is essentially expressed in this quote is: art is one domain of many. Initially, art has the same value for creativity as sport or cooking: all of them – according to the prevailing opinion here – are purposeful human activities, i.e., active processes leading to tangible results that can be described as creative in one way or another. Art is neither an exception here, nor is it seen as a possible origin of creativity or as an existential part of it. This approach towards artificial creativity is based on the concept of an expert system, as it has existed since the 1980s in particular.[88]

The second approach is more concerned with a fundamental understanding of creativity and considers complementary, ontological questions such as the possibility of an artificial consciousness: the author Pamela McCorduck, renowned primarily for her texts on the significance and history on artificial intelligence, summarizes the arguments "as to why machines [...] cannot be said to think"[89] in four categories. Next to emotional or ethical reservations there are "Arguments of insuperable differences"[90]. For McCorduck, this *insuperableness* lies in the very essence of creativity:

> "The reasoning says that machines can't be said to think because intelligence requires creativity and originality, and no machine has been or can

87 Veale et al., "Systematizing Creativity: A Computational View", p. 2.

88 Cf. chapter 5.1.4.

89 McCorduck, *Machines Who Think. A Personal Inquiry into the History and Prospects of Artificial Intelligence*, p. 199.

90 Ibid.

> be creative and original. [...] Intelligence, this argument runs, requires autonomy, and no machine can ever be autonomous. [...] the only so-called intelligent tasks machines can accomplish are one of a kind; [...] it won't be able to transfer that savvy [...]. Intelligence means coping with a variety of tasks successfully and with originality. Even if a machine could do these things, it would not be conscious of having done so, and consciousness is a significant part of intelligent behavior".[91]

Even though opinions within the discourse differ widely, there seems to be an essential understanding that creativity does not equal creativity. There is hence a concluding tendency to draw a distinction. For example, journalist Geoff Colvin (2015) acknowledges the ability of computers to be creative in principle but reserves the *high-value creativity* for humans.[92]

One applied example is AARON, a computer program which has been developed and continuously improved since the 1970s by the British artist Harold Cohen. The system is capable of producing abstract images that have made it to the Tate Gallery. Yet, Cohen himself does not consider the program to be creative, partly because it cannot independently learn or discover new styles.[93] Rather, new styles must be written by humans in appropriate code form. Nevertheless, Cohen provokes people's exclusive claim to be creative by asking what it is then, what AARON produces, and how this can be distinguished from the real thing, the artwork produced by humans.[94]

A possible answer to this is provided by cognitive scientist Margaret Boden, who proposed a hierarchical classification of the concept of creativity into three levels, which differ significantly in their degree of unconventionality and complexity.[95] The basal level is called *combinatorial* creativity. Within known and familiar ideas, unfamiliar combinations are created, and analogies are made. This allows, for example, future scenarios and appropriate behaviour patterns can be developed. What has already been learned can be applied to unknown situations, since, according to Boden, analogies create similarities to familiar situations. The second level is known as the ground

91 Ibid.

92 Geoff Colvin, *Humans are Underrated. What High Achievers Know That Brilliant Machines Never Will* (New York: Penguin, 2015).

93 Harold Cohen, "The Further Exploits of AARON, Painter", *Stanford Humanities Review* 4, no. 2 (1995): 141-158.

94 Ibid.

95 Boden, *The Creative Mind: Myths and Mechanisms.*

explorative level. For Boden, this is the ability to create new, surprising ideas within the existing field. The value of explorative creativity lies in the demonstration of new possibilities within an existing framework that no one previously suspected or knew of.[96] Boden describes the third form of creative work as *transformative* creativity. According to Boden, transformative creativity strives to replace the old with something new, whereby it automatically becomes a danger to the established, but can hardly encounter a general understanding.[97]

From a discursive point of view, it seems reasonable to speak of (artificial) creative approaches rather than (artificial) creative abilities. Ultimately, technical feasibility is of secondary importance for discourse. More interesting is the power of the discursive truth, which propagates the existence of artificial creativity. As part of the creativity narrative of IT, the phenomenon of artificial creativity is also subject to the assumption that the question of how this phenomenon expresses itself is more relevant than the question of *what* artificial creativity is. Discursively speaking, something is creative if it appears to be creative – just as the interpretive approach above expressed it with the words *to be deemed creative.*[98]

Accordingly, the creativity narrative in IT is of importance, since its dominant position in the creativity discourse (which includes the special discourse of artificial creativity research) determines what can be perceived as (artificially) creative.

96 Ibid.

97 Ibid.

98 One aspect of the Chinese Room thought experiment may function here as an analogy: the simulative character of (apparent) intelligence does not allow an observer to distinguish it from supposedly "real" intelligence. A *pretending as if* is sufficient. Again, the question of *how* and *by whom* is perhaps more relevant than *what*. In terms of creativity, the situation may be similar: if IT simulates artificial creativity to an extent that can produce the same effects as human creativity from an external point of view, this seems to be a variant of creativity that has become a discursive truth. Cf. John. R. Searle, "Minds, brains, and programs", *Behavioral and Brain Sciences* 3, no. 3 (1980): 417-45.

7 RESULTS AND DISCUSSION

7.1 RESULTS

The discursive elaboration of a presumed specific creativity narrative in IT allows conclusions to be drawn about relevant actors, their intentions and motivations, corresponding representations, organisations, verbal and non-verbal forms of expression as well as contexts of justification, i.e., the specifics of creativity from the perspective of and with regard to IT.

A total of four current socio-cultural and economic currents preconditioned the contextual foundation for the analyses, which had to be taken into account, were accordingly considered in the course of the analyses. It is not my intention to provide conclusions or evaluations about these aspects. Even though my analyses of the creativity narrative in IT once again underlined their significance, the four contextualisations remain a means to an end in order to address the relevance of the topic and to simultaneously situate it in the actual state of things. They will subsequently be outlined in preparation of the representation of results.

Based on this contextualisation, five focal points were retrospectively selected as cornerstones of the analysis and further subdivided into aspects that are constitutive for the narrative. Applying a diachronic analysis, the *unique characteristics of Silicon Valley*, the *societal transformations and scientific currents of IT's self image* as well as an *account on the connection between artificial intelligence and creativity* were exposed and construed. Building on the analysis of the historically constituted creativity narrative in IT, I then outlined the way the meaning of this narrative and its immanent logics function and present themselves today. This was done by focusing on the *social organisation of a productive practice* and the *habitat and habitus*, hence including the non-verbal aspects of a discourse on creativity.

7.1.1 CONTEXTUAL FRAMEWORK

The first current to consider is *the everlasting creativity as social norm*. Creativity is not a hype anymore but a matter of course, a social norm. I have illustrated this using the resolution of the so-called Business Roundtable as an example, according to which it now becomes a prime purpose of every company to promote the creative ability of every individual.

Secondly, the *creation of a digital world* is another relevant factor. The use of the concept of a digital world as a result of the fundamental digital transformation is becoming more and more widespread.[1] The inhabitants and visitors – hence its programmers and users – of this world have to care less about the existing framework developed by politics and society. Rather, they must abide by and take the rules of the IT game into account. Even if there are increasing calls for stronger regulations or even break-ups of large IT companies, this does show that awareness of the emergence of a world outside the state and controlled by IT companies is growing, but at the same time many of the apprehended structures already exist.[2]

Thirdly, *changing conditions of work and labour* have been identified as a crucial current. The way people work and the conditions under which they do so are being discussed and negotiated in ongoing lively and expressive discourses. In the course of digitalisation and the emergence of the digital world, the very concept of work is being questioned and renegotiated. From this it could be deduced that the likewise increasing and threatening automation of jobs thus once again reinforces the imperative character of an economic understanding of creativity. Because being creative appears as an effective solution to not become obsolete on the job market.

Fourthly, the *dawn of creative machines* is a context to be considered, i.e., the possibilities and limitations of an AI system to be by all or no means creative.

---

1 Reckwitz, for example, also uses the term *digital world* in his most recent publication. Cf. Reckwitz, Andreas. Das Ende der Illusionen. Politik, Ökonomie und Kultur in der Spätmoderne. Berlin: Suhrkamp, 2019.

2 See journalist Carsten Knop of the Frankfurter Allgemeine Zeitung in commenting the topic of digital sovereignty: Without digital sovereignty, we are threatened with a world in which a few companies or states determine the technologies and thus the parameters according to which we trade and shape change, discuss political issues, make decisions and develop ourselves as individuals in a self-determined or even non-self-determined manner. In fact, we are currently running the risk of entering such a world without having had a broad and open debate on the consequences in time.

It is therefore a subject of both semantic and ontological nature, which repeatedly pushes the boundaries of familiar discourses, as recent discussions within trans- and posthumanist discourses show.[3]

7.1.2 CONCLUSIONS OF ANALYSES

For the early phase of IT, the diachronic analysis initially pinpoints a specific but subtly implicit understanding of creativity that already resonated and had a constitutive effect on the development of IT. This refers in particular to those aspects of the creativity narrative that support the specific *otherness* of IT, such as the opposition to the economic East Coast mentality. From the very beginning, however, there was a simultaneity in IT between a liberal understanding of the market on the one hand and philanthropic ideas on the other, coupled with a robust self-image of fundamentally improving the world through one's own ability to do so, as Doug Engelbart's role shows, among others.

IT's incipient self-description as "being creative" leads to a new self-awareness and pride in its idiosyncratic form of creativity; a sense of superiority to *conventional* managers emerged. From IT's point of view, outsiders (hence the establishment) cannot understand the inside; while those being part of the inner IT circle pretend to know how things could be done better.

However, this is neither primarily about developing something new per se nor about serving a genuine *idea of creation*, but about uncovering, linking and exploiting potentials with existing trajectory paths, i.e., innovations. As has been shown, the role of creativity should not be underestimated in this. Initially, the aim was to strive for one's own creativity in a utopian sense, but due to the influence of the counterculture of the 1960s and appropriate technologies such as the computer and other small technologies, the appropriate infrastructure emerged to realise one's own utopia creatively and playfully for the purpose of improving the world.

Certainly, this approach was quickly appropriated by market-economic efforts and functioned as a valorisation and quasi-marketing product, all under the guise of the countercultures' liberal-artistic connotation of creativity:

3 This recently became true for German-speaking expert groups as well, cf. Loh, Janina. Trans- und Posthumanismus zur Einführung. Hamburg: Junius, 2018; Loh, Janina. Roboterethik. Berlin: Suhrkamp, 2019; Misselhorn, Catrin. Grundfragen der Maschinenethik. Ditzingen: Reclam, 2019.

The analysis further depicts a deterministic-normative picture of the creativity narrative in IT that offers freedom only within its own boundaries. The development of a specific *otherness* shows IT's lack to recognise the outside, hence anything which is not inherent to its own logic. The creativity narrative of IT takes on a constitutive role here, in that creativity still lives on a liaison with the concept of freedom by being clichédly attributed to art and artists or certain ideals of counterculture that are kept alive in stories and ascriptions. Using creativity as intermediary effectively cloaks the marketing aspect.

This is not new per se, even if it has now been examined specifically for IT. In Gerald Raunig's words, however, a certain paradox is noticeable. This paradox is already evident in the strong influence of both military interests in Silicon Valley (more general in IT-industry) and free-spirited ideas (the culture): technology is connectable to the military, and hippies' appropriate technology through the connotation of creativity whereby the usage of technology is morally justified, as exemplified by Stewart Brand's Whole Earth Catalog. Simultaneously, a new self-awareness of IT arose resulting in the already above mentioned but fundamental construction of an *outside* (the "non-creative") with the affirmative self-description as being creatively empowered serving as justification for such a differentiation.

Again, with the help of the concept of creativity, IT further focuses on the exploitation of potential and possibilities, which reaches a new peak by the rise of venture capitalism. The inherent idea of an iterative-contingent principle is of special interest with regard to IT's creativity narrative[4]. The iterative aspect, in turn, is not thought of as a temporal component (hence the repetition of the same process), but as a quantitative one: by spreading the risk over different, potentially innovative ideas, the chance of having success with at least one idea and using this investment to compensate for the others is increased. For IT creatives, this means a shift in the idea of what is understood as being creative and therefore of what being successful means. They are no longer successful when a new product or service actually works, but when such an idea has been successfully financed before it is actually implemented or even developed. The promise and potential became the true (quantitatively measurable) value. Here, too, the narrative of creativity is hence increasingly occupied with the outer façade. What's more is the fundamental simplicity of being capable to finally measure creativity in quantitative terms, hence

4 ...whereby the concept of contingency does not refer to Luhmann here but is thought of in connection with him.

money: the more potential an idea, product or service might have and the better its story is, the higher the funding.

With recourse to IT's tendency towards the separation of being either inside or outside its sphere, a strong uniformity is recognisable that is promoted in particular by the quantitative approach of the creativity narrative, but at the same time it is also obscured.

For this reason, I have used IT's well-known implementation of a culture of error in the process of the analysis to highlight the importance of adhering to implicit rules and norms of IT. When a Yahoo employee enthusiastically tells us that he no longer distinguishes between work and private life, this shows the almost total monopolisation of labour. Sarcastic contributions by former employees who are asked to describe their "typical Silicon Valley day" again exemplify the discrepancy between inside and outside, or the propagated ideal state and individual reality. Although the ironic and sarcastic nature of the contributions hypothesise that at least some people are aware of this discrepancy, this does not seem to apply to the general assessment of the fundamental nature of IT. For it is implicitly assumed that a closed *inside* exists within which employees circulate from one tech company to another without the fear of falling from the inside to the outside.

The extreme example of a venture capitalist who did not obey to these internal yet unwritten rules and became socially isolated in the process only to finally committing suicide underlines the dogmatism in a drastic way – especially against the background of the (also contingent-iterative) error culture, according to which failures are a good part of the story of everyone's biography. As shown, it just cannot happen to be the wrong type of failure.

Finally, the discourse on artificial creativity complements the analysis of IT's creativity narrative with an independent and quasi-inverted logic: discussing artificial creativity is not just about using one's own creative potential or (institutionally speaking) expanding it through acquisitions or strengthening the potential of other third parties through products or services, but about *creating creativity*. For this, a more precise understanding of the term's technical perspective was necessary, and answers were sought and partially found in research on human creativity. This in turn led to a connection to ontological questions about the potential of an artificial consciousness and the resulting research into differentiating factors between humans and machines.

IT companies themselves, on the other hand, take a developmental approach: it is possible, they claim, to construct autonomous systems that produce novel and useful results that deserve the label "creative". Here, the influence of the IT-specific understanding of creativity, which is focused on quantitatively measurable results, becomes apparent. Even more so, the influence of the creativity narrative of IT on a general interpretation of creativity becomes apparent considering the amount and type of public and expert feedback on topics regarding the existence of artificial creativity.

Ultimately, however, technical feasibility is of secondary importance for the discourse. It is the power of the discursive truth that propagates the existence of artificial creativity that is of higher importance here. As part of the creativity narrative of IT, the phenomenon of artificial creativity is also subject to the assumption that the question of how this phenomenon is expressed is more relevant than the question of what artificial creativity actually is. Discursively speaking, something is creative if it appears to be creative. Accordingly, the creativity narrative is important in IT because its dominant position in the creativity discourse (which also includes the specific discourse of artificial creativity research) determines what can be perceived as (artificially) creative.

7.2 DISCUSSION

If creativity is perceived as a reification, hence a quantitatively measurable variable that is, moreover, a means to the end of cloaking the uniform character of IT and with simultaneous consideration of the four contextual currents (creativity as a social norm, the emergence of a digital world, changing conditions of work and labour and the emergence of potentially creative systems), it cannot only be discussed merely within the framework of a general critique of economics in consideration of a creative imperative. The influence of the creativity narrative of IT is, in my view, more extensive than that. Creativity acts as a mediator and justification for an industry that is totalitarian at its core, characterised by a clear dichotomy of inside and outside and committed to the logic of quantification.

7.2.1 THE IDEALISED IT SUBJECT AND THE TOTAL ENTERPRISE

Sociologist Erving Goffman coined the term *total institutions* for his field as early as the late 1950s.[5] But even if the term became widespread in the course, employing the term *total enterprise* is not without risk and certainly problematic unless it is preceded by some clarifying sentences. The problem lies not in the historical weight of the term, but in its possible intention. For some time now, large IT companies such as Google or Facebook have been the object of criticism from right-wing groups and conspiracy theorists such as the *Alt-Right* movement or extremist supporters of a so-called *white supremacy* myth. These groups accuse the corporations in question of censoring and, in their view, publishing and actively supporting *left-wing extremist positions* while blocking and deleting their own "conservative" views.[6]

However, no analysis of ultra-right Internet platforms is required to come across exaggeratedly populist lead stories that fuel fear by depicting a dystopian future scenario, as for example the conservative and moderate right-wing news website The Federalist did with the following heading and sub-headline: "Okay, Google: How Do You Prepare A Country For Totalitarianism? – To be ready for dictatorship, people have to embrace its habits and practices voluntarily, or at least show little resistance. Google is doing its part".[7] Hence, headlines and summaries alone already speak of totalitarian

5 Cf. Goffman, Erving. On the Characteristics of Total Institutions. New York: Holt, Rinehart and Winston, 1961.

6 A current example is the case of a former Google engineer who was given a platform on Fox News to argue that he had been fired for his "conservative" views and that Google is actively manipulating positions contrary to their own vision of the world – the accusations go as far as the allegation of vote rigging. However, the tv-show is silent about what the former quoted Google employee understands by conservative and what ultimately led to his dismissal: The employee was known as a supporter of the Alt-Right movement and wanted to collect money on the company's internal message boards for a bounty on the man who had assaulted a well-known right-wing radical on the day of Donald Trump's swearing-in ceremony as president. Cf. w. d. *Former Google employee accuses tech giant bias*, YouTube, posted by Fox Business, 6th August, YEAR, https://www.youtube.com/watch?v=deAea89VI; Frauke Steffens, "Das Internet der Faschisten", *Frankfurter Allgemeine Zeitung*, last modified 7th August, 2019, https://www.faz.net/aktuell/politik/ausland/internet-der-rechtsextremen-rassisten-treffen-sich-im-netz16321835.html?printPagedArticle=true#void.

7 Cf. Robert Tracinski, "Okay, Google: How Do You Prepare A Country For Totalitarism?" *The Federalist*, last modified 9th August, 2017, https://thefederalist.com/2017/08/09/h

structures of companies such as Google in media, which are also read and quoted by right-wing extremist groups.

To the best of my knowledge, however, they do neither include the concept or narrative of creativity in their argumentation nor the notion of a *total enterprise*, which would otherwise not have been justifiable for the subsequent argumentation in terms of mutual semantic narrowness.[8]

In the digital society, data has become the leading currency, which leads to an infinite process of data production and increased competition.[9] The more data are produced and collected, the better measures of service provision and self-improvement can be applied.[10] This can be seen, for example, in the development of the healthcare sector. In a document about IBM's AI system "Watson", which is also used in oncology and other areas of medical technology, it is stated that in one's life, an average human being (in Western societies) generates 0.4 terabyte of clinical data, 6 terabyte of genomic data and 1100 terabyte of so-called exogenous data, e.g. behavioural, socio-economic or environmental factors.[11]

The growing amount of data suggests manifold possibilities of comparability between individuals. Data seems harmless. They appear as a means of a neutral and, above all, unadulterated description of reality, with no valorisation. On the basis of this quantification, individuals, by their patterns, are ordered into new hierarchies: not only is generated income relevant to top the hierarchy, but also the size of the volume of data produced.

---

ey-google-how-do-you-prepare-a-country-for-totalitarianism/. The article itself makes an effort to appear balanced and profound through a long chain of arguments and numerous examples, though. But the substance of this article is not up for debate here; rather, it should be pointed out that a link exists between a notion of totalitarian structures at tech companies and right-wing supporters and whose recognition is necessary in order to clearly distinguish one's own argumentation from these currents.

8 There exists, however, a long research article of the Swiss online magazine *Republik* called *the total enterprise* ("Das totale Unternehmen") about the *management of power* of the Swiss company Migros, in which reports about *dependencies, lobbying* and *homeland identity* are released. Cf. Simon Schmid et al., „Das totale Unternehmen", *Republik*, last modified 17th January, 2019, https://www.republik.ch/2019/01/17/das-systematische-unternehmen.

9 Steffen Mau, *Das metrische Wir. Über die Quantifizierung des Sozialen* (Berlin: Suhrkamp, 2017), p. 26.

10 Cf. ibid.

11 IBM, internal document.

This is important because it ultimately generates discursive truths[12] that make quantification, hierarchisation and, ultimately, human *clustering* through the increasing use of digital technologies a real possibility.[13] With an abundance of data, we are made more calculable, but possibly we ourselves are also acting more calculable: the *quantification of the social* thus has the potential to produce a new regime of inequality, Steffen Mau notes in this regard.[14]

However, the idea of quantifiability and clustering is by no means new and can be found in an illustrative place in Florida's description of a concept on the creative class[15] and neither is the formulation of a criticism on this.[16]

IT, however, is no longer limited to digital spheres, but has the claim of general validity. Amazon, for example, is expanding into the physical book market and opened its first analogue book store in 2015, with a total of 17

---

12 IBM, internal document, p. 14ff.

13 For the mentioned example from medicine, the argumentation is that this creates a significant opportunity to collect and use factual patient-generated information in order to achieve a better treatment option. An article in the Harvard Business Review (HBR) uses a hypothetical patient to illustrate what such clustering of individuals may look like. Since the respective and hypothetical person is an African-American woman who lives below the poverty line, her risk of cardiovascular disease increases, as can be seen from various factors such as her gender and socio-economic status. The latter suggests that she is less likely to have insurance and is less likely to report symptoms (among other aspect) and is therefore more likely to die from a given disease. These are important clues for treating physicians - who, according to the HBR, are more likely to be male, white, and affluent. Cf. Olympia Duhart, "Why More Hospitals Should Prioritize Cultural Competency", *Harvard Business Review*, last modified 26th May, 2017, https://hbr.org/2017/05/why-more-hospitals-should-prioritize-cultural-competency#.

14 Mau, Das metrische Wir, p.286.

15 Florida's assessment of the concept of creative class would not be possible without indexes and clustering, as Charles Landry summarizes. He thus names exemplary: "the Talent Index measured as percentage of people with a higher degree or above; the Gay Index, a measure of over- or under- representation of coupled gay people relative to nation as a whole", to name just two examples. Cf. Charles Landry, "Lineages of the Creative City", *Creativity and the City, Netherlands Architecture Institute*, [accessed 25th August, 2019], http://charleslandry.com/panel/wp-content/uploads/downloads/2013/03/Lineages-of-the-Creative-City.pdf, p. 12.

16 Again, already in 2005 and with regard to the concept of Creative Cities, Landry critically points out that cities "tend to restrict its meaning to the arts and activities within the creative economy professions calling any cultural plan a 'creative city' plan, when this is only an aspect of a community's creativity". Cf. ibid.

stores in 2019.[17] Not only does the digital have an influence on the analogue[18] (as can be seen, for example, in the decline of small, owner-managed bookstores that had to close due to competition from online retailers), the digital is also increasingly being analogised itself.

Through data-generated quantifiability, IT organisations claim to know what is right.[19] At *Amazon books*, for example, the selection of books on site is determined by the algorithms of the Amazon webpage and the books sold there. Only what is successful is offered. This type of selection is called *curation*. In this case, this curatorial activity means that only items are offered that have received *4 stars & above* at Amazon, are *top-seller* or *new & trending* on amazon.com.[20] The Frankfurter Allgemeine Zeitung (FAZ) notes that there is of course no place here for the unusual, and notes that everything from the customer to the e-book reader to the store customer just goes round in circles, reinforcing each other and creating a filter bubble.[21] On the shelf of the *100 books to read in a lifetime* are just two titles by non-English-speaking original authors[22] and the oldest book is (appropriately) George Orwell's 1948 novel *1984*. For the FAZ, this is the epitome of the bankruptcy declaration of independent reading and the display of the dominance of discoveries capable of majority support. With Foucault, Amazon uses user data to produce knowledge. Not only is access to knowledge restricted, (as the commentary on Google Books makes clear) it also produces specific knowledge that determines what is right and what is wrong, what is valuable and what is not. In the late modern era, technologies are extensively transformed into infrastructures of the special, they make singularities (speaking with Reckwitz) visible and fabricate them

---

17 Amazon, "amazonbooks", *Amazon*, [accessed 26th August, 2019], https://www.amazon.com/b?ie=UTF8&node=13270229011.

18 As can be seen, for example, in the decline of small, owner-managed bookstores that had to be closed due to competition from online retailers.

19 Well-known examples are recommendations like Spotify's "mix of the week" or Amazon's suggestions, which are based on patterns of user behaviour.

20 Cf. Andreas Platthaus, „Entdecke die Bücher, die Kunden lieben", *Frankfurter Allgemeine Zeitung*, last modified 17th August, 2019, https://www.faz.net/aktuell/feuilleton/buecher/amazons-buchhandlung-mit-1000-empfehlungen-ins-regal-16336766.html#lesermeinungen.

21 Cf. Ibid.

22 These are: Haruki Murakami's novel *The Wind-Up Bird Chronicle* and Marjane Satrapi's comic *Persepolis*. Cf. Platthaus, "Entdecke die Bücher, die Kunden lieben".

automatically,[23] because they can determine what is unique and special. If Google Books is an example, social media sites are another, even more concise one: under the guise of the creativity narrative in IT, which propagates uniqueness for the users of social media if only they act creative,[24] it is concealed that in reality it is about the greatest possible denominator, triggered by the desire for quantification, classification and comparability. A paradoxical situation evolves: out of the desire to be unique and special, only a minimal modification of what is already familiar arises, in order not to deviate too much from the creativity prescribed by IT and thus not to be successful in the sense of likes and followers. Attention is being sought.[25] Although this circumstance was criticised at a very early stage,[26] it continues to prevail. Attention is conformal, but presents itself differently, because the attribution of creativity conceals any conformity.

All this seems to happen under the aegis of the creativity narrative of IT, or more precisely: to become possible in the first place. The apparent voluntariness of the creative self-expression and the grateful acceptance of "curated" music lists, music videos, etc. happens at the price of surveillance and the provision of one's own data.[27]

This practice is also very efficient in working life, as Steffen Mau notes. In his critical analysis of technological surveillance in the working environment, Mau argues that thanks to the combination of data and technologies, a sophisticated control machinery has emerged, especially in the service sector of creative workers, which gains its effectiveness from not knowing whether you are being controlled or not.[28] Without calling it by its name, Mau describes

23 Reckwitz, *Die Gesellschaft der Singularitäten*, p. 73.

24 If YouTuber reach a certain number of subscribers on their channel, YouTube (or rather Google) will send them a plaque including a letter referring to the recipient's unique creativity, which is why other people are interested in their content.

25 Here in the sense of Bernhard Waldenfels' *Phenomenology of Attention*. Cf. Bernhard Waldenfels, *Phänomenologie der Aufmerksamkeit* (Frankfurt: Suhrkamp, 2004).

26 For example, an article in the Guardian in 2012 states: "the Instagram [...] filters are the antithesis of creativity. They make all pictures look the same. They require no thought or creative input: one click and you're done." Cf. Kate Bevan, "Instagram is debasing real photography", *The Guardian*, last modified 19th July, 2012, https://www.theguardian.com/technology/2012/jul/19/instagram-debasing-real-photography.

27 However, many people are generally aware of the latter and view it critically, cf. for example Facebook's data scandal in recent years.

28 Mau, *Das metrische Wir*, p. 244.

the concept of the panopticon, which can be of use for the argumentation of this chapter.

The concept of Panopticon, introduced by Michel Foucault features the very aspect of a prison capable of supervising inmates without them knowing if they are currently under surveillance or not, resulting in an inmate's behaviour that acts on the assumption of constant supervision.[29]

In discussing digitisation, Byung-Chul Han developed the notion of the *Digital Panopticon*.[30] According to Han the *Digital Panopticon* supersedes the Panopticon of disciplinary society, working even more efficiently. The digital in general as well as social media in particular evolves into *Digital Panopticons* that keep the social under surveillance. In its beginnings, the Internet has been praised for its boundless freedom. To Han, now it is a means to social control. What makes it so effective is its permissivity.[31] Unlike in the Panopticon of disciplinary society, the inmates of the Digital Panopticon expose themselves voluntarily.[32] In the desire for attention and recognition, the

29 Cf. Michel Foucault, *Überwachen und Strafen. Die Geburt des Gefängnisses* (Frankfurt am Main, Suhrkamp, 2015). For Foucault, Panopticism represents the generalised functional model of the ideal-typical prison of the disciplinary society - the Panopticon - designed by Jeremy Bentham. (cf. Ibid., p. 263). Its logic aims at the most effective control, organisation and governance possible of the individual's diversity (cf. Ibid., p. 264). Thus, it perfects the effects of disciplinary power (cf. Ibid., pp. 173-292), so that they can be extended to the whole of society (cf. Ibid, 268). The specific architecture of Bentham's Panopticons creates a special kind of observation that makes it irrelevant whether the individual is actually observed or merely feels observed. The Panopticon creates a permanent effect despite sporadic implementation (cf. Ibid., 258). Accordingly, the prisoner must never know whether he is under surveillance but must be sure that he can be monitored at all times (cf. Ibid., 259). The central effect of the Panopticon is thus the creation of the prisoner's awareness of being permanently visible (cf. Ibid., 258).

30 Byung-Chul Han, *Psychopolitik. Neoliberalismus und die neuen Machttechniken* (Frankfurt am Main: Fischer, 2016), p. 18.

31 Cf. Ibid., p. 26. Here, Han refers to Foucault again, who introduced the concept of permissiveness in his works on governmentality, as the permissiveness of disciplinary power is one of the central points of critique of studies of governmental on the concept of neoliberalism. Cf. only Michel Foucault, *The Birth of Biopolitics: Lectures at the Collège de France, 1978-1979 (Lectures at the College de France)* (New York: Picador, 2010).

32 Han's remarks cannot be adapted to this situation without criticism. Since Han's reference to Foucault operates in the context of poststructuralist subject-conceptions, his assumption of a voluntary self-exposure of individuals is, in my opinion, too shortsighted here. What remains unconsidered is how the disposition to this voluntary self-

Digital Panopticon does not create a sense of surveillance. On the contrary, it creates a sense of freedom.[33] Instead of being separated individually, the inmates are encouraged to communicate permanently through social media and, as a result, are revealing themselves.[34] *Smart power*[35] calls upon individuals to continuously communicate their needs, desires and opinions. They continually produce data about themselves. The voluntary nature of self-disclosure is what makes the Digital Panopticon so effective.[36] The consequence of this total networking and total communication[37] is a total compliance regarding the induced transparency. Han, in a thoroughly elevated and exaggerated way, considers psychopolitics as the end of free will[38]: through the mass generation of subject-related data, it is thus possible to influence the subject and its actions on a pre-reflexive level. Hence, it will be ultimately governable.[39] The beginning of this new type of control society was located in 1984 by Han: contrary to Apple's message, the year 1984 did not mark the end of the surveillance state. Instead, it was the beginning of a control society whose efficiency exceeded that of Orwell's surveillance state many times over.

In disciplinary power, the body was disciplined, yet now nobody sits in a panoptic cell anymore. One does not experience the observation physically,

---

exposure in the subject emerges. Since the subject is always both a product and a generator of itself within the framework of the process of subjectivation, Han's reflections on the self-exposure of the subject remain somewhat naïve. Cf. Norbert Ricken, „Zur Logik der Subjektivierung. Überlegungen an den Rändern eines Konzepts", in *Techniken der Subjektivierung*, eds. Andreas Gelhard, Thomas Alkemeyer and Norbert Ricken (München: Wilhelm Fink, 2013), pp. 29 - 48. However, it seems fruitful to look at Hans' approaches in a more differentiated way in order to take the paradoxality of subjectivation and the possibility of influencing the psyche on a pre-reflective level into account, which Han dreads in the context of the Digital Panopticon. See Judith Butler, *Psyche der Macht. Das Subjekt der Unterwerfung* (Frankfurt am Main: Suhrkamp, 2017), pp. 8-10.

33 Cf. Han, *Psychopolitik*, p. 55.

34 Cf. Ibid., p. 18.

35 Cf. Ibid., p. 27.

36 In fact, experience in the digital is different from experience in the analogue since it lacks embodiment. Han's emphasis on the freedom in the digital panopticon, which is not perceived as surveillance, should nevertheless be put into perspective as the potential surveillance situation has long since become a commonplace. Cf. Zuboff, *The Age of Surveillance Capitalism*.

37 Cf. Ibid., p. 20.

38 I intentionally only refer to Han here, as the concept of the free will is a rather failing term in the context of Foucault's works and the poststructuralist school of thought.

39 Cf. Ibid., p. 67.

therefore it comes along more subtly; it can be hidden more easily. *Thanks* to the creativity narrative of IT however, the (imperative) desire for performance and recognition is observation and discipline at the same time. The first happens in order to get one's own performance reflected at all; the latter happens in the form of the performance evaluation predetermined by the narrative.

In a Digital Panopticon, communication now completely coincides with control.[40] The control is held by those who not only provide the infrastructure – the Digital Panopticon itself, so to speak – but also, through the dominant narrative of creativity, call for participation in this new kind of posed and simulated uniqueness. The creativity narrative equally feeds on the total structures of individual IT companies as it constitutes them. It is deceptive to the extent that it carries these structures subtly and hypocritically.

7.2.2 CREATIVITY AS A TOOL FOR CLOAKING HYPOCRISY

As pointed out and criticised above, data has become the leading currency in the digital world, and the growing amount of data allows for multiple possibilities of comparability between individuals. Critique is manifold and vigorous (though mostly entrenched in specialised discourses): Shoshana Zuboff speaks of surveillance capitalism and Byung-Chul Han, drawing on Foucault, proposes the notion of the digital panopticon. The reason why I mentioned these examples is the complex role the creativity narrative of IT has to play in here. Due to the suggestive power of the narrative, a utopia of freedom and uniqueness (or singularity, to speak with Reckwitz's terminology) is promised, which in reality implies the near opposite by means of the creativity narrative's constitution: namely quantification, and thus predictability, comparability, uniformity and economic efficiency. This in turn has an impact on the analogue world, such as when Amazon opens a physical bookstore whose inventory and recommendations are curated almost exclusively by algorithms, which in turn are traceable to quantifiable online ratings on books.

With this, the critique of capitalist economy as well as the critique of creativity and of the creative dispositive go hand in hand with a critique of certain usages of technology. Albeit criticism of economy and the role of creativity

40 Cf. Ibid., pp. 56f.

within differs in its various school of thoughts, interpretations and conclusions (where Boltanski and Chiapello fear the appropriation of creativity (and other originally positively connotated concepts such as openness to others or novelty)[41] by capitalism, Lazzarato claims that creativity cannot and will never be appropriated by capitalism, for example), they all highlight the importance of creativity, with newer approaches including the entanglement of technology (Reckwitz) or even include the inherent IT logic (Zuboff) – albeit in the latter's case without a distinct reference to creativity.

As shown, the creativity narrative equally feeds on the overall structures of individual IT companies as it constitutes them. It is deceptive in that it subtly and hypocritically sustains these structures by both invoking and evoking the predominance of IT communities (the *inside*) that in turn is based on tales and stories about connecting creativity to concepts like freedom, genius, and the thriving for one's own capabilities. All this happens under the banner of creativity as understood by IT.

The study from 2001 mentioned in chapter 2.2, which deals with the question of creativity in Silicon Valley, still distinguishes between technological and artistic creativity. However, this distinction no longer seems to apply in IT terms. It is vital to not fall into the misconception that IT (i.e., its actors and productive participants) is occupied with art in a wider sense. Rather, a quite simplified, abbreviated and effective concept of art regarding its publicity is used and referred to. Recourse is mostly made to artists and works that are generally known and enjoy great public popularity. Here, too, the logic of simplistic quantification takes effect in its final consequence: what is known and popular is what most people would describe as such. Interestingly, however, IT does not seem to succeed in emancipating itself from art (i.e., the popular term). Although the technologies they produce are shaking up all our lives and redefining them in parts, it remains insufficient as to what they themselves are capable of.

Although this dichotomy lives on and technological development has taken on a dizzying pace in recent decades (culminating in the emergence of the digital world, as illustrated in chapter 4), it is still a knighthood for the grandees of IT to be seen as artistic, to emulate the great artistic geniuses and to be conventionalised as creative geniuses themselves.

Why is that at all? One answer may lie in the nature of IT's creativity narrative. The iterative and contingent ductus of venture capital, in which there

41 Cf. Boltanski and Chiapello, *The New Spirit of Capitalism*, p.97.

is talk of success especially when something is seen as creative, and in which one receives financial support for a promise, for what is to become one day, not for what already is or actually will be. The economically infused charge of IT's notion of creativity needs the story, the promise; and the story in turn needs creativity to elevate itself, to charge itself with ideals that justify this elevation and separate an inside from the outside. If nothing else, the creativity narrative of IT is a proven and efficient means of cloaking: a garment thrown over the true figure, disguising its real intentions in the process.

I am not primarily concerned with ascribing or accusing blame. As pointed out, critique of the economy is diverse and heterogeneous, although it seldom or never chooses the whole range of topics that I believe are necessary for a contemporary approach to critique. For this, it would be necessary to take the different considerations and schools of thought on economics, creativity, technology and IT itself into account. Nevertheless, the question remains: what is it all for? Was it not actually once about something completely different when the term creativity was mentioned? It is about an artistic creativity as a counter-design, which actually should no longer be called that because of the appropriation of the concept of creativity by the narrative of IT. Does not this other concept of creativity have to look for a different semantic shell in order, if not to escape the appropriation, then at least to negate it and escape IT's logic of the creativity narrative? These are open questions to which I cannot find an answer, but whose urgency has become emphatically apparent through the examination of the creativity narrative of IT. However, it would be short-sighted to grant the arts per se; similarly trivial as IT's approach to art. Therefore, it seems reasonable to at least approach this *other*; that particular approach to creativity that may seem to be in opposition to the creativity narrative in IT. This *artisticness* (in order to not call it artistic creativity) incorporates another way of being and thinking that reveals itself through uncertainty, sensitivity and revelation and in the end cannot count on recognition – also and precisely because it is not quantifiable but understands the incommensurability between its various shapes as a necessity.

Another way of thinking would be, in Dieter Mersch's words, thinking in the aesthetic.[42] The aesthetic goes beyond all concepts and genres in the mode

42 Cf. Dieter Mersch, *Epistemologien des Ästhetischen* (Zürich/Berlin: diaphanes, 2015), p. 53.

of experience. It is essentially procedural.[43] Its knowledge is revealed in execution. Unlike in propositional, discursive thinking, no dichotomies (of truth and falsehood) are produced in the aesthetic. Accordingly and in contrast to IT's understanding of creativity, the *real* is not yet subjected to any structuring of distinctions and symbols.[44] Instead, the knowledge practice of aesthetics is characterised by a fundamental openness.[45] It is permanently on the lookout, open to the unsuspected or the alteritarian and does not hope for progress in knowledge or an increase in objectivity and the stabilisation of models.[46] It conducts experiments whose outcome remains uncertain.[47] The particular, like the processual, is essential for art and aesthetic practice.[48] After all, aesthetic epistemes reveal what fails to work, and what remains incommensurable, resisting the usual classification.[49] In art, contrary to propositional thinking, there are no paradigms that can be standardised and generalised.[50] Each work of art creates its own *singular paradigm*.[51] Such a paradigm eludes comparison.[52] It is the refusal of any commensurability that distinguishes art from the creativity narrative in IT. As shown, IT is not interested in singular paradigms. Because these paradigms cannot be generalised, they cannot be quantified and thus cannot be marketed, valued (again in a quantifiable way), classified or scaled. IT measures creativity quantitatively: creative is what achieves economic success. IT needs and wants to be understood. Despite or precisely because of its apparently revolutionary innovations, its narrative of creativity ultimately remains trapped in the still somewhat familiar.

A way out requires actual alterity, i.e., a partial intercultural otherness, which is, however, the opposite of the totalitarian dichotomy of inside and outside propagated by IT, made possible and legitimised by creativity acting as intermediary and cloaking device.

Through its exclusive adherence to this concept, IT refuses to accept the process openness and undirectedness of the (aesthetic) research process. Mer-

43 Cf. Ibid., pp. 128-133.
44 Cf. Ibid., pp. 52f.
45 Cf. Ibid., p. 67.
46 Cf. Ibid., p. 61.
47 Cf. Ibid., p. 147.
48 Cf. Dieter Mersch, *Nichtpropositionalität und ästhetisches Denken* (2013) p. 2.
49 Cf. Ibid., pp. 9ff.
50 Cf. Mersch, *Epistemologien des Ästhetischen* p. 164.
51 Cf. Ibid., p. 116; 157.
52 Cf. Ibid., p. 158.

sch provides a new perspective on the new saying that the new that can be understood cannot be entirely new, just as, conversely, the completely new could not even be recognised and described as new without referring it to something familiar. Creativity, from this point of view, seems to be useless for IT; or better: immune from IT – especially in the light of emerging concepts like artificial creativity. Only with the further development of learning systems could it be possible to autonomously create such an indifferent creativity, which as such will never be understood by anyone. But those singular paradigms that the other way of thinking in the aesthetic practice of knowledge creates remain hidden from IT, which is bound up in the logic of the propositional and distinguishable. Thus, a decisive part of the new (the *really new*) eludes it. For its concept of creativity can only grasp what becomes linguistically tangible and, accordingly, describable and constructible on the basis of existing categories. In contrast, the epistemes of art elude the logic of discursivity.[53] Art is capable of undermining discourses. It opens up that other way of thinking transcending all oppositions between determination and indeterminacy.[54]

This neither-nor, this in-between, thus the *interspace*[55] between differentiated poles that are determination and indeterminacy is not easy to endure. But it is a way out in order to negate the superficial purpose of IT's understanding of creativity as a cloaking device. One must be able and willing to not only endure the unsteady and fragile that is the *indifferent* or *other way of thinking*, but deliberately embrace it. Only in this way, however, is it possible to create a counter-design to the uniform, quantified and rampant logic of the creativity narrative of IT.

On the other hand, it may probably help to wait and see – as no dominance lasts forever: Even Salomon Friedlaender in the early 1920s already complained about a *monstrous overevaluation of the differentiated*.[56] And returning to the very beginning of this dissertation, in 2001 the Hudson River began

53 Cf. Ibid., pp. 139f.

54 Cf. Mersch, *Nichtpropositionalität und ästhetisches Denken*, pp. 6f.

55 According to Salomon Friedlaender, this space is called *indifference*. At first it seems that indifference is nothing but the plain background from which the interesting (perceptible, because distinguishable) figure stands out. Friedlaender saw it differently. For only in the middle between the poles one has the possibility to turn to the whole beyond the differences. That is why indifference is not boring, but *creative*. Cf. Salomon Friedlaender, *Schöpferische Indifferenz* (München: Ernst Reinhardt Verlag, 1926).

56 Cf. Ibid., p. 4.

to slowly recover from the mussel invasion and native species returned in large numbers. Although far away from a complete recovering, diversity seems to have been restored.[57]

57 Rebecca Kessler, „Musseled-Out Native Species Return to the Hudson", *Sciencemag*, last modified 21st January, 2011, https://www.sciencemag.org/news/2011/01/musseled-out-native-species-return-hudson.

BIBLIOGRAPHY

Adams, Tony E., Stacy Holman Jones and Carolyn Ellis. *Autoethnography: Understanding Qualitative Research.* New York: Oxford University Press, 2015.

Adams, W. H. Davenport, "Imitators and Plagiarists (Part 2 of 2)," The Gentleman's Magazine 272, June (1892).

Amabile, Teresa M. and Beth A. Hennessey. "Creativity." *Annual Review of Psychology* 61, January (2010): 569-598. https://ssrn.com/abstract=1601146.

Amabile, Teresa M. and Julianna Pillemer. "Perspectives on the social psychology of creativity." *The Journal of Creative Behavior* 46.1 (2012): 3.

Anderson, John J. "Dave tells Ahl – the history of Creative Computing." *Creative Computing* 10, no.11(1984):66. https://www.atarimagazines.com/creative/v10n11/66_Dave_tells_Ahl__the_hist.php.

Anderson, Neil, Kristina Potočnik and Jing Zhou. "Innovation and Creativity in Organizations: A State-of-the-Science Review, Prospective Commentary, and Guiding Framework." *Journal of Management* 40, no. 5 (2014): 1297–1333. doi:10.1177/0149206314527128.

Baecker, Dirk. *4.0 oder die Lücke die der Rechner lässt.* Leipzig: Merve, 2018.

Baraldi, Claudio. „Doppelte Kontingenz." In *GLU. Glossar zu Niklas Luhmanns Theorie sozialer Systeme.* Frankfurt am Main: Suhrkamp, 2015.

Bauman, Zygmunt. *Liquid Life.* Cambridge: Polity, 2005.

Besant, Hanisha. "The Journey of Brainstorming Regent University School of Business & Leadership." *Journal of Transformational Innovation* 2, no. 1 (2016).

Blumenberg, Hans. *Wirklichkeiten in denen wir leben: Lebenswelt und Technisierung.* Stuttgart: Reclam, 1981.

Bochner, Arthur and Carolyn Ellis. *Evocative Autoethnography: Writing Lives and Telling Stories.* New York: Routledge, 2016.

Boden, Margaret A. „Creativity and artificial intelligence. "*Artificial Intelligence* 103, no. 1 and 2 (1998): 347-356. doi: 10.1016/S0004-3702(98)00055-1.

Boden, Margaret A. *The Creative Mind: Myths and Mechanisms.* London: Routledge, 2004.

Boltanski, Luc and Ève Chiapello. *The New Spirit of Capitalism.* London / New York: Verso, 2007.

Brand, Stewart. *Whole Earth Catalog.* Menlo Park: Portola Institute, 1968.

Bush, Vannevar. "Science: The Endless Frontier." *Transactions of the Kansas Academy of Science (1903-)* 48, no. 3 (1945): 231-264, doi: 10.2307/3625196.

Butler, Judith. *Psyche der Macht. Das Subjekt der Unterwerfung.* Frankfurt am Main: Suhrkamp, 2017.

Cardoso, Amílcar, Tony Veale and Geraint A. Wiggins. "Converging on the Divergent: The History (and Future) of the International Joint Workshops in Computational Creativity." *AI Magazine*, Fall 2009, 15-22.

Castells, Manuel. *Das Informationszeitalter. Band 1: Der Aufstieg der Netzwerkgesellschaft,* Leverkusen: Leske und Budrich Verlag, 2004.

Catmull, Edwin. *Creativity, Inc.: Overcoming the Unseen Forces That Stand in the Way of True Inspiration.* New York: Random House, 2014.

Cheyfitz, Kirk. *Thinking Inside the Box: The 12 Timeless Rules for Managing a Successful Business.* New York: Simon and Schuster, 2003.

Chomsky, Noam. "On the Nature, Use and Acquisition of Language." In *Mind and Cognition*, edited by William G. Lycan. Cambridge, Mass.: Basil Blackwell, 1990.

Clarke, Arthur C. *The Lost Worlds of 2001.* Kolkata: Signet, 1971.

Cohen, Harold. "The Further Exploits of AARON, Painter." *Stanford Humanities Review* 4, no. 2 (1995): 141-158.

Colton, Simon and Geraint A. Wiggins.– "Computational creativity: The final frontier?" In *Frontiers in Artificial Intelligence and Applications* 242, January (2012): 21-26. doi: 10.3233/978-1-61499-098-7-21.

Colvin, Geoff. *Humans are Underrated. What High Achievers Know That Brilliant Machines Never Will.* New York: Penguin, 2015.

Crutchfield, R.S. "Conformity and creative thinking." In *The Atherton Press behavioral science series. Contemporary approaches to creative thinking: A symposium held at the University of Colorado, edited by* H. E. Gruber, G. Terrell, & M. Wertheimer, 120-140. New York: Atherton Press, 1962.

Eco, Umberto. *Einführung in die Semiotik.* München: Wilhelm Fink Verlag, 2002.

Edelmann, Thomas. „Kreativität ist nur ein Wort – Wie Design zum Vorbild wurde." In *Kreativität in Gestaltungsprozessen,* edited by M. Jarchow, 21-40. Neumünster: Wachholtz, 2011.

Eliot, T. S. *The Sacred Wood: Essays on Poetry and Criticism*. London: Methuen & Company Ltd., 1920.

Ellingson, Laura L. and Carolyn Ellis. "Autoethnography as constructionist project." In *Handbook of Constructionist Research*, edited by J.A. Holstein and J.F. Gubrium, 445-466. New York: Guilford Press, 2008.

Ellis, Carolyn. *The ethnographic I: A methodological novel about autoethnography*. Walnut Creek: AltaMira Press, 2004.

Feigenbaum, Edward and Pamela McCorduck. "The fifth generation: Japan's computer challenge to the world." *Creative Computing* 10, no. 8 (1984): 103. http://www.atarimagazines.com/creative/v10n8/103_The_fifth_generation_Jap.php.

Ferrey, Michel, "Silicon Valley: a cluster of venture capitalists?" Paris Innovation Review. Last modified September 21, 2017. http://parisinnovationreview.com/articles-en/silicon-valley-a-cluster-of-venture-capitalists.

Fisher, Adam. *Valley of Genius: The Uncensored History of Silicon Valley (As Told by the Hackers, Founders, and Freaks Who Made It Boom)*. New York: Twelve, 2018.

Florida, Richard. *Cities and the Creative Class*. New York: Routledge, 2005.

Florida, Richard. *The Rise of the Creative Class, Revisited*. New York: Basic Books, 2012.

Michel Foucault, Michel. *The Birth of Biopolitics: Lectures at the Collège de France, 1978–1979 (Lectures at the College de France)*. New York: Picador, 2010.

Foucault, Michel. *Überwachen und Strafen. Die Geburt des Gefängnisses*. Frankfurt am Main, Suhrkamp, 2015.

Freud, Sigmund. "Eine Schwierigkeit der Psychoanalyse." *Imago. Zeitschrift für Anwendung der Psychoanalyse auf die Geisteswissenschaften*. Bd. V (1917), 1–7.

Frey, Carl Benedikt and Michael A. Osborne. "The future of employment: How susceptible are jobs to computerisation?" *Technological Forecasting and Social Change* 114, January (2017): 254-280. doi: https://doi.org/10.1016/j.techfore.2016.08.019.

Freiberger, Paul and Swaine, Michael. *Fire in the Valley. The Birth and Death of the Personal Computer*. Dallas: The Pragmatic Programmers, LLC, 2012.

Friedlaender, Salomon. *Schöpferische Indifferenz*. München: Ernst Reinhardt Verlag, 1926.

Friedman, Milton. *Capitalism and Freedom*. Chicago: University of Chicago Press, 2002.

Gallie, Walter B. "Art as an essentially contested concept." *Philosophical Quarterly* 6, no. 23 (1956): 97-114. doi: https://doi.org/10.2307/2217217.

Ganahl, Simon. „Ist Foucaults ‚dispositif‘ ein Akteur-Netzwerk.“ *Forschungsstelle für Sozial-und Wirtschaftsgeschichte* (Ed.): *foucaultblog. Universität Zürich* 1 (2013). *doi: https://doi. org/10.13095/uzh. fsw. fb*, 9.

Gardt, Andreas. „Diskursanalyse–Aktueller theoretischer Ort und methodische Möglichkeiten.“ In *Diskurslinguistik nach Foucault. Theorie und Gegenstände*, edited by Ingo H. Warnke, pp. 23-48. Berlin/New York: de Gruyter, 2007.

Gillmor, C. Stewart. *Fred Terman at Stanford. Building a Discipline, a University, and Silicon Valley*. Stanford: Stanford University Press, 2004.

Goertzel, Ben and Cassio Pennachin, eds., *Artificial General Intelligence*. Berlin/Heidelberg: Springer, 2007.

Goffman, Erving. *On the Characteristics of Total Institutions*. New York: Holt, Rinehart and Winston, 1961.

Goldschmidt, Walter. "Anthropology and the Coming Crisis: An Autoethnographic Appraisal." *Anthropologist* 79, no. 2 (1977): 293-08. doi: https://doi.org/10.1525/aa.1977.79.2.02a00060.

Gompers, Paul A. "Optimal Investment, Monitoring, and the Staging of Venture Capital." *The Journal of Finance*, no. 50 (1995): 1461-1489, doi:10.1111/j.15406261.1995.tb05185.x.

Gompers, Paul and Josh Lerner. "The Venture Capital Revolution." *Journal of Economic Perspectives* 15, no. 2 (2001): 145-168. doi: 10.1257/jep.15.2.145.

Groys, Boris. *Über das Neue*. Frankfurt am Main: Fischer, 2002.

Guilford, Joy P. "Creativity," *American Psychologist* 5, no. 9 (1950): 444–454, doi: 10.1037/h0063487.

Gumbrecht, Hans Ulrich. "Das Denken muss nun auch den Daten folgen." *Frankfurter Allgemeine Zeitung*. Last modified March 12, 2014. http://www.faz.net/aktuell/feuilleton/geisteswissenschaften/neue-serie-das-digitale-denken-das-denken-muss-nun-auch-den-daten-folgen12840532.html?printPagedArticle=true.

Hall, Sir Peter. *Cities in Civilization*. New York: Pantheon Books, 1998.

Han, Byung-Chul. *Psychopolitik. Neoliberalismus und die neuen Machttechniken*. Frankfurt am Main: Fischer, 2016.

Hawkins, Jeff and Sandra Blakeslee. *On Intelligence*. New York: Times Books, 2004.

Heidegger, Martin ed., *Edmund Husserls Vorlesungen zur Phänomenologie des inneren Zeitbewußtseins*. Halle: Max Niemeyer Verlag, 1928.

Hiltzik, Michael. *Dealers of Lightning: Xerox PARC and the Dawn of the Computer Age*. New York: HarperCollins Publishers Inc., 1999.

Hoy, Matthew B. "Alexa, Siri, Cortana, and More: An Introduction to Voice Assistants." *Medical Reference Services Quarterly* 37, no. 1 (2018): 81-88. doi: 10.1080/02763869.2018.1404391.

Isaacson, Walter. *Steve Jobs* (London: Abacus, 2015) p. 212.

Jansen, Stefan A. "Magnetismus der Metropole als Stätte der Kreativen. Ein Überblick bildungs-, migrations-, politikökonomischer Analysen zur Dynamisierung von Metropolen." In: *Rationalität der Kreativität?*, edited by Stefan A Jansen, et al. Wiesbaden: VS Verlag für Sozialwissenschaften, 2009, p. 67-92.

Joas, H ans. *The Creativity of Action*. Chicago: University of Chicago Press, 1996.

Jordanous, Anna. "A Standardised Procedure for Evaluating Creative Systems: Computational Creativity Evaluation Based on What it is to be Creative." *Cognitive Computation* 4, no. 3 (2012): 246-279. doi: https://doi.org/10.1007/s12559-012-9156-1.

Jung, Rex E., Brittany S. Mead, Jessica Carrasco and Ranee Barrow. "The structure of creative cognition in the human brain." *Frontiers in Human Neuroscience* 7: July (2013): 330. doi: 10.3389/fnhum.2013.00330.

Haraway, Donna. "Situated Knowledges: The Science Question in Feminism and the Privilege of Partial Perspective." *Feminist Studies* 14, no. 3 (1988): 575-599.

Hayano, David M. "Auto-Ethnography: Paradigms, Problems, and Prospects." *Human Organization* 38, no. 1 (1979): 99-104. doi: https://doi.org/10.17730/humo.38.1.u761n5601t4g318v.

Holt, Knut. "Brainstorming – From Classics to Electronics." *Journal of Engineering Design* 7, no. 1 (1996): 77-82. doi: 10.1080/09544829608907928.

Hutchinson, Eliot Dole. "Materials for the study of creative thinking." Psychological Bulletin 28, no. 5 (1931): 392–410. doi: 101037/h0070088

Kaiser, David. *How the Hippies Saved Physics: Science, Counterculture, and the Quantum Revival.* New York: W.W. Norton & Company, 2011.

Kerchner, Brigitte and Silke Schneider. „,Endlich Ordnung in der Werkzeugkiste'. Zum Potenzial der Foucaultschen Diskursanalyse für die Politikwissenschaft – Einleitung." In *Foucault: Diskursanalyse der Politik*, edited by Brigitte Kerchner and Silke Schneider, 9-30. Wiesbaden: VS Verlag für Sozialwissenschaften, 2006.

Krämer, Hannes, „Praktiken kreativen Arbeitens in den Creative Industries." In: *Kreativität und Improvisation,* edited by Udo Göttlich and Ronald Kurt. Wiesbaden: Springer VS, 2012, p. 109-132.

Kotter, John. *Leading Change*. Boston: Harvard Business School Press, 1996.

Landry, Charles. *The creative city: A toolkit for urban innovaters*. London: Earthscan, 2012.

Lanier, Jaron. "Whoever owns our data will be our fate." *Frankfurter Allgemeine Zeitung*, April 24, 2014. https://www.faz.net/aktuell/feuilleton/debatten/the-digital-debate/almighty-google-whoever-owns-our-data-will-determine-our-fate-12908348p2.html.

Latour, Bruno. "Reassembling the social. An introduction to actor-network-theory." *Journal of Economic Sociology* 14, no. 2 (2013): 73-87.

Leslie, Stuart W. "The Biggest 'Angel' of Them All: The Military and the Making of Silicon Valley." In *Understanding Silicon Valley: The Anatomy of an Entrepreneurial Region*, edited by Martin Kenney, 48-67. Stanford: Stanford University Press, 2000.

Levy, Steven. *Hackers*. Sebastopol: O'Reilly, 2010.

Link, Jürgen. „Noch einmal: Diskurs. Interdiskurs. Macht." *kultuRRevolution. Zeitschrift für angewandte Diskurstheorie*, no. 11 (1986): 4-7.

Lorey, Isabell. „Vom immanenten Widerspruch zur hegemonialen Funktion. Biopolitische Gouvernementalität und Selbst-Prekarisierung von KulturproduzentInnen." In *Kritik der Kreativität*, edited by Gerald Raunig and Ulf Wuggenig, 121-136. Wien: Verlag Turia + Kant, 2007.

Loh, Janina. *Trans- und Posthumanismus zur Einführung*. Hamburg: Junius, 2018.

Loh, Janina. *Roboterethik*. Berlin: Suhrkamp, 2019.

Löw, Martina. *Raumsoziologie* (Frankfurt am Main: Suhrkamp, 2000)

Luhmann, Niklas. *Soziale Systeme. Grundriß einer allgemeinen Theorie*. Frankfurt am Main: Suhrkamp, 1987.

Mau, Steffen. *Das metrische Wir. Über die Quantifizierung des Sozialen*. Berlin: Suhrkamp, 2017.

McCorduck, Pamela. *Machines Who Think. A Personal Inquiry into the History and Prospects of Artificial Intelligence.* Natick: A K Peters, 2004.

Misselhorn, Catrin. *Grundfragen der Maschinenethik*. Ditzingen: Reclam, 2019.

Mersch, Dieter. *Nichtpropositionalität und ästhetisches Denken*. 2013.

Mersch, Dieter. *Epistemologien des Ästhetischen*. Zürich/Berlin: Diaphanes, 2015.

Miller, Timothy S. The Hippies and American Values (Knoxville: University of Tennessee Press, 2011).

Minsky, Marvin L. *Computation: Finite and Infinite Machines.* Englewood Cliffs: Prentice-Hall, 1967.

Negri, Antonio. *Marx and Foucault. Essays Volume 1*. Cambridge: Polity Press, 2017.

Oelze, Berthold. „Ideen zu einer phänomenologischen Soziologie der Kreativität." In: *Rationalität der Kreativität?*, edited by Stefan A Jansen, et al. Wiesbaden: VS Verlag für Sozialwissenschaften, 2009, p. 79-98. doi: https://doi.org/10.1007/978-3-531-18989-5_5

Omohundro, Steve. "Autonomous technology and the greater human good." *Journal of Experimental & Theoretical Artificial Intelligence* 26, no. 3 (2014): 303-315. doi: 10.1080/0952813X.2014.895111.

Parjanen, Satu. "Experiencing Creativity in the Organization: From Individual Creativity to Collective Creativity." *Interdisciplinary Journal of Information, Knowledge, and Management* 7 (2012).

Perry, Paul. *On the bus: the complete guide to the legendary trip of Ken Kesey and the Merry Pranksters and the birth of the counterculture.* New York: Thunder's Mouth Press, 1990.

Preston, John and Mark Bishop, *Views into the Chinese Room: New Essays on Searle and Artificial Intelligence.* Oxford: Clarendon Press, 2002.

Raunig, Gerald. „Kreativindustrie als Massenbetrug." In *Kritik der Kreativität*, edited by Gerald Raunig and Ulf Wuggenig, 67-78. Wien: Turia + Kant, 2007.

Reckwitz, Andreas. *Die Erfindung der Kreativität*. Frankfurt am Main: Suhrkamp, 2012.

Reckwitz, Andreas. *Die Gesellschaft der Singularitäten*. Berlin: Suhrkamp, 2017.

Ricken, Norbert. „Zur Logik der Subjektivierung. Überlegungen an den Rändern eines Konzepts", in *Techniken der Subjektivierung*, edited by Andreas Gelhard, Thomas Alkemeyer and Norbert Ricken, 29-48. München: Wilhelm Fink, 2013.

Ritter, Joachim. *Historisches Wörterbuch der Philosophie.* Basel: Schwabe & Co. AG, 1995.

Rossiter, John R. and Gary L. Lilien. "New 'Brainstorming' Principles." *Australian Journal of Management* 19, no. 1 (1994): 61–72. doi:10.1177/031289629401900104.

Salvucci, Dario D. and Niels A. Taatgen. *The Multitasking Mind.* New York: Oxford University Press, 2010.

Saussure, Ferdinand de. *Course in General Linguistics*. London: Peter Owen, 1974.

Searle, John R. "Minds, brains, and programs." *Behavioral and Brain Sciences* 3, no. 3 (1980): 417-45.

Jochen Schmidt, Jochen. *Die Geschichte des Genie-Gedankens in der deutschen Literatur, Philosophie und Politik 1750-1945*. Darmstadt: Wissenschaftliche Buchgesellschaft, 1985.

Smith, Richard Candida. *Utopia and dissent: art, poetry and politics in California*. Berkeley: University of California Press, 1995.

Strayer, David L., Nuria Cid and Heather M. Malcom. "Long-term changes in a population of an invasive bivalve and its effects." *Oecologia* 165, no. 4 (2011): 1063-1072. doi: https://doi.org/10.1007/s00442-010-1792-0.

Sturgeon, Timothy J. "How Silicon Valley Came to Be." In *Understanding Silicon Valley: The Anatomy of an Entrepreneurial Region*, edited by Martin Kenney, 15-47. Stanford: Stanford University Press, 2000.

Swaine, Michael and Paul Freiberger. *Fire in the Valley. The Birth and Death of the Personal Computer.* Dallas/Raleigh: The Pragmatic Bookshelf, 2014.

Touraine, Alain. *Die postindustrielle Gesellschaft*. Frankfurt am Main: Suhrkamp, 1969.

Turkle, Sherry. *The Second Self: Computers and the Human Spirit.* Cambridge: MIT Press, 2004.

Turner, Fred. "Where the Counterculture Met the New Economy: The WELL and the Origins of Virtual Community." *Technology and Culture* 46, no.3 (2005): 488, [accessed August 22, 2019]. https://muse.jhu.edu/.

Turner, Fred. *From Counterculture to Cyberculture: Stewart Brand, the Whole Earth Network, and the Rise of Digital Utopianism*. Chicago: The University of Chicago Press, 2006.

van den Berg, Karen. "Kreativität. Drei Absagen der Kunst an ihren erweiterten Begriff." In *Rationalität der Kreativität? Multidisziplinäre Beiträge zur Analyse der Produktion, Organisation und Bildung von Kreativität*, edited by Stephan A. Jansen, Eckhard Schröter and Nico Stehr, 207-224. Wiesbaden: VS Verlag, 2009.

Veale, Tony, F. Amílcar Cardoso and Rafael Pérez y Pérez. "Systematizing Creativity: A Computational View." In *Computational Creativity. Computational Synthesis and Creative Systems,*" edited by Tony Veale and F. Amílcar Cardoso, 1-19. Cham: Springer, 2019, doi: https://doi.org/10.1007/978-3-319-43610-4_1.

von Osten, Marion. „Unberechenbare Ausgänge." In *Kritik der Kreativität*, edited by Gerald Raunig and Ulf Wuggenig, 103-120. Wien: Turia + Kant, 2007.

Waldenfels, Bernhard. *Phänomenologie der Aufmerksamkeit.* Frankfurt: Suhrkamp, 2004.

Waldschmidt, Anne, Anne Klein, Miguel Korte and Sibel Dalman-Eken. "Discourse in Everyday Life – The Everyday Life of Discourse: Towards an Empirical Grounded Methodology of Discourse Research in Social Sciences." *Forum Qualitative Research* 8, no. 2 (2007).

Wiener, Anna. "The Complicated Legacy of Stewart Brand's 'Whole Earth Catalog,". The New Yorker. Last modified November 16, 2018, https://www.newyorker.com/news/letter-from-silicon-valley/the-complicated-legacy-of-stewart-brands-whole-earth-catalog.

Wolfe, Alexandra. *Valley of the Gods*. New York: Simon & Schuster, 2017.

Zuboff, Shoshana. "The human factor." *Frankfurter Allgemeine Zeitung*, July 18, 2014. https://www.faz.net/aktuell/feuilleton/debatten/the-digital-debate/digital-economy-the-human-factor-13050472.html.

Zuboff, Shoshana. *The age of surveillance capitalism: the fight for a human future at the new frontier of power.* New York: PublicAffairs, 2018.

Online Sources

Adobe. „Adobe Studie: Kreative Problemlösungskompetenz ist Wegbereiter der Zukunft, doch überholten Lehrplänen fehlt dafür die Fantasie." *Adobe Newsroom*. Last modified February 19, 2018. http://www.adobe-newsroom.de/2018/02/19/adobestudie-kreative-problemloesungskompetenz-ist-wegbereiter-der-zukunft-doch-ueberholten-lehrplaenen-fehlt-dafuer-die-fantasie/.

Amazon. "amazonbooks." *Amazon*. [Accessed August 26, 2019]. https://www.amazon.com/b?ie=UTF8&node=13270229011.

Association for Computational Creativity. [Accessed January 14, 2019]. http://computationalcreativity.net/home/.

Bevan, Kate. "Instagram is debasing real photography." *The Guardian*. Last modified July 19, 2012. https://www.theguardian.com/technology/2012/jul/19/instagram-debasingreal-photography.

Biermann, Kai. „Zweifel als Motor des Fortschritts." *Zeit Online*, April 14, 2010. https://www.zeit.de/digital/internet/2010-04/republica-2010-berlin.

Bloomberg. "Venture Capital: Sand Hill Road Rules the Valley." *Bloomberg*. Last modified December 4, 2014. https://www.bloomberg.com/news/articles/2014-12-04/venture-capital-sand-hill-road-rules-silicon-valley.

Bowling, Matt. "Stanford Research Park: The Engine of Silicon Valley." *The Palo Alto History Project*. [Accessed on March 19, 2019], https://web.archive.org/web/20100116012546/http://www.paloaltohistory.com/stanfordresearchpark.html.

Brand, Stewart. "Spacewar: Fanatic Life and Symbolic Death Among the Computer Bums." *Spacewar*. [accessed June 22, 2019], http://www.wheels.org/spacewar/stone/rolling_stone.html.

Bush, Vannevar. "As We May Think," *The Atlantic*. [Accessed April 26, 2019]. https://www.theatlantic.com/magazine/archive/1945/07/as-we-may-think/303881/.

Business Roundtable. "*Statement on the Purpose of a Corporation*." Last modified, August 2019. https://opportunity.businessroundtable.org/wp-content/uploads/2019/08/Business-Roundtable-Statement-on-the-Purpose-of-a-Corporation-with-Signatures.pdf.

Cannistraro, Alan. "Generating Ideas at Apple." *Medium*. Last modified January 15, 2016. https://medium.com/self-starter/generating-ideas-at-apple-71e575a1e2e3.

Casper, Gerhard. „Die Luft der Freiheit – On and Off." Stanford University Office of the President. [Accessed on May 1, 2019]. https://web.stanford.edu/dept/pres-provost/president/speeches/951005dieluft.html

Cifarelli, Luisa. "The EPS Historic Site." *EPS*. [Accessed August 8, 2019]. http://epn.eps.org/historic-sites-booklet#p=37.

Cohen, Judy Radler. "A Brief History of Venture Capital." *Financial Poise*. Last modified November 21, 2018. https://www.financialpoise.com/a-brief-history-of-venture-capital/.

Copeland, Jack. "What is Artificial Intelligence?" *AlanTuring.net*. Last modified May 2000.

http://www.alanturing.net/turing_archive/pages/reference%20articles/what_is_AI/What%20is%20AI11.html.

Daub, Adrian. "The undertakers of Silicon Valley: how failure became big business." *The Guardian*. Last modified August 21, 2018. https://www.theguardian.com/technology/2018/aug/21/the-undertakers-of-silicon-valley-how-failure-became-big-business.

DeMet, George. "The Search for Meaning in 2001." The 2001 Archive. [Accessed June 22, 2019]. https://2001archive.org/resources/the-search-for-meaning-in-2001/.

Dowd, Maureen. "Confirm or Deny: Jaron Lanier." *The New York Times*. Last modified November 8, 2017. https://www.nytimes.com/2017/11/08/style/confirm-or-deny-jaron-lanier.html.

Duhart, Olympia. "Why More Hospitals Should Prioritize Cultural Competency." *Harvard Business Review*. Last modified May 26, 2017. https://hbr.org/2017/05/why-more-hospitals-should-prioritize-cultural-competency#.

Efrati, Amir. "Google Beat Facebook for DeepMind, Creates Ethics Board." *The Information*. Last modified January 26, 2014. https://www.theinformation.com/articles/Google-beat-Facebook-For-DeepMind-Creates-Ethics-Board.

Enacademic. "Habitat." *Enacademic*. [Accessed April 7, 2019]. https://enacademic.com/dic.nsf/enwiki/776335#cite_note-4.

Ende, Michael. In Werner Onken, «Die ökonomische Botschaft von Michael Endes 'Momo'. Mit einem Brief von Michael Ende an Werner Onken vom 3. September 1986.» *Sozialökonomie.info*. [Access April 9, 2019], https://www.sozialoekonomie.info/Weiterf%C3%BChrendes/weiterfuehrendes-3-werner-onken-die-oekonomische-botschaft-von-michael-endes-momo.html.

Engelbart, Douglas C. "Augmenting Human Intellect: A Conceptual Framework," *Doug Engelbart Institute*. [accessed April 22, 2019]„ http://dougengelbart.org/content/view/138.

Failory. "The Ultimate Startup Failure RatevReport." *Failory*. Last modified 2019. https://www.failory.com/blog/startup-failure-rate.

Farber, Dan. "What Steve Jobs really meant when he said 'Good artists copy; great artists steal'." *cnet*. Last modified January 28, 2014. https://www.cnet.com/news/what-steve-jobs-really-meant-when-he-said-good-artists-copy-great-artists-steal/.

Fast Company, http://www.fastcompany-digital.com/fastcompany/201404?pg=1#pg1.

Fisher, Adam. *Valley of Genius*. [Accessed April 20, 2019]. https://www.valleyofgenius.com/secondary-sources.

Fisher, Lawrence M. "Company News; Xerox Sues Apple Computer over Macintosh Copyright." *The New York Times*. 1989, https://www.nytimes.com/1989/12/15/business/company-news-xerox-sues-apple-computer-over-macintosh-copyright.html?scp=3&sq=apple+xerox&st=nyt.

Gates, Bill. "Unleashing the Power of Creativity." *National Public Radio*. Last modified September 19, 2005. http://www.npr.org/templates/story/story.php?storyId=4853839.

Gee, Alastair. "More than one-third of schoolchildren are homeless in shadow of Silicon Valley." *The Guardian*. [Accessed May 28, 2019]. https://www.theguardian.com/society/2016/dec/28/silicon-valley-homeless-east-palo-alto-california-schools.

Goertzel, Ben. "AI Can Help Create a Better World – If We Build it Right." *SingularityHub*. Last modified August 13, 2018. https://singularityhub.com/2018/08/13/ai-can-help-create-a-better-world-if-we-build-it-right./.

Google Scholar. "Creativity 1940-1950." [Accessed April 4,2019]. https://scholar.google.de/scholar?q=creativity&hl=de&as_sdt=0%2C5&as_ylo=1940&as_yhi=1950.

Google Scholar. "Creativity 1950-1960." [Accessed April 4, 2019]. https://scholar.google.de/scholar?q=creativity&hl=de&as_sdt=0%2C5&as_ylo=1950&as_yhi=1960.

Google Scholar. "Creativity 1960-1970." [Accessed April 4, 2019]. https://scholar.google.de/scholar?q=creativity&hl=de&as_sdt=0%2C5&as_ylo=1960&as_yhi=1970.

Google Scholar. "Creativity 1970-1980." [Accessed April 4, 2019]. https://scholar.google.de/scholar?q=creativity&hl=de&as_sdt=0%2C5&as_ylo=1970&as_yhi=1980.

Google. "Artificial Intelligence at Google: Our Principles," *Google AI*, [accessed April 9, 2019], https://ai.google/principles.

Google careers. "5 surprises about Google Zurich." *Google careers.* [Accessed August 24, 2019]. https://careers.google.com/stories/5-surprises-about-google-zurich/.

Gordy, Sam. "IBM & NASA: Working Side-by-Side to Land on the Moon." *IBM*. Last modified July 19, 2019. https://www.ibm.com/blogs/think/2019/07/ibm-nasa-working-side-by-side-to-land-on-the-moon/.

Greenspan, Alan. "The Challenge of Central Banking in a Democratic Society." *The Federal Reserve Board*. Last modified December 6, 1996. https://www.federalreserve.gov/boarddocs/speeches/1996/19961205.htm.

Guilford, Joy P. "Creativity." *American Psychologist* 5, no. 9 (1950): 444–454. doi: 10.1037/h0063487.

Gusenbauer, Michael. "Google Scholar to overshadow them all? Comparing the sizes of 12 academic search engines and bibliographic databases." *Scientometrics* 118, no. 1 (2019): 177-214, doi: https://doi.org/10.1007/s11192-018-2958-5.

Hafiz, Asma. "12 Awesome Yet Affordable Coworking Spaces in Palo Alto (2019)." Coworking Mag. [Accessed August 8, 2019]. https://coworkingmag.com/unitedstates/coworking-space-palo-alto/.

HanaHaus. "Workspace Palo Alto." HanaHaus. [Accessed August 9, 2019]. https://www.hanahaus.com/whatweofferpaloalto.

Harris, Aisha. "Is HAL Really IBM?" *Slate*. Last modified January 7, 2013. https://slate.com/culture/2013/01/hal-9000-ibm-theory-stanley-kubrick-letters-shed-new-light-on-old-debate.html.

Horvitz, Eric and Mustafa Suleyman. "Introduction from the Founding Co-Chairs." *Partnership on AI*. Last modified September 28, 2016. https://www.partnershiponai.org/introduction-from-the-founding-co-chairs/.

IBM. "Trusting AI." *IBM AI Research*. [Accessed May 7, 2019]. https://www.research.ibm.com/artificial-intelligence/trusted-ai/.

IBM. "IBM Client Center THINKLab." *IBM*. [Accessed August 8, 2019]. https://www.ibm.com/ibm/clientcenter/zurich/research/.

IBM Research – Zurich. "Fact Sheet." *IBM*. [Accessed August 8, 2019]. https://www.zurich.ibm.com/pdf/employment/ZRL_FactSheet.pdf.

IBM. "IBM Q Experience is quantum on the cloud." *IBM Q*. [Accessed August 20, 2019]. https://www.research.ibm.com/ibm-q/technology/experience/.

IBM. "System 360. From Computers to Computer Systems." IBM. [Accessed June 4, 2020] https://www.ibm.com/ibm/history/ibm100/us/en/icons/system360.

Ifi Claims Patent Services. "2018 Top 50 US Patent Assignees." Ifi Claims Patent Services. Last modified January 2, 2018. https://www.ificlaims.com/rankings-top-502018.htm.

Jordanous, Anna. "What is Computational Creativity?" *The Creative Post*. Last modified April 10, 2014. http://www.creativitypost.com/science/what_is_computational_creativity/.

Kahney, Leander. "John Sculley On Steve Jobs, The Full Interview Transcript." *Cult of Mac*. Last modified October 14, 2010. https://www.cultofmac.com/63295/john-sculley-on-steve-jobs-the-full-interview-transcript/63295/.

Kaufman, Scott B. "Dreams of Glory." *Psychology Today*. Last modified March 11, 2014. https://www.psychologytoday.com/us/articles/201403/dreams-glory.

Kessler, Rebecca. "Musseled-Out Native Species Return to the Hudson." *Sciencemag*. Last modified January 21, 2011. https://www.sciencemag.org/news/2011/01/musseled-out-native-species-return-hudson.

Khabsa, Madian and C. Lee Giles. "The Number of Scholarly Documents on the Public Web." *PLOS ONE*. May 9, 2014. https://doi.org/10.1371/journal.pone.0093949.

Koulopoulos, Thomas. "*181 CEOs of the Largest U.S. Corporations Just Altered the Role of Corporations for Decades to Come.*" *Inc.*. Last modified August 19, 2019. https://www.inc.com/thomas-koulopoulos/181-ceos-of-largest-us-corporations-just-altered-role-of-corporations-for-decades-to-come.html?cid=hmside3.

Krishna, Arvind. "IBM Marks More Than a Quarter Century of Patent Leadership with Record Year." *IBM Research Center*. Last modified January 8, 2019. https://www.ibm.com/blogs/research/2019/01/2018-patent/.

Landry, Charles. "Lineages of the Creative City." *Creativity and the City, Netherlands Architecture Institute*. [Accessed August 25, 2019]. http://charleslandry.com/panel/wp-content/uploads/downloads/2013/03/Lineages-of-the-Creative-City.pdf.

Lanier, Jaron. "Whoever owns our data will determine our fate." *Frankfurter Allgemeine Zeitung*. Last modified April 24, 2014. https://www.faz.net/aktuell/feuilleton/debatten/the-digital-debate/almighty-google-whoever-owns-our-data-will-determine-our-fate-12908348.html.

Lapowsky, Issie. "Elizabeth Warren fires a warning shot at big tech." *Wired*. Last modified March 8, 2019. https://www.wired.com/story/elizabeth-warren-break-up-amazon-facebook-google/.

Leonard, Jennifer. "Stewart Brand on the long view." *Jennifer Leonard*. [accessed April 28, 2019] https://web.archive.org/web/20071212213039/http://www.renegademedia.info/books/stewart-brand.html.

Lichtenstein, Jesse. "The Real." *The New Yorker*. Last modified March 29, 2004. https://www.newyorker.com/magazine/2004/03/29/the-real.

Lindner, Roland. „Amerikas Tech-Giganten demonstrieren ihre Macht." *Frankfurter Allgemeine Zeitung*. August 1, 2019. https://www.faz.net/aktuell/wirtschaft/diginomics/us-konzerne-feiern-apple-ist-wieder-eine-billion-dollar-wert16311893.html?printPagedArticle=true#pageIndex_0.

Logan, Stuart. "What is a venture capitalist?" *Quora*. Last modified June 7, 2017. https://www.quora.com/What-is-a-venture-capitalist.

Löhr, Julia. "'Die Deutschen sagen immer nur: Oh Gottogott!'" *Frankfurter Allgemeine Zeitung*, July 9, 2019. https://www.faz.net/aktuell/wirtschaft/diginomics/wirtschaftsminister-peter-altmaier-im-silicon-valley-16275487.html.

Lombardo, BJ and DJ Roddy. "Cultivating Organizational Creativity in an Age of Complexity." *IBM Institute of Business Value.* Last modified September, 2010. http://cdn.creativityatwork.com/wp-content/uploads/2011/08/IBM-creative-leadershipstudy-2011.pdf.

Markoff, John. "Technology; A Celebration of Isaac Asimov." *The New York Times*. Last modified April 12, 1992. https://www.nytimes.com/1992/04/12/business/technology-a-celebration-of-isaac-asimov.html?pagewanted=all&src=pm.

McCarthy, John, Marvin L. Minsky, N. Rochester and C.E. Shannon. "A Proposal for the Dartmouth Summer Research Project on Artificial Intelligence." Last modified August 31, 1955. http://www-formal.stanford.edu/jmc/history/dartmouth/dartmouth.html.

McCracken, Harry. "Google CEO: AI is a bigger deal than fire or electricity." *Fast Company*. Last modified January 19, 2018. https://www.fastcompany.com/40519204/google-sundar-pichai-ai-is-a-bigger-deal-than-fire-or-electricity.

Metz, Cade. "Google's AI wins first Game in historic Match with GO champion." *Wired*. Last modified March 9, 2016. https://www.wired.com/2016/03/googles-ai-wins-first-game-historic-match-go-champion/.

Mindq. "What is Brainstorming and how is it helpful?" *mindq*. [Accessed on April 4, 2019]. https://www.imindq.com/uses/brainstorming.

Moore, Amy. "Complete guide to Apple Park." *Macworld*. Last modified February 20, 2018. https://www.macworld.co.uk/feature/complete-guide-apple-park-3489704/#toc-3489704-4.

Mortensen, Pete. "What Matters Next: Creativity is Just Connecting Things." *Medium*. Last modified March 31, 2016. https://medium.com/matter-driven-narrative/what-matters-next-creativity-is-just-connecting-things-ebd5f24fb0fd.

Naughton, John. "Why Silicon Valley wants to thwart the grim reaper." *The Guardian*. Last modified April 9, 2017. https://www.theguardian.com/commentisfree/2017/apr/09/silicon-valley-wants-to-cheat-grim-reaper-google.

O'Brien, Chris. "At Apple Campus 2, security will be a priority." *Los Angeles Times*. Last modified October 1, 2013. https://www.latimes.com/business/la-xpm-2013-oct-01-la-fi-tn-security-will-be-priority-at-apple-campus-2-20130927-story.html.

Parrish, Robin. "Inside Apple HQ." *AppleGazette*. Last modified April 5, 2012. https://www.applegazette.com/feature/inside-apple-hq/.

Patton, Phil. "A 3- Wheel Dream That Died at Takeoff.", *The New York Times*. Last modified June 15, 2018. [Accessed May 5, 2019], https://www.nytimes.com/2008/06/15/automobiles/collectibles/15BUCKY.html?mtrref=en.wikipedia.org&gwh=81F084FFB2375D70DBEF22E236401615&gwt=pay.

Pelke, Nikolas. „Kreative Handwerker sind die Zukunft." *Mittelbayerische*, July 16, 2018. https://www.mittelbayerische.de/region/nuernberg-nachrichten/kreative-handwerker-sind-die-zukunft-21503-art1670797.html.

Platthaus, Andreas. „Entdecke die Bücher, die Kunden lieben." *Frankfurter Allgemeine Zeitung*. Last modified August 17, 2019. https://www.faz.net/aktuell/feuilleton/buecher/amazons-buchhandlung-mit-1000-empfehlungen-ins-regal-16336766.html#lesermeinungen.

PROSECCO. "Introduction to Computational Creativity." *Promoting the Scientific Exploration of Computational Creativity*. [Accessed August 21, 2018]. http://prosecco-network.eu/introduction-computational-creativity/.

Pulcrano, Dan. "Back to the Garage." *Metro*. September 16-22, 1999. http://www.metroactive.com/papers/metro/09.16.99/cover/bushnell1-9937.html.

Richard Crawford '74. "Brad Handler '95 on eBay, Founding a Travel Empire, and Luck." *UVA Lawyer.* [Accessed April 19, 2019]. https://www.law.virginia.edu/static/uvalawyer/html/alumni/uvalawyer/spr12/handler.htm.

Richter, Felix. "Google Leads the Race for AI Domination." *statista*. Last modified May 17, 2017. https://www.statista.com/chart/9443/ai-acquisitions/.

Röhl, Klaus. „Diszipliniert Foucault: (K)ein Hammer, genannt Diskurs." *RSOZBLOG.de, Weblog von Prof. em. Dr. Klaus F. Röhl, Ruhr-Universität Bochum*. Last modified March 16, 2015. https://www.rsozblog.de/diszipliniert-foucault-kein-hammer-genannt-diskurs/#fn4-3465.

Rosenbaum, Ron. "'Secrets of the Little Blue Box': The 1971 article about phone hacking that inspired Steve Jobs." *Slate*. Last modified October 7, 2011. http://www.slate.com/articles/technology/the_spectator/2011/10/the_article_that_inspired_steve_jobs_secrets_of_the_little_blue_.html.

Samsung Newsroom. "20 Things You Didn't Know about Samsung's Headquarters in Suwon." *Samsung Newsroom*. Last modified September 29, 2014. https://news.samsung.com/global/purposely-leaked-20-things-about-samsungs-digital-city.

Savio, Mario: *Sproul Hall Steps, December 2, 1964*, (accessed April 11, 2019), http://www.fsm-a.org/stacks/mario/mario_speech.html.

Schinko, Christian. „Kreativität als Schlüsselkompetenz der Zukunft: Schulen stehen unter Zugzwang." *Cancom info*. Last modified May 28,

2018. https://www.cancom.info/2018/05/kreativitaet-an-schulen-das-muss-bei-der-foerderung-beruecksichtigt-werden/.

Schmieder, Jürgen. „Unter der Sonne." Sueddeutsche Zeitung. Last modified June 25, 2019. https://www.sueddeutsche.de/wirtschaft/silicon-beach-unter-der-sonne-1.4498321.

Schmid, Simon. Dennis Bühler, Tina Tuor and Yves Bachmann. «Das totale Unternehmen.» *Republik*. Last modified January 17, 2019. https://www.republik.ch/2019/01/17/das-systematische-unternehmen.

Senger, Amy and Steven Mandzik. "Photos from inside Apple Headquarters." *1x57*. Last modified April 11, 2012. http://1x57.com/b/photos-from-inside-apple-headquarters/.

Shane, Scott. "Start Up Failure Rates: The Definitive Numbers." *Small Business Trends*. Last modified December 24, 2018. https://smallbiztrends.com/2012/12/start-upfailure-rates-the-definitive-numbers.html

Shead, Sam. "Google's 400 million acquisition of London AI startup DeepMind just got very interesting." *Business Insider*. Last modified July 21, 2016. https://www.businessinsider.de/googles-400-million-acquisition-of-deepmind-is-looking-good-2016-7?r=US&IR=T.

Stanford University. "The Founding Grant with Amendments, Legislation, and Court Decrees." *Stanford University*. Last modified 1987. https://wasc.stanford.edu/sites/g/files/sbiybj10311/f/foundinggrant.pdf.

Stanford University. "Stanford. Faculty Handbook." *Stanford University*. Last modified September 1, 2017. https://facultyhandbook.stanford.edu/1-university#1.1.

Stanford University. "The Founding of the University." *Stanford University*. Last modified February 15, 2019. https://facts.stanford.edu/about/.

Steffens, Frauke. „Das Internet der Faschisten." *Frankfurter Allgemeine Zeitung*. Last modified August 7, 2019. https://www.faz.net/aktuell/politik/ausland/internet-der-rechtsextremen-rassisten-treffen-sich-im-netz-16321835.html?printPagedArticle=true#void.

Stokel-Walker, Chris. "Atari Teenage Riot: The Inside Story of Pong and The Video Game Industry's Big Bang." *BuzzFeed*. Last modified November 29, 2012. https://www.buzzfeed.com/chrisstokelwalker/atari-teenage-riot-the-inside-story-of-pong-and-t.

Thisisbillgates, "I'm Bill Gates, co-chair of the Bill& Melinda Gates Foundation. Ask Me Anything." *reddit*. Last modified February 27, 2017. https://www.reddit.com/r/IAmA/comments/5whpqs/im_bill_gates_cochair_of_the_bill_melinda_gates/dea731b/.

Tiku, Nitasha. "Three years of misery inside Google, the happiest company in tech." *Wired*. Last modified August 13, 2019. https://www.wired.com/story/inside-google-three-years-misery-happiest-company-tech/.

Tom Boredpanda staff. "The Best Place to Work: Google and their Office in Zurich." *Boredpanda*. [Accessed August 22, 2019]. https://www.boredpanda.com/the-best-place-to-work-google-and-their-office-in-zurich.

Tracinski, Robert. "Okay, Google: How Do You Prepare A Country For Totalitarism?" *The Federalist*. Last modified August 9, 2017. https://thefederalist.com/2017/08/09/hey-google-how-do-you-prepare-a-country-for-totalitarianism/.

Ulrich, Dave and Justin Allen. "Private Equity's New Phase." *Harvard Business Review*. Last modified August 9, 2016. https://hbr.org/2016/08/private-equitys-new-phase.

Valaitis, Alex. "The Truth About Silicon Valley." *Medium*. Last modified February 25, 2018. https://medium.com/@Alex.Valaitis/the-truth-about-silicon-valley7ba5de6c36a2.

Vollmer, Gerhard. „Die vierte bis siebte Kränkung des Menschen. Gehirn, Evolution und Menschenbild." [Accessed July 9, 2019]. http://www.gkpn.de/vollmer.htm.

Vivek Wadhwa, Vivek. "Silicon Valley can't be copied." *MIT Technology Review*. Last modified July 3, 2013. https://www.technologyreview.com/2013/07/03/177476/silicon-valley-cant-be-copied/.

Walesh, K. & D Henton. "The creative community-leveraging creativity and cultural participation for Silicon Valley's economic and civic future." *San Jose, CA: Collaborative Economics*, 2001.

w. a. "Computers: Carry Along, Punch In, Read Out." *Time Magazine*. June 21, 1982. http://content.time.com/time/magazine/article/0,9171,925484,00.html.

w. a. "Study Reveals Global Creativity Gap." *Adobe*. Last modified April 23, 2012. https://www.adobe.com/aboutadobe/pressroom/pressreleases/201204/042312AdobeGlobalCreativityStudy.html.

w. a. "The Race For AI: Google, Intel, Apple In A Rush To Grab Artificial Intelligence Startups." *CBInsights*. Last modified February 27, 2018. https://www.cbinsights.com/research/top-acquirers-ai-startups-ma-timeline/.

w. a. "History of the Telephone Tax and Campaigns." *National War Tax Resistance Coordinating Committee*. [Accessed April 15, 2019]. https://nwtrcc.org/programs-events/hang-up-on-war/history-of-the-telephone-tax-and-campaigns/.

w. a. "History of the Telephone Tax and Campaigns." *National War Tax Resistance Coordinating Committee*. [Accessed Mai 14, 2019]. https://nwtrcc.org/programs-events/hang-up-on-war/history-of-the-telephone-tax-and-campaigns/.

Wiener, Anna. "The Complicated Legacy of Stewart Brand's 'Whole Earth Catalog'." *The New Yorker*. Last modified November 16, 2018. https://www.newyorker.com/news/letter-from-silicon-valley/the-complicated-legacy-of-stewart-brands-whole-earth-catalog.

Wolf, Gary. "Steve Jobs: The next insanely great thing." Wired. Last modified January 1, 1996. https://www.wired.com/1996/02/jobs-2/.

Zorn, Dirk and Christian Ebel. „IT-Ausstattung an Schulen: Finanzierung ist eine milliardenschwere Daueraufgabe." *BertelsmannStiftung*. Last modified November 2, 2017. https://www.bertelsmann-stiftung.de/de/themen/aktuelle-meldungen/2017/november/it-ausstattung-an-schulen-finanzierung-ist-eine-milliardenschwere-daueraufgabe/.

Zuboff, Shoshana. "The human factor." *Frankfurter Allgemeine Zeitung*. Last modified July 18, 2014. https://www.faz.net/aktuell/feuilleton/debatten/the-digital-debate/digital-economy-the-human-factor-13050472.html.

Blogs

Becca. "Startup investment: What is a VC?" *twine* (blog). Last modified April 17, 2017. https://www.twine.fm/blog/vc-startup-investment/.

Nevala-lee, Alec "My ten creative books #3: The Whole Earth Catalog." *Alec Nevala-Lee*. Last modified August 1, 2018. https://nevalalee.wordpress.com/2018/08/01/my-ten-creative-books-3-the-whole-earth-catalog/.

Tomaszewski, Michael. "Creative Thinking: Definition, Examples & How to Boost Creativity Skills." *zety* (blog). Last modified July 5, 2019. https://zety.com/blog/creative-thinking-skills.

Treat, Jessica. " What is a typical day like in Silicon Valley?" *Quora* (blog). [Accessed May 22, 2019]. https://www.quora.com/What-is-a-typical-day-like-in-Silicon-Valley#MoreAnswers.

Videos

Humboldt Institute for Internet and Society. *Digitaler Salon: Zahlen, die malen*. YouTube, posted by Humboldt Institute for Internet and Society. February 5, 2019.

https://www.youtube.com/watch?v=t74HlOVFW-I.

w. d. *Macworld 1997-Full Version*. YouTube, posted by JoshuaG. March 6, 2006. [Accessed August 2, 2019]. https://www.youtube.com/watch?v=PEHNrqP kefI.

w. d. *Former Google employee accuses tech giant bias*. YouTube. Posted by Fox Business, August 6, 2019. https://www.youtube.com/watch?v=__deAea89VI.

Picture Index

Fig. 1: IBM. NASA & IBM.
https://www.ibm.com/blogs/think/2019/07/ibm-nasa-working-side-by-side-to-land-on-the-moon/.

Fig. 2: IBM. IBM100- System360. https://www.ibm.com/ibm/history/ibm100 /us/en/icons/system360/. IBM, After 1964.

Fig. 3: Computer History Museum. The PARC Computer Science Laboratory (CSL). https://www.computerhistory.org/revolution/input-output/14/348/186 8. Computer History Museum. Ca.1970.

Fig. 4: Office Snapshots. Awesome Previously Unpublished Photos of Google Zurich. https://officesnapshots.com/photos/8449/. Office snapshots 2019.

Fig. 5: Office Snapshots. Google Zurich Offices. https://officesnapshots.com/ photos/11833/. Office Snapshots. 2019.

Cultural Studies

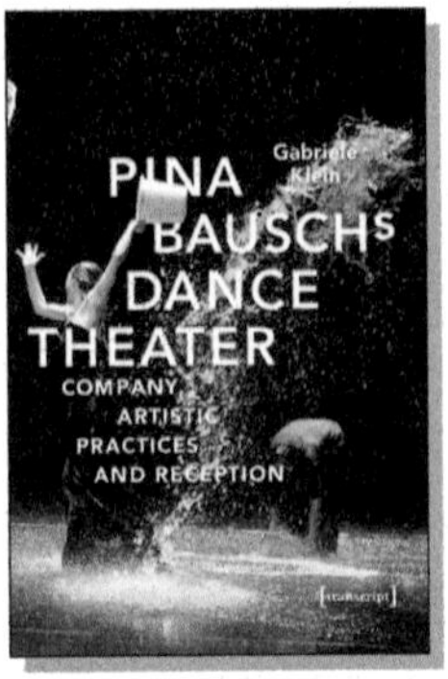

Gabriele Klein

Pina Bausch's Dance Theater

Company, Artistic Practices and Reception

2020, 440 p., pb., col. ill.
29,99 € (DE), 978-3-8376-5055-6
E-Book:
PDF: 29,99 € (DE), ISBN 978-3-8394-5055-0

Ingrid Hoelzl, Rémi Marie

Common Image

Towards a Larger Than Human Communism

2021, 156 p., pb., ill.
29,50 € (DE), 978-3-8376-5939-9
E-Book:
PDF: 26,99 € (DE), ISBN 978-3-8394-5939-3

Elisa Ganivet

Border Wall Aesthetics

Artworks in Border Spaces

2019, 250 p., hardcover, ill.
79,99 € (DE), 978-3-8376-4777-8
E-Book:
PDF: 79,99 € (DE), ISBN 978-3-8394-4777-2

All print, e-book and open access versions of the titles in our list are available in our online shop www.transcript-publishing.com

Cultural Studies

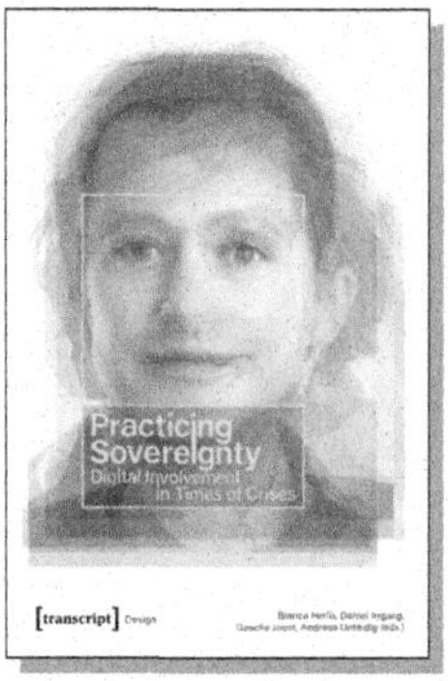

Bianca Herlo, Daniel Irrgang,
Gesche Joost, Andreas Unteidig (eds.)
Practicing Sovereignty
Digital Involvement in Times of Crises

January 2022, 430 p., pb., col. ill.
35,00 € (DE), 978-3-8376-5760-9
E-Book: available as free open access publication
PDF: ISBN 978-3-8394-5760-3

Tatiana Bazzichelli (ed.)
Whistleblowing for Change
Exposing Systems of Power and Injustice

2021, 376 p., pb., ill.
29,50 € (DE), 978-3-8376-5793-7
E-Book: available as free open access publication
PDF: ISBN 978-3-8394-5793-1
ISBN 978-3-7328-5793-7

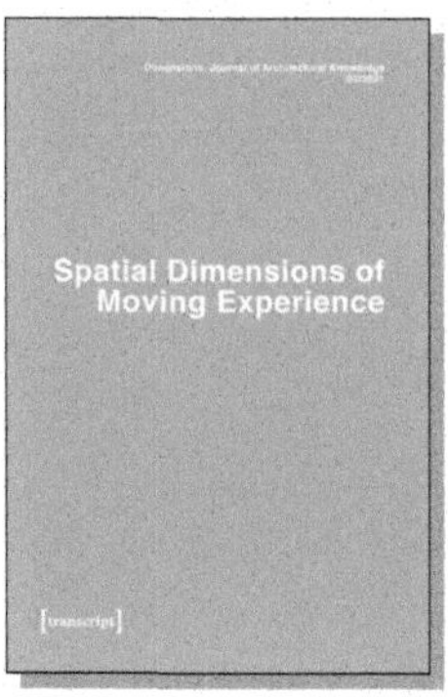

Virginie Roy, Katharina Voigt (eds.)
Dimensions. Journal of Architectural Knowledge
Vol. 1, No. 2/2021:
Spatial Dimensions of Moving Experience

2021, 228 p., pb., ill.
39,00 € (DE), 978-3-8376-5831-6
E-Book: available as free open access publication
PDF: ISBN 978-3-8394-5831-0

All print, e-book and open access versions of the titles in our list are available in our online shop www.transcript-publishing.com